TURBULENCE AND
FLOW IN FILM

TURBULENCE

————————AND

FLOW IN FILM

The Rhythmic Design

Yvette Bíro

Translated from the Hungarian
by Paul Salamon

INDIANA UNIVERSITY PRESS

Bloomington and Indianapolis

This book is a publication of

Indiana University Press
601 North Morton Street
Bloomington, IN 47404-3797 USA

http://iupress.indiana.edu

Telephone orders	800-842-6796
Fax orders	812-855-7931
Orders by e-mail	iuporder@indiana.edu

The paper used in this publication meets the minimum
requirements of American National Standard for
Information Sciences—Permanence of Paper for
Printed Library Materials, ANSI Z39.48-1984.

Manufactured in the United States of America

Library of Congress Cataloging-in-Publication Data

Bíró, Yvette.
  [Idoformák. English]
  Turbulence and flow in film : the rhythmic design /
Yvette Bíró ; translated from the Hungarian by Paul Salamon.
    p. cm.
  Filmography: p.
  Includes bibliographical references and index.
  ISBN-13: 978-0-253-35086-2 (cloth : alk. paper)
  ISBN-13: 978-0-253-21965-7 (pbk. : alk. paper)
  1. Motion pictures—Philosophy. 2. Motion pictures—
Aesthetics. I. Title.
  PN1995.B477413 2008
  791.4301—dc22

                                   2007035718

1 2 3 4 5   13 12 11 10 09 08

Time past and time future
What might have been and was has been
Point to the end, which is always present.

T. S. Eliot

CONTENTS

Preface   ix

Acknowledgments   xiii

1   **Volatile Time**   1

2   **Setting the Pace**   29

3   **Intricate (Extended) Story Structures**   51

4   **Detours**   69

5   **Seeing in Time: *Quasi una pausa***   101

6   **Repetitions or Reprise**   129

7   **Odysseys**   151

8   **Everyday Rituals**   181

9   **Endgames**   203

10   **Strategies of Time**   231

Notes   241

Selected Bibliography   247

Filmography   253

Index   259

Preface

This book was born as a further elaboration of one essay written in the mid-nineties, "Hurry up Slowly" (*Festina Lente*) which bore the provoking subtitle "In Praise of Slowness" (translated from the Hungarian: "Siessunk lassan" [Budapest: Uj Világ, 1997]). At that time I first approached the problems of modern film time, particularly the questionable and overly privileged trend of using fast speed. My intention was to discuss the neglected value of attention to detail and the power of a more patient, calmer way of storytelling. The timeliness of my discussion does not seem to be obsolete. However, the more closely I tried to examine the role of rhythm and tempo in film, the more I discovered that the relationship between slowness and fastness has to be seen in a more complex way; handling time needs a more intricate elaboration. Instead of merely perceiving the oppositions of rushing and streaming movements in film, I realized I need to understand their mutual connection and interdependence and how their function and application is necessarily inseparable.

The terms "turbulence" and "flow" became the more precise naming of my subject matter, intending to illuminate some of the basic devices, patterns, and modes in which this intertwining takes place. Indeed, rhythmic design appeared to be an extraordinarily manifold phenomenon, based on more factors than simply a quick or slow pace. I realized with pleasure and excitement how the changing pulsations of events and emotions alter meaning, affecting not just the ambiance and physical impressions of a film, but the overall tone and nature of the work as well.

This insight led me to a more profound analysis of the notion of time. Modern life and modern filmmaking bring about the unavoidable experience of complex, multilayered structures and we have to get used to them. The comprehension of a diluted, stretched out, and simultaneously existing present opens up the horizon and calls for refined articulation. Susanne K. Langer has recognized the specificity of cinema in the *eternal now*, by which she meant the comprehensive energy of a vast territory making possible the union of differences, contrasts, even antinomies.

As I tried to take into consideration these pulsing components, the map became more dynamic; ever-changing and unpredictable, this feature alone lent to the film's disarming power. As I built the structure of my arguments, I formed the intention to focus on those occasions, both potentials and necessities, in which the ambition for expressivity dares to break the simplistic rules of sheer cause-and-effect logic. When digressions, interruptions, and repetitions venture into seemingly foreign territories (dreams, memories, fantasies), they are not only permitted but also inevitable in the creation of a truly continuous whole. Marvel, surprise, the unknown, and even uneventful matters are no less the substance of the narrative than mere rapid succession. Thus I was drawn to the appealing task of evaluating the contribution of these components.

Also, the joyful discovery of the new Asian cinema, the stream of works by Tsai Ming-liang and Wong Kar-wai or the Iranian Abbas Kiarostami, not neglecting the "old" Ozu, emphasized even more the best traditions of classical American and European cinema, offering another perspective on their undeniable values. Discussing them together, I wanted to stress the best and lasting traits of cinema art: maintaining a fluctuating continuity in these authors' recognizable endeavor. Methods, processes, and proportions may change, yet the *new* does not lose its originality if origins or precursors are named. On the contrary: naming these origins calls attention to the deep roots of particular points of view and prestigious solutions.

Temporality, the resemblance between the composition of film and music, has been much less investigated than the visual and narrative aspect, except perhaps in writings on the golden age of silent film. I believe this likeness deserves more thought since strong emotional impact cannot be created without careful structural composition or without significant articulation of "ascents" and "descents" providing a vital heartbeat to the story. This is the reason in this book I want to center on these often disregarded principles and ways of efficient practice. When referring to older or newer examples I came to realize how meaningful and sensible the rhythmic design could be, suggesting in its "musical" language what cannot be seen or told.

Great painters, such as Paul Klee, always knew that the spatial and temporal cannot be separated. Form also entails movement, or, as Klee says, a given measure "may result in two constructive procedures: establishing large horizontal layers, or, in the opposite way, a construction of heights, a systematic montage in a vertical direction."[1] Yet, there is no reason to go this far to illuminate definitions, since we should not forget that it was Sergei Eisenstein, one of the most insightful film geniuses, who said and developed much about this particular talent of film. In his analyses of montage, and in particular of vertical montage (based often on his own achievements), he found many subtle examples of the apparent "disorder" of details. Finally, Ingmar Bergman has also stated, "Film is mainly rhythm; it is inhalation and exhalation in continuous sequence. Music works in the same fashion: I'd say that there is no art form that has so much in common with film as music."[2]

The continuity of film thus becomes a true paradox, not simply in the technical sense that film consists of gluing together tiny pieces, but in a deeper sense that is even more significant. The narrative is never a smooth river. Twists and turns, bifurcations, repetitions, and unforeseeable obstacles loom large in its path. All the ruptures, cuttings-away, beats, and pauses are the proof and trial of the fullness of the narrative, its saturation. The wanderings and eruptions bring about the most specific configurations: particular configurations under which a rich and emotionally authentic experience comes to life.

Therefore we should keep in mind that fragmentation is not the monopoly of the modernists' *ars poetica*. Storytelling, by principle, relies on the current of turbulence and flow. Fragments should be and are able to lead to a real whole since they represent more than themselves.

When I am lingering on both the prose of everyday and the unexpected scandal of the extraordinary, my interest turns precisely to their needed and possible peaceful coexistence. Following bold odysseys and deliberate withholding, feverish adventures and shrewd retardation, I do hope that we will be more open to accept and embrace the sacrilegious enterprise of good storytelling.

Paris–New York, 2003–2004

Acknowledgments

I obviously owe much to the various writers and cineastes mentioned throughout the book, but I would like to express my profound gratitude to those filmmakers whose films are analyzed here. They not only gave me permission to use some of the photos from their films but were generous enough to discuss with me the relevant problems tackled in my approach. Chris Marker, Agnès Varda, Theo Angelopoulos, Alain Cavalier, Gus Van Sant, the late Krystof Kieslowski, and my friends and colleagues Miklós Jancsó, Jiri Menzel, and Bela Tarr have greatly contributed to a better understanding and appreciation of their oeuvres.

TURBULENCE AND
FLOW IN FILM

Gus Van Sant, *Elephant,* 2003

I Volatile Time

The Many Layers of the Present
Chronos and Tempus
The Sense of Complexity
The Characters' Shifting Consistency
Inspiring (Borrowed) Notions

No single god rules time. In Greek and Roman mythology the ideas of change and continuity, speed, and measure are embodied not only in Chronos, but also in other minor gods (and goddesses). Hermes, Saturn, Uranus, Vulcanus, and Jupiter represent different qualities of the essence of time divided up by nature and man. And indeed, when we think of winged speed and weighty immobility, of fire's arrhythmia and bright equilibrium, how can we assume that all these qualities could be squeezed into a single category? Time's power, slow in building and quick in destroying, is only one of the many antinomies involved in the concept of time. In offering explanations of the stormy relationships between the gods and the world, between man and nature, the myths tell stories about the restless laws of being, movement, and the streaming flow of time.

Timeless time, cyclical time, aleatoric time . . . one French philosopher discusses fifty-eight different concepts of time in his book on the forms of time.[1] I shall not discuss them all here, but rushing time, the effects of accelerated time on our lives and on our culture deserve some thought, all the more so since this phenomenon poses new, unanswered questions.

Thinking about time is as old as thinking itself. Philosophers talk about the aporia of time, since its nature is irresolvable and contradictory and its various interpretations appear elusive. In the wake of the far-reaching effects of the achievements of modern science and the changes in contemporary culture, our knowledge of systems on the move has expanded considerably. Our orientation in space and time has become flexible in its complexity; it accommodates the multiplicity of different layers, complementarities, and even antinomies. The nature of time has become increasingly intricate, as our modern perspective has evolved through an incredibly fine-grained analysis of events and the workings of the micro and macro worlds. The concept of complexity itself has acquired an active, self-evident role in every aspect of our daily existence. This in turn, has affected our culture's direct perception, thinking, and artistic representation as well.

Consequently, in any dynamic system, including a narrative one, the privileged, if not monopole position of speed—as opposed to the almost anachronistic extreme of a slow pace—can no longer be the sole celebrated ideal. Keeping the possibilities of a more tension-filled structuring in mind, we have become used to more varied rhythm patterns.

We should add, however, that the greatest and most inventive artists have always had the capacity to see the world and time in a comprehensive way. This is true of Shakespeare, Rabelais, Mozart, Beethoven, Dostoevsky, Proust, Beckett, Joyce, Borges, Kandinsky, Schoenberg, and many others. The subversive, enlightening sensibility of these artists has remained unsurpassed to this day. In their works they anticipated and conveyed things that, later on, science came to verify and prove theoretically, with the help of mathematics and sophisticated technical apparatus. But, as Einstein pointed out, the problem is not that we haven't yet come to a full understanding of the cosmos as a whole; on the contrary, it's a miracle that we are able to understand any of it, and that we are making steady progress in this endeavor. But man is part of the cosmos, after all. As Bergson says, "The whole has the same nature as the self, and we understand the former through a deepening of our knowledge of ourselves."[2] We can recognize the complicated laws of interconnections, even if we can't work them out entirely.

"Until recently, however, there was a striking contrast. The external universe appeared to be an automaton following deterministic causal laws, in contrast with the spontaneous activity and irreversibility we experience. The two worlds are now drawing closer together," wrote the recently deceased Nobel Prize–winning I. Prirogine and his coauthor, Isabelle Strengers, in their book, titled *Order out of Chaos*.[3]

This celebrated book, instead of simply contrasting the micro and macro worlds, talks about the complexity of "recovered time," the laws of time, about a certain new balance, the relational connection between stability and instability. What is the essence of its off-the-beaten-track finding?

The authors' first concern is the relationship between permanence and change, between irreversible and reversible processes. In other words, they replace the mutually exclusive, single concept of time with a multifaceted time. Bergson had already reminded us that, besides the time measured by the clock, there are other times, for instance, those that measure inner processes or contents. Yet, all these different times pass simultaneously, and thus they define universal change. We have to accept the idea of complementarities, and not merely in this context.

If this is true of nature, and of science investigating nature, then why shouldn't it be valid for the arts that also make it their business to investigate our living environment and human nature? We live in an age of interdisciplinary research. Theories of the natural sciences and the humanities are advanced in an exciting atmosphere of mutual inspiration. New paradigms have led to new interpretations. In light of these developments it is natural to ask: how do the new, complex laws of this "restless time" apply to artistic representation?

The avalanche of events that formerly was considered an anomaly and an aberration is now the paradigm of a complex state of affairs. It is no longer looked upon as unusual, perverse, or absurd, but is accepted and acknowledged as the law of our living environment, for our environment is indeed alive and as such it is subject to constant revision, deconstruction, and reconstruction. The "whims" of weather, such as hurricanes, heat waves, floods, and earthquakes, are natural phenomena that can be understood only as complex systems. We also need to consider social, economic, and individual human systems. As a result of these considerations, the concept of chaos, although still debated, has become more and more accepted, applied in an ever-increasing number of fields, while gradually shedding its negative connotation.

The newly emerging idea is that the diverse happenings of our fluctuating, pulsating life are held in motion by various kinds of time interconnected in a vast, intricate system that defies reduction to the homogeneous simplicity of any single time. Yet, it remains a question whether the functional structure of the cosmic-natural system, the fluctuating "branching" of the vast universe, or even the dynamic instability of microphysical particles, can be harmonized with the similarly disordered state of the inner human microcosm. Can the pace of structures described by physics and the indeterminate pulse of human changes be identical? Can the two come into contact?

Be that as it may, if the new scientific discoveries have changed our conception of time, it is difficult to contemplate the temporality of representation without incorporating the lesson of these new developments.

> It is hard to avoid the impression that the distinction between what exists in time, what is irreversible, and, on the other hand, what is outside of time, what is eternal, is at the origin of human symbolic activity. Perhaps this is especially so in artistic activity. Indeed, one aspect of the transformation of a natural object, a stone, to an object of art is closely related to our impact on matter. Artistic activity breaks the temporal symmetry of the object. It leaves a mark that translates our temporal dissymmetry into the temporal dissymmetry of the object.[4]

To put it in a simpler way: the human creative process leaves its mark on the object and on the world in general and, as a result, that which the thing has become differs from that which the thing has been: the *before* and the *after* differ. Time is an inherent part of every forming process.

Ruskin, on the other hand, says: movement in time becomes form, and spatial forms are manifestations of temporal processes. If this is true of the fine arts, why wouldn't this conception that links the temporal with the spatial be just as valid when it comes to dramatic representation portraying man in action, and why wouldn't it be especially applicable to portrayal by moving light, that is, to the film?

We are living in a world of multiple, unstable processes, giving the system a strongly temporal, historical dimension. The traces and memories of past events affect the ongoing present and its further potentials. Consequently, sooner or later an inevitable accumulation of outside and inside forces takes effect, creating complexity and tension that will bring about sudden changes. This abrupt acceleration and outbreak is turbulence, leading to new levels of complexity.

As a consequence of perturbation, no phenomenon will be

exactly the same as it has been. By "choosing" and realizing one of the many possibilities, we arrive at a new level where we find a different mix of order and disorder. If we are dealing with open systems, stability and immobile states of equilibrium will be replaced by change, by a further fluctuation of the process. Applying this to our own, narrower field, it is obvious that by its very nature human life is characterized by a certain stability, an effort to maintain or repeat the original conditions, but at the same time it is also marked by change, by the occurrence of unpredictable turbulences. It is interesting that change and metamorphoses form a part and the foundation of continuity. Our life is an unstoppable and paradoxical process. This might explain why a seemingly smooth continuity followed by a sudden confusion and an inevitable reordering or regrouping is the daily fare of us all. In the course of his long history man—pressed by the weight of this process, by a series of external and internal necessities—seems to have done nothing more than recreating, mastering, and deploying, day after day, the conditions of his existence.

It was known even before Freud that in the latent motivational background of human action the hidden and the open, the suppressed and the conscious operate in a peculiar way, and can have unexpected manifestations. Nonetheless, we try to accept disorder and diversity, and strive to express these in works of art. The diversity of film is due, among other things, to its characteristic effort to create a certain complexity, so that taking heterogeneity; it can conjure up simultaneity in the place of a mere linear sequence.

The Many Layers of the Present

Let's take the telling example of Gus Van Sant's 2003 film, *Elephant*. Here, the infamous Columbine High School massacre is shown on a surprisingly wide-open field, in a most understated, almost documentary style. We are following the unfolding of an ordinary day. The movements of nameless protagonists, and numerous events and happenings, run parallel to each other. Teenagers come and go in the hallway; they eat cafeteria food; bulimic girls gossip in the bathroom while trying to give up the lunch they have just devoured; kids sit bored in classrooms, and others play soccer during the break. There is nothing extraordinary going on, everything takes place in a most banal dimension. We are observing the patient recording of a group's simple existence. We accompany our heroes in their long march through the empty, endless, labyrinth-like hallways. The camera usually follows these figures from behind, showing the steady rhythm of their movement.

The director's gaze is unusually calm. Undisturbed. He wouldn't miss even the most insignificant moment in the nothing-is-happening life of these characters, for indeed they are facing nothingness embodied in a stretched-out time. There is nothing to finish, nothing to accomplish. So, the short interruptions still lead smoothly to the actions of the next character. Captions indicate their names, as they appear, on their way somewhere—to the library, the photo lab, or the gym—and the camera, always staying at a respectful distance, walks with them tirelessly. It moves on a course parallel to theirs, as it were; they exist in the same time.

Of course, this deliberate calm creates a certain tension, without, however, any perceptible change in the rhythm or in the pace of events. Fragments upon fragments of minute, ordinary actions are performed and shown in an unhurried pace that fills us with increasing suspicion. This feeling is hard to define. What is the source of this increasingly chilly atmosphere that surrounds us? Of course, we know the story. We know what's coming. This is why we can register certain signs here and there (the spleen, the sadness, or jealousy of the kids), then the more explicit, short little flashes of viewing Nazi documents, of getting weapons through the Internet, and a rather ominous moment when the kid with the most gentle face is writing down notes, sizing up the cafeteria with a view toward a future use. Of course, all this illustrates the mysterious nature of accumulation: how odd that we should hardly perceive the approach of danger (turbulence), yet somehow we do sense it, experience it. We collect the signals that anticipation can feed on. Not one of these is strong enough to serve as a direct explanation of the massacre. These scattered moments mentioned above blend into a faceless time of other time-killing projects.

Then, when the "explosion" occurs, when the massacre is executed in a methodical fashion, even this takes place unhurriedly, tangentially as it were (many times off camera), without any nervous or nerve-racking exaggeration.

The judicious message of the film is that there is no "explanation," no decisive cause, and no single, clear, rational, tangible motivation. A multiplicity of causes, factors, and circumstances is whirling and mixing with inclinations and weighing pressures in a chaotic temporality. For this reason the director, throughout the entire narration, emphasizes simultaneity as opposed to linear succession. Any given day is a single time unit existing in the undulation of a single flow of time in which the before and the after are kept purposely in the dark. Which kid we followed when and where, in his or her meandering, doesn't seem to matter all that much. For the ordinary day is not so ordinary after all. Things turn out to revolve around some hidden center of gravitation (a black hole), rather than proceeding along lines of linear development. Only later on, when we are deep into the story, do we realize that certain scenes are repeating themselves; they are presented merely from different angles and perspectives. For example, the first character, John, turns up in the same situation twice or even three times when his friend is taking pictures of him in the hallway. But now, suddenly we also have to remember that when he first arrived late at school he already met the two armed kids dressed in military-style clothes, and that he barely paid attention to them; then, toward the end, surprisingly, he meets them again when once again they head toward the entrance, and he *already* knows what has happened inside, since he warns others outside not to go in, for there is going to be big trouble in there. Yet it is then that he runs into these two grim characters in their conspicuous military getup, with their ominous baggage. What time are we in? What happened when? What have we anticipated, and what have we merely recalled?

So the present is all stirred up, and in its ruffled state it is burdened simultaneously by the past (by the innocent-looking "preparation"), but also by the future (by the coming terrible event that we already have knowledge of), and all this contributes to the justified, clever enigma of the representation.

At any rate, the rhythmic contour of the film as a whole gives an indication, gently and without resorting to any loud gestures, of the intimate connection between flow and turbulence. Leaving a "boring" calm behind, we accelerate toward an end where sudden changes, temporal and spatial shortcuts, and ever more pulsing scenes take their turns. From a consistently maintained slow pace we get to the release of hitherto suppressed forces, but here too Van Sant carefully avoids belaboring the point. His commendable originality lies exactly in the restrained balance with which he handles this piece of incomprehensible reality. Thus he is equally above the suspicion of didacticism and of cheap and loud dramatizing. His message is that turbulence never has a single cause; it cannot be traced back to some reductive principle, but only to the interplay and coincidence of many tiny contingencies.

In our attempt to understand the causal connection of events we contemplate the relationships of permanence and change, of *imperceptible* accumulation and its consequences, and of symmetry and asymmetry of time. And since in these concepts we cannot discover any strict, mandatory, direct connection, or any rigidly disparate, mutually exclusive principle, the unsettling effect of the indeterminable relationship between reversibility and irreversibility makes itself felt as inevitability. Was the eruption an accident? Obviously not. Necessary then? Again, obviously not. We are sailing somewhere between the two when we are navigating around the sources of *before,* and perhaps this is exactly the region we should call complexity.

Similarly, the circumstances of *after* are also very complex and intricate. True, the fatal event shocks everyone involved, we know nothing will be the same as before, but then the traces of the trauma fade and even become invisible, and in the end things return to business as usual, as the saying goes. The school will probably get a new principal to replace the murdered one, and the kids will continue their meandering through the hallways that hold out no promise of any ecstasy. Their meandering will be the same, *yet different.*

So the present has "expanded," since it accommodates an existence of multiple (parallel, crisscrossing) layers and a future that points beyond itself. In other words, the present is not stable at all; it is the dimension of unceasing change.

Chronos and Tempus

The reason this region of change is so odd and unique resides in the fact that in it the micro and macro worlds mix in a very peculiar way, making it rather hard to calculate the effect of change on the individual. The physical reality of everyday existence, the normal macro world, belongs simply to our direct experiences. This is stronger than we are, and it operates incorrigibly. *Chronos,* as we denote the concept of the clock, of physical time, proceeds according to its own rigid laws: time is passing; Monday is fol-

lowed by Tuesday, night by morning. But the processing of impressions and experiences, this human time we call *Tempus,* this
reality, a micro-level compared to the big one, is unforeseeable.
The interconnection of so many causes played out on the field of
acceptance-rejection results in such a complex, ballooning mass
that Tempus will (might) get the upper hand over Chronos.

Are the arts capable of capturing the constantly shifting re-
fractions of this undulation? At any rate, the complexity of the arts
rests on a dynamic base, in which the smallest collusion will direct
time in a privileged direction. Narrative representation operates
on the principle of time's arrow, that is, according to the law of
linearly advancing movement. Events and the reactions to them
always mean a liveliness that assumes the passage of time.

This explains why it is natural that the meaning of a work of
art is not independent or permanent. It harbors countless possible
interpretations and not just because these depend on various contexts, but also because it is by nature polyvalent. If we think only
of the outlook of modernity's great subversive artists like Proust,
Joyce, Borges, and others, we can see how their stories develop
through a kaleidoscopic vibration of time units, through the compulsory "recoiling" of the labyrinth, and the creation of new constellations. Although not toward a clearly defined goal, they still
move from the vague to the more distinct, from the improbable
to the more verifiable.

Borges's metaphor about the staircase that ends in the (open)
space, leading not to a door but to vertigo, is an excellent demonstration of the bewildering range of possibilities, of the complexity
of the unforeseeable about which modern science has so much
to say. "Although it does not lead to the expected door, it can
sometimes turn into a passage that opens onto previously unrecognized and unconstituted territory," says N. Katherine Hayles.[5]
pointing out, correctly, that the concept of dynamic *principium*
cannot be mechanically constricted. Forward movement cannot

be restricted solely to the horizon of physical space; it extends to the depth, to the "vertical" dimension of grasping the unknown.

The essence of every creation of art is its novelty, its reflection of a unique, inimitable perspective. This is why room has to be made for chance, the appearance of which, of course, can always give rise to trouble, unexpected turbulence, or chaos. But we should remember that today scientists are talking about two different types of chaos: one that is characterized by an "orientation" toward order, and another that tends toward an increasing disorder, and a lower level of equilibrium. These two, however, are not mutually exclusive, since what the state of movement means is precisely that we are not advancing smoothly toward "harmony." Without the shocks of disorder there is simply no dynamism. For this reason, art, if it wishes to avoid idealistic or mechanistic reduction, is forced to accommodate both types of chaos. Félix Guattari, a French philosopher-psychologist, has coined the term *chaosmose* to describe the chaotically complex inner world of the subject. I don't think Guattari's experiment, mostly with the similarity/identity of psychosis and aesthetic expression, is entirely justified, but he is probably right in saying that the subjective processing of existence in the world involves more than a series of simple, gradual recognitions. "Irruptions," the intrusions of parts of the past, are inevitable, and through the osmosis of digressions and fantasies they lead to disorder, that is, to complexity.

Perhaps, we just have to admit that in our so-called inner world the micro and macro laws hold an equal sway. After all, we live in the external world, and we cannot tear ourselves away from its determining factors. The way we move around and go about our daily business is part of the operation in the "normal" world. But our subjective experiences, our perceptions, and our stored and retrieved memories, all these belong to an entirely different dimension. Features, formed by personal destiny and character, make for a whole different sort of operation.

The human experience of time is genuinely sensitive to the emotional quality of time. Our perception is essentially affected by the emotional weight and content of external occurrences. This experience is also characterized by an ability to discern the simple measurability of physical time. The valuations of particular events and states are not always the same for everyone. There exist simultaneously in the world and in us many possible interpretations and, consequently, many possible reactions. Since people live separately as sovereign individuals, each governed by separate (often changing) laws, it is inevitable that there will be many independent timelines running parallel with each other. Even Einsteinian physics talks about different kinds of time depending on the space and specific situation, and this should apply all the more in the individual, subjective dimension. For, naturally, it's not only the difference between and complementarity of the categories of physical and psychological time that is decisive, but also the uniqueness of the individual's time experience shaped by the given moment, by the present as much as by the past. Even the simplest linear dimension contains numerous layers of time, so we can imagine how many such layers the nonlinear dimension must have! This means that every activity is teeming with unknown variables, even if at the first level the *before* and the *after* are clearly separated.

After what Saint Augustine has said on this subject, we cannot quote often enough the most accurately described paradox of time: the contradictory nature of the three kinds of present. The past is no longer, since it is gone; the future is not yet, since it is only promising its own arrival; finally, the present ceased to exist at the moment it commenced when it immediately became past. How, then, could time have an independent existence when its component parts are all nonexistent? Should we say that the moment is given as a temporal atom, suspended between two nothings? But then we would have to say that the moment possesses no time. It's a vicious circle; time shows itself only by denying itself. Being is becoming, we say; succession and simultaneity are not mutually exclusive concepts.

In any case, for the purposes of my argument it is most important to question every transition, from rest to movement, and also the other way around, from movement to rest. Also, every change in rhythm and tempo has to be questioned, for these characteristics form the basis of further complexities, which in turn can throw light on new components, linking thereby a new set of relations to the given initial state. This is how changes of speed can reveal the existence of new complexities. Thus Whitehead's remark about the emergence of new states, "the many become one and are increased by the one," is to the point. In other words, the new state, with its growth and multiplication, doesn't mean quantitative change; rather, it indicates the multilayered nature of phenomena, always enriching the picture of the given situation.[6]

If every rich narration depends on its ability to show life beneath the surface, complete with its inherent dynamism, the stratification of any given state is determined by the motivations underlying the actions, by the movement of consciousness between past and future, by memory and dream work, by the number and nature of associations, and so on. This is how we get to "disorder," to the lack of equilibrium, which then produces change. For effects can be created only through some sort of difference, some discrepancy in sensations on the move, and these effects will in turn become further differences.

Human and natural systems develop through a series of instabilities, amplified undulations, and crises. This design is the unfolding story of action in drama, and the story, whether linear or nonlinear, forms the basic rhythm of all narration. We have to be able both to follow the unfolding story—the storyline—*and* to understand the unique behavior of certain *characters* if we want to give an account of the nature of the transformation process, the source of which is the lack of equilibrium. The reason why this is so important in narrative storytelling and drama is that the absence of equilibrium is the origin of all conflicts, the engine that will keep our story running. It is precisely this "uneven" running that creates rhythm, defined according to *Webster's Seventh New Collegiate Dictionary* as "an ordered recurrent alternation of strong and weak elements in the flow."

Complex and active processes are made possible only by those ceaselessly arriving impulses that keep these processes off balance. Forces that exert their effect from and in many directions manifest themselves through a series of speed-up and slow-down phases. Inescapably, but not without reason.

The Sense of Complexity

We have come to the indispensable requirement of complexity, a concept that today, far from being part of a hackneyed rhetoric, is subject to manifold definitions. Complexity is a system of relations, amid *hidden* possibilities of interaction, capable of producing diversity, but also chaotic behavior, chance disturbances, and jumps. The modern scientific conception is that in Nature simplicity doesn't even exist, only simplification that humans create, for practical purposes, by a reductionist separation and division of basic phenomena. To support this view, Wittgenstein is cited. On his view, the simple object is already embedded in a complex Nature, only on a different level, for if we proceed further we might be able to grasp the interrelationships among the behavior patterns of individual components. In this cluster of relations the contingent, the uncertain, and even the contradictory are complementary and antagonistic at the same time.

The acclaimed neurologist Antonio Damasio calls it "a nesting principle," which consists of having parts of simpler reactions incorporated as components of more elaborate ones. "That is why the metaphor of a tall building with many floors only captures some of the biological reality. . . . A better image is that of a tall, messy tree with progressively higher and more elaborate branches coming off the main trunks and thus maintaining a two-way communication with their roots."[7]

If the excessively generalizing scientific abstraction has disregarded singularity, individual locality, and temporality, it is high time that we should think about and create our representations by taking these conditions in account. This is exactly where the function of art has to find its *raison d'être*. After all, every living being is *unique*, producing unique things and beings, living and developing in a *specific* environment, says the French philosopher Edgar Morin, and singularity deserves keen observation. Only through specific, individual phenomena can we deeply understand diversity. In spite of this, the resulting multiplicity doesn't necessarily mean hopelessly unmanageable disarray; it can also mean a certain unity. There is maybe no more substantial requirement in the world of art than this respect for singularity and uniqueness that despite all heterogeneity embraces unity. It is not only particular life situations that reveal the ambivalence of change and identity; this flexible duality also holds for human characters. This is why we can say that character is nothing but destiny, for defining features shape a character's career, even if they don't determine it completely. We should consider separately that which is permanent in a human character or in its destiny, and that which is variable because it is irreversible.

The Characters' Shifting Consistency

In *The Marriage of Maria Braun* (1979), Maria Braun, in Fassbinder's perception, is the paradoxical emblem of loyalty. From a grotesque wedding, which takes place during an air raid, in a shower of bombs, to the final reunion, Maria Braun is, in her own way, the most consistent soul: she remains faithful to her beloved

Rainer Werner Fassbinder, *The Marriage of Maria Braun*, 1979.
Used by permission Criterion/Photofest.

man. But the road she travels is far from being straight or simple. On the contrary, it takes sudden and fatal turns, thus both turbulence and flow are present in her journey. Moreover, whenever any outburst or explosion occurs, it cannot be traced back to one single motive.

First, in the beginning, all her actions seem to be "normal," if not resigned. She accepts with discipline her lot. During her mourning period (groundless, as it turns out), she starts an affair with a GI and is ready for a new kind of life. But when her supposedly dead husband unexpectedly appears in the middle of an intimate and happy moment with the new lover, she gets tangled up in an involuntary manslaughter. The scene is violent; she acts under the fiery impulse of bewilderment and fear. Her eruption is understandable, yet it doesn't ensue from her original temperament. After this turbulent episode she regains her well-established character. She accepts without any apparent agitation the sacrifice offered by the beloved husband, and goes on with icy determination, even at the cost of infidelity for her success. Then, later again, when it turns out that she was duped, and her freedom is but a purchased independence, she (accidentally? or by intentional, sudden carelessness?) puts an end to the whole game, or rather, she allows the "caprice of fate" to cut both of their lives short. The brilliant success story ends in wild and complete destruction.

What, then, is permanent in her character, and what in it is variable, because irreversible? Her toughness, her hunger for success is obviously an immovable fixture. But, at the same time, doesn't she collapse under her self-assigned task? Doesn't she become increasingly vulnerable and disoriented? The cleverly calculating life energy loses its way in confusion, while the goal fades away. The snarled relations in the family; the disappearance of her husband from prison; her love affair with her boss; the sudden death of the latter; all these are enough to unsettle her but not enough to get her to react directly to these events. It is undeniable that all more or less significant events or changes, even if she suppresses her reactions to them, leave their traces and marks on her. The sum total of these effects is stored up in unstable inner processes. This is where we get to the micro status. But the dynamic of this is everything but arrhythmic. There can be great temporal discrepancies between cause and effect, between perception and reaction, but this distance doesn't alter their significance. In addition, temporal distance means more: the smaller scale shifts onto a different level; large-scale instabilities or reorganizations appear, even causing ferocious, cascading events.

The singular nature of the reactions is definitely manifested in temporality: the slow and quick reactions are articulated in the representation as well, for the dispositions of particular individuals determine who, how, when, and in what ways people respond to what happened.

In the case of Maria Braun, for example, the always dominant goal-consciousness, the cold determination, and then the rising tide of anger and hunger for revenge suggests in a different pace the development of pent-up emotions. At this point, the dimension of her actions expands, becoming incomparable to her initial determination. The determining causes have the same roots, yet, on account of their accumulative nature, they lead to other, graver effects. And the other way around: the apparent or bitter indifference of the husband, who accepts the discipline together with the circumstances, shows emphatically little change. Always putting his duties before his emotional needs, he is the one who, in spite of the shocks and tribulations, faithfully carries out what he has given himself. His change is less visible than that of his wife, yet he too has a latent history bearing the traits of a deliberately cool character.

The dialogue between man and the world is uninterruptible, and it is hard to know when a small event will turn out to be fatal, or will have a far-reaching effect that sets things in motion much later. The sudden appearance of the husband; Maria's excited, overly joyful reaction to the event; her provocative undressing, while the man keeps his hat on, listening to the loud broadcast of the soccer match; her hurried, flustered running around the house, from the bathroom to the kitchen; and his restrained silence: all these events reveal an unbalanced, baleful atmosphere, intimating something menacing. Yet it is impossible to foresee what is in store. In any case, consciousness, and especially the unconscious, certainly have irreversible properties. Here the contingent and the necessary, the stable and the unstable are intertwined. Of course, we are interested mostly in the sources of proximate causes, in the roots of motivation. How and why have we ended up where we are now? There is, however, never a single answer to these questions.

This is why it's so important to investigate the accidental or inevitable interplay of multiple, innumerable, and heterogeneous factors. They form the essence of every change. The mechanical application of causality simplifies matters. The micro world is not only incredibly multifaceted, but it exists in almost unchartable, immeasurable undulations, connections, and disruptions. The lived content is not permanent and immobile, but it is subject to a ceaseless formation process. We live under the uneven pressure of event sequences that give life to suddenly emerging forces, and this explains the chronic lack of balance. However, it is exactly the latter that will serve as the triggering cause of further movements. Our restlessness derives from our attempt to deal with this lack of balance, to offset and eliminate this disturbing "disorder." We take action in order to reduce disorder, to achieve a happier, relatively tension-free, harmonious state of existence. This, however, we usually achieve at the cost of transgressions when overstepping the "allowed, customary" threshold, as the effects become more complex than the given structure itself.

In the case of the above-mentioned Fassbinder film, the husband's sacrifice, by going to prison instead of the guilty, though adulterous wife, is an exceptionally unselfish act that "transcends" the hero's original capacities. However, precisely through this extreme gesture can we get insight into the underlying and hidden forces. To put it in another way: all solutions, strong decisions, and behavior will lead to new situations of stability, which by turn and principle become again temporary and, naturally, gives rise to further troubles.

The other question, nevertheless, regards the presence of a certain given, almost stubborn, permanence. Man is characterized by hard-wired response patterns and recurring obsessions. On the one hand, everything is irreversible; what happened cannot be undone, that is, we move on and leave behind disaster, grief, and pleasure. Yet, on the other hand, the originally given features, the indestructibility of traces, and the return of memories also signify that we cannot become entirely different from what we were born to be, or from the rather rigid form of the person we have turned into. In spite of the transient element, the basic structure is present, and even if it has gone through alterations, the original "blueprint" has not changed by erasing itself.

Which one is stronger? This is an unpredictable and also unstable variable. We should stress once again that complexity is a delicate balance indeed, of which it is true to say that not only do order and disorder meet here but also that any given state is open to the possibility to significant qualitative changes and to the possibility of decay and homogenization as well.

In the case of *The Marriage of Maria Braun*'s characters, both wife and husband belong to the category of unusually strong, vigorous personalities, revealing innate inclinations and a solid ground that governs their actions. However, even they cannot distract themselves from the constraining, forceful external conditions that define their lives.

Inspiring (Borrowed) Notions

For a long time, chaos had a negative connotation attached to it. If order is a good thing, then chaos is bad because it is incapable of producing or maintaining order. Yet, the phenomenon itself is hardly new, only it has become more generally accepted in our increasingly multifaceted and global culture. The mass of comprehensive social, technological, scientific, and visual information whirling under the umbrella of the World Wide Web continually confronts us with the incidental, concepts of nonlinearity, and chaotic disorder. Our daily practice tends to bring us face to face with information galore, rather than with any evidence of a respectable, solid, and immovable order. The unforeseeable and the unpredictable have become integral parts of our perception and even of our planning. The irregular phenomena are not exceptions; they form an organic part of our lives, and so modern artistic endeavors must take them into account and understand their meaning.

Complexity requires not only that we acknowledge all these but also that we are able to apply them creatively. Beyond the ample examples of fragmentation, interruption, and asymmetry found in modern art, the interplay of the above-mentioned small and large dimensions, and the lack of transparency in cause and effect relations, will gain new importance.

There are discoveries and notions in modern sciences that can be startlingly found in modern artworks as well. Let's first of all think of the so-called high sensitivity to inciting incidents, which, of course, is also the starting point of drama. I refer to this kind of special "openness" that makes possible immediate and unexpected behavior toward the environment, becoming thus the nucleus of an interesting story. This "high sensitivity" is revealed in Ozu's *There Was a Father* (1942), when the teacher leaves his profession and position after an unfortunate accident, the drowning of a student, that happens during a class excursion that he led. It is a grievous event, undeniably, but the teacher's reaction seems to be "exaggerated," beyond the evident, throwing light on the fact that particular situations or "causes" may tilt people off their normal balance.

It seems rather appropriate to call the ominous act a "strange attractor," since it happens incidentally, far from necessity, yet its consequence becomes utterly crucial, changing the entire path of the hero. Similarly, the role of the "catalyzer" recurs rather frequently in stories, and we understand that the duration of their presence, the quantity of their actions is not in proportion with the impact they will have. Here what matters is the gravity of the case, and the particular quality it represents.

All these not-so-new phenomena and their names, although derived mostly from modern science, have become useful guides in dealing with complex works of art since they also have a role in weaving stories.

Indeed, how could anyone imagine any exciting, stimulating story without a peculiar initial situation, without a high sensitivity to inciting incidents, without peculiar constellations and actors vigorously reacting to these? Minor challenges or larger tests can suddenly set a seemingly calm existence in motion, only to lead to disproportionately large effects. The dramatic nature of these new developments became clear when a few decades ago physicists coined the term "strange attractors," those factors that induce a system to "wander," to go through different phases in the course of which the behavior of the particles become restless and irregular.

Turbulence in drama is even more pronounced than in the life of an everyday environment where things usually stand ready to tip out of balance, waiting only for a little "push" to start the change. The appearance of the strange attractors is precisely the challenge that will form the basis of action. But here, we are talking about the interplay of two different factors. It is hard to imagine that anyone could become a dramatic actor without the above-mentioned high sensitivity. Attraction is effective only on those who are capable of responding to it. Isn't this exactly the role of "inciting incidents," the well-known device of dramatic exposition designed to set a given situation into motion, as a result of which the hero, willy-nilly, has to act? This can be a sudden disaster; falling in love or breaking up; pressing external circumstances; or slander. The point is that the usual order is upset, and it cries for action. "The time is out of joint," says Hamlet, "O cursed spite, that ever I was born to set it right!"

The hero of Jean-Luc Godard's *Breathless* (1960), Laszlo Kovacs, interpreted by Belmondo, in a state of cynical pennilessness, casually swipes a nice-looking car just to get the thrill of speeding. On the road, also by chance, by pure happenstance, he gets into an argument with a policeman whom, for lack of any better solution, he shoots. The murder, this not very sensible mode of attaining freedom, becomes in the twists and turns of the remaining story (fleeing, the chase, and a desperate hunt for money) the unexpected strange attractor to which the hero responds in his own way. This action visibly diverts him from pursuing the course really close to his heart (enjoying his affair with the pretty woman). He becomes erratic and capricious, doing things that are sometimes against his own interest; at other times, on the contrary, he does things that serve his naked self-interest. It is fair to say that Belmondo's character is introduced as someone who "stands ready" for this tipping over, and we should interpret this at the same time as the "state of high sensitivity." It is understandable that by the end of the story we are heading toward an increasingly greater and more accelerated turbulence. Things are closing in around the hero, and the young woman, with her own uncertainties, chooses a course of drastic actions. So in the denouement, the hero's will, combined with the external "chance" circumstances, generate the long-drawn-out, and in the end, ambiguous punishment.

Crises, disturbances of a state, and the further consequences, as well as the antecedents, can never be explained by a single action and reaction, nor even by a clearly delineated phenomenon, but only by a whole set of events showing chaotic behavior. If the inciting incidents are charged with high sensitivity to begin with—and this is the essence of every situation worth noticing— then the response to these cannot be simple, swift, and perfectly satisfactory either.

Often, it is the opening scenes that provide the strongest inciting incident or starting point from where we inevitably get into great upheavals and bewildering complexities. The beginning of Fritz Lang's *The Big Heat* (1953) is one of the most spectacular and concise inciting incidents. A shot is fired, somebody shot himself in the head, and from this point on it is the labyrinth created by the investigation, intrigues, lies, pretenses, false insinuations, accusations, and revenge that set the course for all the lines of the story. We are not simply asking why, but become curious about the motives behind the actions of all these characters, while, as is wont to happen in thrillers, the investigation throws light on the corrupt conditions of the entire city. The successive episodes might seem chaotic, since they do not lead gradually toward a resolution or final clarification. Lang's trademark is that in his films situations can reverse themselves in the most unexpected ways; an action can turn suddenly against the perpetrator as a result of chance, but never because of arbitrary play.

Here too, the multiplicity of causes is the subject of demonstration. It is these external and internal events that, hidden in the background, activate things and become that dense cluster of unexpected turns I referred to earlier. According to this, and also in the case of classic films of the premodern era, the "unfolding story," the faster or slower flow of action, requires the recognition of many different components.

Understandably, all this is deeply connected to our experience of time, to our need to comprehend better the diverse time structures. If it is the various inciting incidents, acting as zones of attraction, that "hijack" the action from its presumably regular orbit, then the other borrowed notion of physics is the role of the catalyzers, a category better known than the attractors. These indicate the presence of factors that, without transforming themselves during the reactions, modify the speed of reactions and thus affect the changes. In human relationships (and, of course, in works of art representing these), we are thoroughly familiar with this peculiar function, which speaks of the exceptional importance of the active-passive effect.

With Fellini, Bergman, and Antonioni, for instance, we can see quite often the temporary appearance of characters that, by the nature of their position, have a marginal role in the hero's life, yet whose example and fate will become decisive, albeit without any conscious intention on their part. We have to think only of the trauma of the suicide of the reporter (Alain Cuny) in *La Dolce Vita,* or, in a completely different vein, the harmless, passing aggression of the youngsters in *Wild Strawberries,* the "model" of which not only conjures up old memories in the hero, but also has a mind-altering effect on the old scientist. *La notte* too is unimaginable without the effect of the agonizing friend (Bernhard Vicki) appearing in the opening scenes. Although we don't get to spend a lot of time with him and we don't find out much about him either, still his death weighs much heavier in the subsequent story of the couple than most of the things that happen to them.

When Lotman says that "what is extra systemic in life is represented as polysystemic in art"[8]—he claims nothing less than that the subversive element in a work of art acquires a new context, and adds an additional meaning to the world. Complexity is built on a brave combination of elements of different kind and rank: instead of accepting a single logic, methodology, or system of relationships, it is not only allowed but also constructive to adopt multiple viewpoints and other alternative structural principles.

Applying this principle to the temporality of film means that it is no longer possible to build the mechanism of the action or the entire story and image logic on the sheer continuum of deterministic development. The cause and effect relationship only knows the rigor of steady rules. Instead, time has to be left for digression, interruption, and rest—even to the point of standstill—and for the repetition of variations so that its vividness be authentic. These are the moments when turbulences occur, disrupting the even flow.

In the following chapters I'll try to examine these phenomena with the hope that more diversified, complex, even playful and imaginative storytelling strategies not only have outstanding models in the history of film but also may have the power to enchant the spectator.

I cannot resist citing here Barthes's quarter-century-old famous definition of the two different codes that build narrative structures. They are the proaieritic and the hermeneutic codes, as Barthes explains: "[These are the codes] of actions, Voice of the Empirical and the code of enigmas and answers, the Voice of Truth. The first concerns the logic of actions, how their completion can be derived from their initiation, how they form sequences. . . . The other could be seen as temporary blockage, with the 'dilatory space,' the space of suspense." This was Barthes's distinction between the principle of the consequential and the consecutive order. The difference resides in the strength of the function they represent. If the first one is cardinal, the second is more "attenuated, unilateral, parasitic." He calls them moments of rest, "luxuries" that are however, not useless, as they give fresh impetus to the discourse and anticipate, revive the tension. But without "filling in between the 'hinge-points' no intuitive expectation, enigma and lively ambiance could be created."[9]

The interruptions, the parasitical-looking digressions, transcend the hierarchical dichotomy. The connection between logical development and enigmatic accidents belongs to the essence of the flow. Codes may differ in their quality and function but this is exactly that forms the condition of multifaceted versatility. The two codes proceed together, and they equally carry the burden of meanings. Without acknowledging the flexibility and richly stratified nature of time we cannot comprehend the essence of change. This is why I think it so important to understand the role of more complex systems—and within them, the role of slow pace that often appears to be a disruption—as opposed to a preference for mechanical, fast-flowing causality and speed. The tension of opposites is not a characteristic foisted upon things from outside, but an inherent reality.

Ignis mutat res, as the old saying goes: fire sparked by clashes gets things moving.

Buster Keaton, *The General,* 1927

2   Setting the Pace

Always Faster?
Living in Time
Rushing
Streaming

Always Faster?

The experience of accelerated time and its trivial pursuits have become common currency. We have gotten used to the frequent transgression and destruction of the boundaries between time and space. It appears that speed is idolized as a virtue, not only in respect to our daily activities but also in our intellectual lives. We need speed and constant acceleration to experience the ecstasy of time and our power over it. As we rush and hurry from place to place, the success of our achievement is measured primarily in the shortness of time devoted to each task. As if instantaneous arrival seems to be the essential purpose of our journeys.

Not surprisingly, in our world of rampant haste, film was bound to join this marathon. Amid the varied experiments and preferences of contemporary filmmaking one feature clearly dominates all: the obvious acceleration of tempo. Quickness has aggressively invaded every aspect of life. Just as the mere ability to represent motion was a thrilling moment in the early days of motion pictures, so the representation of speed in film has become all-encompassing. Of course, this is not an isolated phenomenon. Changes in narrative conventions are closely related to the new realities and demands of our culture and postmodern existence.

Following the initial thrill over the conquest of space and time, the price of victory must still be faced. What are the costs of all these wonders? What price is to be paid for our sudden giddiness? What is the nature and extent of the attendant damage?

Alvin Toffler described the concept of *future shock* and a subsequent apocalyptic vision in his famous book on the subject, and the term has since become a phase in current use.[1] Toffler's central thesis rested on the disturbing link between two phenomena: "the death of permanence," that is, too much change, and the absurdly ephemeral nature of "transience."

For Toffler, the abnormal acceleration and unmanageable flow of events represented the premature arrival of a future where the new culture hoists itself onto the old, suppressing the values of the past. This putsch-like "takeover" leads to frustration, confusion, and broken lines of communication. The transitory nature of things is the most unnerving aspect of change. The emergence and disappearance of phenomena is all but simultaneous, fundamentally defining our relationship to the environment.

While acceleration is an undeniable social force, its consequences can be devastating. If the life cycle of a discovery or accomplishment is constantly halved by the appearance of the next generation of achievements, then birth and death, celebration and oblivion tend to overlap. The victory of yesterday is here and gone within hours.

We could say of course that we have learned to live with these risks over time. And even as we have recognized their dangers, we accept them as the invincible force of acceleration. Nevertheless, the serenity of a more casual tempo is far from popular. The few devotees attracted to this tempo are suspected of some kind of philistine fastidiousness.

* * *

When we look at the current state of visual communication and particularly that of filmmaking, the irresistible march of the cult of speed is all too obvious. Over 90 percent of popular movies overpower their viewers with an assault of fast cars, weapons, and scenes of wild sex and violence. New technologies, such as video and digital cameras, lend authority to hip, fashionable movies, amping them up like a shot of a performance-enhancing drug.

While this forceful trend has proved to be highly effective in many respects, it is also clear that for the most part the cult of speed by any means has led to excess and uncontrolled brutality. Two or three years ago a popular journalist, James Gleick, wrote the book *Faster,* subtitled *The Acceleration of Just about Everything.* The blurb on the book jacket says:

> We are making haste. . . . We have reached the epoch of the nanosecond. . . . we have become a quick reflexed, multitasking, channel-flipping, fast forwarding species, we don't completely understand it, and we are not altogether happy about it.[2]

I believe this unhappiness deserves a moment of reflection. Undoubtedly, in the mass production of film the pursuit of speed for its own sake has already reached a level where it cancels the joy inherent in momentum and purposeful progress. For let us not forget, unchecked contraction of time is accompanied by the "devouring" of space. Eventually, speed holds us captive to abstractions, lifeless citations, and references. We all become addicted victims to messages no longer than news bites.

When holding a fast pace in such high regard, it is worth remembering that speed cannot be appreciated in and of itself. We experience speed always in relation to something else moving at a different rate. Who would not be familiar with the neutralizing effect of constant rapidity relieved only by switching gears experiencing change in the degree of motion? The truth is that speed simply cannot be experienced without the countervailing forces of restraint and slow motion.

Thus we need a more sophisticated and thorough understanding of the importance of temporality. Living in time makes us more sensible to keen observations, to distinct qualities and weight of actions, recognizing values both in fast and slow occurrences: being open to turbulence and flow.

Living in Time

Time, and especially human time, is more than simple linearity. The extension of time has a structure that is intrinsically multidimensional; it has little in common with mere horizontal ordering while its depth and layering cannot be quantified. The passage of our days is not controlled by the dichotomy of movement and rest, flow and interruption alone; this "breathing" is constantly regulated by contingencies and the shifting tension of digressions, the alternating currents of returns and turbulence. Ricœur also examines potential narrative strategies from the point of the ordering of time, the length of units of events, and the frequency of recurrences. If the "story is an operation carried out on the length of time involved, an enchantment that acts on the passing of time, either contracting or dilating it,"[3] as Calvino says, then the mere acceleration of time, this single-minded effort, remains limited by nature, surrendering the magic of the spell itself.

In his book, *Six Walks in the Fictional Woods,* Umberto Eco also contemplates the rich opportunities in spinning a yarn. Following in the footsteps of Borges, he uses the metaphor of the forest to examine the secrets of narration, the converging paths conjured by imagination. He reminds the reader of the pleasures of wandering. For we like walking in the woods because of the possibility of making various discoveries along the way, of being presented with unexpected choices. In fact, we may derive satisfaction from being lost in the foggy depth of the forest. Our goal is not simply to cross the forest in a rush to reach grandma's house as soon as possible. Aimless wandering is also about contented idleness. "There are two ways of walking through a wood," Eco writes. "The first is to try one or several routes (so as to get out of the wood as fast as possible) . . . the second is to walk so as to discover what the wood is like and find out why some paths are accessible and others are not."[4] Put differently, the "forest" itself (our relationship to events and the environment) deserves attention, and the experience of lurking "evil" or failure is not without benefits.

In his musings Eco does not pass over the paradoxical nature of sexual enjoyment. It is universally known that the joy of reaching the goal, the consummation of love is inseparable from the *long* history of give-and-take that precedes it. Cupid's arrow, while a spectacularly effective tool to cover the distance from the beloved, is but the first step on the path of conquest. Much distance must be covered through the endless tension of reserve and withholding before the true encounter and final fulfillment, an orgasm. There is no ecstasy without deferral. Lingering is an art whose craft and technique one spends a lifetime learning and practicing over and over. And if making love is the primal form of combat, its dramatic arc is the natural model for the narrative. Here too, disturbed time is in fact but digression preceding catharsis, an attempt to hold back the final closure.

Delectation morosa, as the ancients said. One must arrive at fulfillment, and the road we take to get there is not without consequences. You cannot just rush ahead if you want to avoid "ejaculation praecox," which caused so much suffering to Jiri Mendel's poor young teenaged hero in his film *Closely Watched Trains* (1966).

In a work of art as well, patience is the source of pleasure. As

Schiller has reminded us, though the goal is there and awaited from the very outset, we are not impatient to reach it but enjoy lingering on each turn and detail along the road. And in Walter Benjamin's words: "Both aspects . . . are equally essential: the playful miniaturization of reality and the introduction of a reflective infinity of thought into the finite space of a profane fate."[5]

Staying with the analogy of a walk through the woods, the thick forest and the clearing hold numerous miracles for the spectator. Every step promises something new; it is worth observing the trees and the play of light on the leaves, noting the life hidden in minute details. Instead of simply following the well-traveled path, we may ponder the options before us. Lingering, instead of being a waste of time, is full of adventure and risk. According to Bachelard, admittedly this state is a form of vacillation vindicating the right to search, grope, and even fail. This vacillation requires a pause before the momentous step is taken so as to consider the moment's challenges, its contingencies and the weight of the decision. Deliberation is always an attempt to become something *else,* to move beyond the present confines and escape the time allotted to us.

The narrative cannot do without this free play. The inclusion and engagement of the viewer is at stake here as well. In the case of the film, the nature of reception is also based on a complex temporality. In fiction the time of action and narration and the time of reception have always represented distinct duration, while they were closely merged in the experience itself. The temporal duration of underlying events hardly ever coincides with the duration of narrative time. And in the presentation of the cinema, this structure gains a thoroughly different rhythm and ordering. The series of moving images, as suggested by the original definition, creates an independent system using bits of events broken into distinct images. Eventually, the time of reception and narration do not automatically coincide, for through the contraction and extension of time the moments of intensity create different emotional effects.

However, the experience of today's moviegoer goes beyond the conventional excursion that offered the taste of events from *somewhere else* and a *different age*. Aside from creating links between memories and associations, the illusion of making contact with alien worlds, the past offers the unprecedented freedom of mobility. At the same time, with TV zapping (channel surfing), video replay, and stop, go, and fast-forward capabilities, today's viewer is increasingly at home in a limitless world of *anywhere* and *anytime*. His imagination is already conditioned for that reality. As new interrelationships undermine the rules of temporality, the viewer surrenders to the temptations of random mobility. Our experience offers some sort of arbitrary license to submerge in virtual reality; an ephemeral, short-lived flirtation without the promise of permanence. The illusion of a joyful slipping into the narrative is often broken.

The sheer number of action-packed scenes and their pulsating succession usually generate momentum and expectation. The relentless rush creates an exciting aura that in earlier times was seen primarily in burlesque and fast-paced comedy. Yet, if you think about it, those forms of entertainment made use of a unique method of timing as well.

Rushing

Without the alternating tempi of acceleration and deceleration, or turbulence and flow, we would never appreciate the meaning inherent in rhythm. We are talking about the coherence and internal antinomies of a vision that defines various methods of proceeding. And it is precisely this combination that may bring an expressive composition to life. As the development of a story synthesizes various components, adapting shorter or longer units, the rhythmic design is clearly pregnant with meaning. The tone of parts, their slow or rapid breathing, is far from extraneous; it is the foundation of phrasing that anchors the work's intellectual and emotional setting. Instead of neutralizing each other, with their clashing and contrapuntal play the two extremes make powerful use of the resulting tension.

Similar to music, film develops its themes in time, and the slow or rushing flow of these rhythms adds as much to the exposition of ideas as the content of the story itself. Hence, the expressive power of rhythm demands as much complexity as any other component of the work; the multiplicity of component parts, complementarily and alternating temporal structures must all be taken into account.

If temporal layering, the manifold reality of the passage and experience of time is so crucial, it must be extended to the composition and structural design of the entire work. One cannot accept crude dichotomies: speed is good, dynamic and captivating; slow is bad, boring and diverting attention from the significant. In this book I would like to elucidate the fallacy of these views. Of course, in themselves both approaches are value free. The question remains always the same: how, why, and what aspects of the work made the application of one or another approach not only possible but also imperative.

Let's take the imperishable pleasures of the burlesque. While directors in the early/heroic age of film found endless delight in the vitality of fast-paced action, they also created a great degree of density in their work. The process has led to a paradox. Even the most elementary definition of speed states that it is the distance covered in a specific unit of time. In other words, if in the same amount of time one covers a larger area and encounters more events as a result, the contraction of space leads to an expansion of temporal experience. The achievements of modern technology appear to annihilate distance. However, film overtakes the speeding automobile, train, and even the airplane. The protagonists of the moving image conquer space with the magic of mythical heroes. They move about in the world with lightning speed, in total disregard for the laws of physics. Consider the endless chase scenes of burlesques from the silent film era, where the wily protagonist, constantly on the run, outwits his enemies with a barrage of cunning and nimble disappearing acts, producing even more breathtaking stunts, and popping up at the most unexpected places. In his films, Buster Keaton—a genius of the technique—overwhelms the viewer with an unstoppable torrent of surprises. Yet, all this rushing is nothing more than a mad chase after something, to reach a specific goal. In Keaton's *Seven Chances* (1925), the hero must find a bride in twenty-four hours to receive his inheritance. However, the tide turns and in short order the hunter becomes the hunted, in this case pursued by a horde of rival candidates. The mad rush through the city streets and the changing scenery of the countryside (in pursuit of and escaping from some ladies), the endless "forward" movement through the streets, people under the incessant prodding of time is suddenly transformed into the physical expression of an abstract concept: acceleration. For all that, the scene would not be so effective if this infernal rush ahead were not occasionally interrupted by well-placed accents. And that calls for a sudden halt! Literally, the main character comes to a full stop in the center of the screen and in a frozen pose reveals his well-defined figure and the face of the clown doomed to standstill. Here, choreography is a poetic device. In Keaton's films this clever solution transforms the helter-skelter flight into a classical paradigm—exploiting its playful, comic and feverish potentials to the full.

The arc and structure of a composition is far from simple accumulation, if for nothing else, because acceleration is generated by diminution, the avalanche of increasingly shorter cuts. Kinetic energy is released through fragmented images, flashes of ephemeral spatial elements. Tempo and density form the relationship of a dialogue. Or rather, they point to the unique discourse between vertical and horizontal axes. With forward movement, the story picks up more and more weight. For, in addition to omissions, ingenious summary requires condensation achieved through bold associations. The time and space lost through condensation is regained in another dimension. Reduced time/space components contain a rich lode of concentrated material. Moreover, thanks to the energy generated by leaps, "negative space" creates renewed tension. As it turns out, the viewer clearly profits at the end: the stage created by the cut is inevitably more saturated than if it were reached through gradual development.

A fast-paced presentation creates fresh energies, allowing a graceful narrative flow liberated of the dead weight of explanation. "Il discorrere e come il correre [discourse is like running a course]," Calvino reminds us of Galileo's remark. We enjoy the rush of thought not only because it demonstrates the deftness and stunning effectiveness of reasoning (play with strategy and deliver a precise strike), but also because it fires up the imagination. Besides an economic use of resources, unexpected associations are discovered, lending renewed energy to viewer and filmmaker alike. Narrative time "is a form of wealth to be spent at leisure and with detachment," says Calvino.[6]

I find Calvino's almost frivolous remark most apt: we enjoy Voltaire's *Candide* today because it works like a successful action movie, as if it were the exemplary forerunner of the genre. True, on each page the reader is bombarded with a torrent of tragedy, torture, and mass murder, escalating and proliferating in endless variations, but events unfold with such grace and speed that, instead of the horror, the dazzling pace of the work fills the reader with cheerful vitality. Undeniably, Voltaire's unique discovery lies in the mad accumulation of high-voltage discharges and interminable eruptions all the way to paroxysm. With clever hyperbole he manages to give an accurate illustration of an absurd world stood on its head, providing the best ground for a philosophical fable.

It is worth recalling that in archaic times speed carried another meaning as well: it stood for abundance and good fortune, a supplication for divine providence to make way and reach a destination. Or is it a mere accident that "speed" is a generic name for some drugs, just as the ability of film to fix light is defined by the same concept? Be that as it may, other meanings of the term refer to a state of excitement and the extraordinary accumulation of energy.

For *good* (adequate, justified, and precise) *speed* does not simply refer to fast-paced movement, but denotes a thousand other meanings. Momentum, effortless gliding, the tension induced by fever or ecstasy all express different content and thus have distinct structures. Moreover, this jumble of actions and mental states may coexist in a complex simultaneity, complementing or contradicting each other, impulses clashing with each other. When the pace is leisurely (large intervals), time slows to a standstill. However, an almost imperceptible transition (reduced interval) appears as a leap, that is, it suggests a frequently recurring new passage and change.

According to silent film director-theoretician Jean Epstein, high speed is the privileged, noble form of motion, its aristocratic symbol, expressing the ideals of an accelerating civilization. Nothing demonstrates the promotion of the relationship better than the Futurists' first breathless manifestos proposing the "new moral religion of speed." And Marinetti proclaimed that the inebriation experienced in a fast, speeding car is like the inebriation of the identification with divinity. Not words of sobriety! But does not one meet the same frenzy in today's enchanted world, where people value the latest tools of communication above everything else and virtually worship them as inalienable idols? Could it be that the latest-model car, the increasingly sophisticated, omniscient computer, and online Internet connection are more relevant to many than poor old meaning and content?

As for the narrative, undoubtedly, the vitality of speed, its ability to spring surprises, its deft and courageous jumps through sudden compression are all highly effective and lend the narrative a deserved quality. On the other hand, leisureliness has a "bad press." At best and with some disdain, we use the term to describe something considered too beautiful, in contrast to rushing energy that is associated with good by definition. Anything that is simply exquisite is automatically suspect; the average viewer quickly dismisses it as "too slow." This commonly used euphemism merely serves to denote boredom. And yet, not that long ago, a leisurely pace was held in high regard as evidence of interior time, of patience and profound perception.

It is not my intention here to negate the importance of speed; far from it. Instead, I advocate for speed as a potential for meaningful expression. A host of masterpieces can be cited to illustrate the many effective applications of *allegro furioso.*

Nearly thirty years ago *Raging Bull* (1980) made an exciting attempt to use subliminal effects and evoke expressions of violence and shock. In this case we are literally talking about image speed in overdrive. We see not only the acceleration of silent film's eighteen-frames-per-second projection to twenty-four frames per second but also the instantaneous flash of fifty to sixty frames, which Scorsese inventively applied for the sake of sensuously characterizing his protagonist. Scorsese was looking for the representation of brute force within the texture of the film itself.

Raging Bull is the story of the middleweight boxing champion Jake La Motta's exemplary "rise and fall." The film evokes his career through the bold juxtaposition of the limits of speed. We are shown extreme opposites. The aggression of boxing and the brutal violence of the game are set against the almost gentle lyricism of motion. The film opens with the slow dance of weightlessness, an affected stylistic device warning us of the coming contrast with floating, controlled motion. We see the slow, choreographed dance of a boxer in the ring—as if swimming through the air. Thus we enter a peculiar time zone, a compressed poetic time meant to illustrate the inner world of our protagonist. For the figure of the boxing champion cannot be reduced to mere functionality. Jake La Motta is a complex character; we follow the shifts and contrasts. Here the sport constituting the most aggressive form of physical confrontation is transfigured into dance.

De Niro's figure slopes and bends softly, like a blade of grass under the wind. Mascagni's grand opera surges—a most effective counterpoint leading to the very core of the theme.

In Scorsese's film, acceleration is not physical reality but a rhetorical device. Nervously shifting perspectives, suddenly sinking, rising and zooming camera movements, and flashing details communicate the infernal rush. In the background, jazz, with virtuoso solo riffs and raw drumming, creates an almost unbearable tension. We are thrown from one extreme to the next. In one moment we are pressed close to the action, and then suddenly removed to a distance in ghostly silence followed by earsplitting noise. Under constant assault, the film makes us wonder: what is this insane pastime where people beat, bruise, and bludgeon each other to a pulp only to claim some kind of victory? What kind of vulnerability and solitude lurks behind all that? In the end the searching eye of the stationary camera records the pain of a deformed figure ready to perform the last act of his wrecked life with a wry smile on his face.

The structure juxtaposes the values of slow and fast and, with a similar contrast of black and white, underlines the burning passions and the lyrical, unreal nature of internal impulses. The way Scorsese shatters the viewer's illusion of time's apparently unassailable solidity offers a demonstration of its relativity. "The gaze"—as Epstein once hoped—"cast on nature through the medium of film, where time is neither unified nor permanent, is more fertile than our rhythms used to abstraction and generalization."[7] Thus the novelty and privilege of film is precisely the freely shaped rhythmic design: rising and falling movement and pace in the articulation.

But one may look at other applications as well. Certain situations or dramatic figures require the strong contrast of sudden shifts and juxtapositions. Ken Loach's *Ladybird, Ladybird* (1994) achieves a similarly captivating effect without the intervention of this particular technique. The film's exceptional tension is maintained by the weight of uncontrolled emotional states. In the story, made monstrous by its very banality, the lead character's children are taken by force due to an incompetent foster-care system, and she can express her feelings only in wild, raging emotional outbursts. A volcanic flow of pain, anger, and powerlessness drives the image-event. Periodic moments of respite are charged with the threat of explosion. Each moment is undermined. The film is composed to this rhythm, rushing on its destructive path toward an impasse.

The power of counterpoint is at work here as well, although on a different plane. The film tells the story with the extreme contraposition of the two protagonists' characters, the man's and woman's behavior and gestures. Though the intensity of their suffering and emotions are similar, the fundamental difference between the two lies in the way they experience their pain and humiliation. The man seems fettered, the woman untamable. This ever-present rhythmic variation, the conflict between acquiescence and blistering emotions, feeds the dramatic tension. Instead of a headlong rush, in this case nervous pace is generated by the opposite characters' behavior and consequently the manner of their performance. The rhythm of the film is defined primarily by the varying degrees of tension, outbursts, and attempts at appeasing, and this is always something more than the simple velocity of movement.

Streaming

Considering the above examples that deal mainly with the problem of rushing and turbulence, it must already have become evident: there is no turbulence without flow. Movement and acceleration develop only through accumulation and sudden transformation. This is why the issue of unfailing sensibility is always fascinating and essential: what are the ingredients of a well-balanced and

Jean Vigo, *L'Atalante,* 1934

telling composition where the simultaneous presence of the two opposite poles is appropriate?

In *Psycho* (1960) and *The Birds* (1963), Hitchcock operates with deliberately slow exposition, the leisurely unfolding of action to reach major turning points. The films achieve their full effect through a rhythmic crescendo and the resulting contrast. However, there are filmmakers who throughout their films prefer to maintain the magic of a slow-moving narrative as if it were the voice of *andante cantabile.* The latest such example is probably Wong Kar-wai's *In the Mood for Love* (2000), which seizes us with its swaying slowness, the soft sequence of uneventful events.

In the Mood for Love represents the surreptitious power of time as it swells with imperceptible ripples and infinite patience. Of course, it is hopelessness and a serene doubt in forward development that captivates us, for the film is an illustration of the eroticism of diffidence. Initially, the theme of the magnetic attraction of the two protagonists emerges from the depiction of the characters' daily life, sharing a small, crowded lodging. Then, gradually, the main theme crystallizes and gathers force as the story concentrates on the leads' movement under slowly shifting, yet almost identical conditions.

The cramped space, the extremely narrow hallways, act simultaneously as a source of constant pressure. It is both a nauseating prison of vigilant tenants hungry for gossip and a backdrop for fateful encounters. In the stairways and the dim corners of corridors, the two characters brush up against each other time and time again. The slightest stir becomes laden with meaning; the smallest movement in the apparently homogenous environment creates a dramatic effect. Then there is another set of stairs, already out in the street, where the woman goes for her take-out dinner. She goes upstairs, he is coming down. They almost touch as they uneasily hide the excitement and embarrassment of their desire. We meet her in beautiful dresses made of colorful silks and flowery patterns—the only references to passing time. Other details remain unchanged: the posture, the line defined by a swaying hip and waist, the fine curve of the nape of a neck. We are enveloped by the soft flow of time and become attuned to a micro environment, the subatomic dimensions of emotional evolvement, radiating an almost mesmerizing aura.

Within the thin storyline, with its elliptical structure, abandoned and enlarged details create a unique texture. The silence of fractured moments, banality of awkward words and interrupted gestures, and short signals of hesitation and anxiety follow each other in leaps and bounds. There is no descriptive narration. The entire story is built on a few defining moments and the finely modulating structure of the duo. Scenes have no beginning or end and lack all dramatic arcs; there is only temporal duration. The serial composition works with the linear alignment of micro structures.

This world of deep melancholy has moments of happiness but, interestingly, these are silent, at a remove, as if they happened only as an imagined event. Our sense of ambiguity is never dispelled; perhaps the protagonists were just dreaming and we simply witnessed projections of their desire. We never learn whether they truly "made it," and if so, how far they got.

The most unsettling effect of *In the Mood for Love* comes from the sense of openness of the almost-events. Every encounter is tentative and incidental, without the weight of consummation. It stimulates the protagonists and the viewer alike but offers no release through fulfillment. This goes beyond the play of syncopated rhythm; it generates an emotional overtone. The fateful uncertainty and woeful distance separates reality from imagination. This is also why the film can get away with shamelessly sentimental music booming at full volume returning again and again, evoking the same motifs. Whatever happens or does not happen in a series of episodes reveals banality in a peculiar, refracted light. The highly calligraphic imagery and choreography, the silky dreaminess of slow rhythms, are rendered ambivalent by careful composition: elegiac and absurd, perceptible only from a distance as in a memorable performance of a foredoomed story.

Browsing through the classics of film history, one recalls the aura of the early Italian neorealistic films. Ermanno Olmi's lesser known *I fidanzati* (*The Betrothed*, 1963), for instance, shows in a moving way this deliberately smooth stylistic approach.

I fidanzati works with a succession of atmospheric scenes, in each case articulated in a well-chosen setting, accompanied by soft and serene movements. The town is uninviting; the Sunday dance is awkward, a forlorn attempt to find more joyful ways to pass the time. Although the blind piano player grinds out evergreen tunes, the scene is not hackneyed because the representation lacks all attempts at caricature. The mood is defined primarily by a sense of deep sorrow, silently accusing eyes, and the hopelessness of communication.

The small story flows peacefully. Even the drama of the sepa-ration of the lovers lacks a loud emphasis. The essence lies in details: in the dreariness of a hotel room, in an endless hot night in a rented apartment, in the sudden flickering of hope when the phone rings, in all the weariness that has seeped into the pro-tagonist's only black suit and shirt, and in a dinner at a restaurant where, for lack of anything better to do, the waiter tells his whole life story.

The opening scene of the film sets the tone: the panning shot of the vast and empty dance hall, the slow filling of the unadorned room with unattractive couples waltzing to a clumsy rhythm. For a long time we see only strangers before finally meeting the taci-turn pair, the engaged couple sitting stiffly, and begin sensing the rising tension of their impending separation.

Life is confined, and this fact is scarcely relieved by shifting locations or displacements. A deliberate evenness is the central message of the film, expressed in the slow waving of the ev-eryday events. Once everything is reduced to the same level, it speaks of life's stolen essence, an absence that can never be redeemed. This melancholy finds its true form precisely in the rhythm: fluctuation is only modest; the subsequent scenes do not glory in anything extraordinary.

In today's cinematography, one of the boldest examples of dealing with a delusive method of the articulation of complex temporal flow is connected with Takeshi Kitano. This director of many talents, originally from television programming and act-ing, operates primarily with the agility and unerring touch of a juggler. From the presentation of tender simplicity through the most violent gangster flick, he not only experiments with ever-newer approaches but also plays with the mixing and merging of such amazing textures that we often have difficulty keeping up with the pace. Wild firefights and playful lyricism, accumulation and emptiness are juxtaposed, until we finally come to appreciate Kitano's version of deadpan humor. He rejects and makes fun of our expectations, always adding a twist and standing familiar clichés on their head.

His *Sonatine,* made in 1993, is perhaps the most revealing synthesis. At every turn he yanks us from one world to another. In a wild chase with handguns blazing away (where Kitano plays an indifferent character with an inscrutable smile on his face), he creates a scene of infantile abandon, of fun and games, until the next fatal shot is fired. It is "as if the film stopped moving forward," he says:

> It founders in some kind of timelessness. . . . In film, in which the story of time and imagery always unfold simultaneously, there are moments that remain outside time, when all synchronicity fails to operate . . . I would like to reach a point where the apparently inseparable bond between time and image is broken. . . . There is no universal time, and what I'd like to achieve is the relativity of time experienced by my characters. The same goes for images as well. If three persons are talking, I suddenly make a close-up of each to demonstrate the uniqueness of each subjectivity. I would like to draw attention to the relativity of perception.[8]

While following this principle, Kitano creates an unusually fluctuating structure, which also means that he takes the alternation and the unity of turbulence and slow streaming to the very extreme. The fist thirty minutes of the film is such an orgy of killing that the viewer is at a loss to figure out who is who, who is killed and for what reason. The whole thing becomes a crazy parody of gangster flicks; not only Kitano, but all his characters perform the single recurring act of the film, precise aiming and firing, with the most self-evident nonchalance. As the operation would not abide the slightest shadow of anxiety, casual indifference reigns. One senses his tongue-in-cheek attitude as the film makes a smooth

transition to fun and games and shows the thugs lying and playing around. The director uses carefully choreographed motions to
show his characters finding pleasure in killing time (when there is
no one else to kill) until the next murder.

   This is the way one can draw attention to the relativity of
"perception." In other words: the viewer's sensations have to
change in the course of time, during the unfolding of the story.

Robert Altman, *Short Cuts,* 1993

3 Intricate (Extended) Story Structures

Parallels
Crossroads
Mosaics
Epic Narration
Orchestration

Parallels

When we look at a story's well-adjusted proportions, we can detect different methods used to create tension. In addition to the purposefulness of the main character's rational behavior, many films provide a number of dominant, complementary events, and characters that enrich the scope of the theme.

Films frequently are composed of parallel stories, woven with many plot threads, which may yield dynamic results while also retaining a "slowing" effect. Robert Altman's oeuvre is the most instructive example. He is particularly fond of polyphonic, multi-narrative plots, constructing many of his films along the rules of musical chorales.

Of all his hallmark works where he applies his favored structural techniques, Altman's *Short Cuts* (1993) appears to offer the best example for justifying a paradoxical treatment of time. What goes on in this rather convoluted, nearly three-hour-long film with myriad episodes and characters revolving around eight couples? The method is built on clashing procedures that end in a challenge each other. As the title indicates, the film weaves the narrative with tight shots, granting relatively little time for development. On the one hand scenes are given short shrift and frequently end "prematurely." And yet, and this is where the film's originality lies, the narrative flow within each episode is unusually slow and reserved. Starting in medias res, with the illustration of a conflict situation, the tense resolution is never rushed. The rhythm in the successive episodes does not follow the classic "rise and fall" model. This chronic aspect of acute drama is presented with astonishing simplicity. This is Raymond Carver's art's most characteristic *stylistic principium,* which Altman applies with superb sensibility. The final impression conveys a hectic, restless, and constantly shifting overall structure built on far more controlled and balanced small components. The wild, frenzied rush of scenes is coupled with a serene treatment that looks behind stereotypes and lingers on trivialities.

The rhythm thus avoids all familiar patterns while it follows a single principle: it develops the tension through opposites that demonstrate the multiplicity of options and, at the same time, it delivers more through the overall effect of the whole. The potential for more danger is suggested even as the denouement of each episode is deliberately left to the imagination.

As we have seen, Altman attempts to make a complex impression on the viewer, and the rich characterization afforded by the multilayered plot serves his purpose well. If, according to the definition in *Webster's Seventh New Collegiate Dictionary,* polyphony is not simply "having many tones or voices," but also is "a style of (musical) composition in which more independent but organically related voice parts sound against one another," it should not come as a surprise that the physical and psychological relations of many characters carry more meaning than the sum of their parts.

With a broad and saturated plot that encompasses an entire

adolescent generation, Peter Bogdanovich's *The Last Picture Show* (1971) is by now considered a classic in the "coming-of-age" category of films. The story of humdrum yet far from emotionally deprived lives of so many parallel characters, unfolding in a nostalgically depicted small town in the middle of nowhere, is pure Americana from the 1950s. However, the awakening adolescent eroticism, first love and its disappointments, jealousies and tragedies, the parents' unhappy adultery, and an expedient compromise add up to more than a tale of stifled individuals who desire for something better in life. It is a rich survey, paying nearly equal attention to all the individual characters. They are obviously interrelated, and without the largeness of the whole picture we could never get the intensity of the elegiac tone. The film shows a multiplicity of distended, amplified dramas, instead of centering on a single one, which suggests the heart-rending and ineluctable end of a doomed way of life with its monotony and pathetically glorious banality.

In John Cassavetes's *Husbands* (1970), frustrated men are motivated by nothing more than an irresistible urge to break out of the pressing confines of marriage and spend a silly day in London to carouse and have a grand time. Obviously, the depiction of the fate of the four protagonists and their respective families employs time and imagination to highlight the most telling feature in each case. Cassavetes has a great understanding of the vitality and power of character, expressed in particular through vigorous acting.

Of course, their whole plot backfires and the homecoming with its bittersweet realignments only serves to underline the (not so tragic) hopelessness of the husbands' lives. The film's power is achieved through these parallels, intersecting then diverging paths, following ironically the play of similar yet distinct strategies. Instead of a rigorous exposition, the drama is based on a series of loosely structured and whimsical ideas. This is how the thin storyline becomes simultaneously voluble and diverse in its intensity, and also highly credible. Here too, in addition to all the escapades, rhythm is an essential means of expression. The flow is driven by boredom, drunkenness, emotional outbursts, and exhausted resignation. In this way, placing the stress on parallel stories, the "husband status" as destiny gains more universal meaning and becomes a slightly bitter and sarcastic illustration of marital conflicts. Without a clearly defined dramatic center, the filmmaker's vision displays similarities; common, concerted actions; and juxtapositions that deepen the story of the film.

We may also recall the playfully tender and ironic *Jonah Who Will Be 25 in the Year 2000* (1976), a film by Alain Tanner and written by John Berger. The film's softly flowing, subtly woven narrative line follows the fate of half a dozen characters looking for their place in the world. The film is enveloped by the warmth of haphazard events. The narrative has an even-tempered cadence; developments are followed with minute attention to detail in an atmosphere of receptiveness. The calm treatment not only allows the viewer to identify with each protagonist but also lets the viewer experience the peculiar nature of the film's world and point of view. This is why the film operates without the usual hierarchy among various subplots. Each scene is left "open" and exists in and of itself, and stretches as far as its internal energy will allow. Cutting onion together around the kitchen table, the arrival of an unexpected guest, the play of children, or a bicycle ride through town in the morning are equivalent events, and all triumph with the power of lucidity and serene compassion. Poetic melancholy emanates from the richly interwoven texture.

Crossroads

The examples above treat the parallel, intersecting exploits of groups of characters forming close relationships. In other cases we see structures where encounters are accidental, far from preordained, and the interest of the story lies in the characteristic feature of each fork in the road and the destinations they may lead to.

In Tsai Ming-liang's films, all the characters are lonely by nature. Their attention, their attachment to things or other persons appears to be resolute but dispassionate, devoid of the desire to make contact. In *Vive L'Amour* (1994), we follow the almost aimless roaming of three young people. Instead of being active participants, they function more like voyeurs. No relationship exists among them. The maximum connection they achieve is exemplified by one boy surreptitiously participating in the lovemaking of the two others by hiding under the bed, eavesdropping and getting worked up by the sounds and the commotion above, seeking self-satisfaction in this fashion. Or, after a bungled suicide attempt, the boy may timidly lean over the sleeping man and snuggle up, making sure not to wake him. Here again the "nonencounters," the inevitable loneliness of these young people, becomes manifest through their accidental yet unaccomplished meetings, their way of only bumping into each other in vain. Urban solitude is the core of the story, told in a mapping out of the crossroads in which they may touch for a moment without having any dealing or real contact.

The loose structure in *Vive L'Amour* is most appropriate for presenting parallel yet never intersecting lives, referring much more to the global picture of contemporary reality than to any kind of crossing or shared activity of particular individuals. However, we should never underestimate another all-encompassing factor, which creates deep coherence: the general ambiance established through the feel and vision of the environment.

Staying with the mix of distinct destinies, Takeshi Kitano's highly successful *Dolls* (2002) has a most unusual structure. Here the director literally throws three short stories into the pot. (One is based on a short story by Tanizaki.) At best, the connections are limited to casual encounters and geographic coincidences. What is essential, however, is the visual metaphor of the lovers as they wander in their utter loneliness through the seasons, along empty back roads in an enchanted and spectacular space, ever slower, in total silence toward their death. As a leitmotif, their fate is meant to invoke death's melancholic beauty, mystery, and irrationality. We are traveling the high road of stylization. Kitano takes his cues from Japanese bunraku puppet theater, where the puppets and their operators are on stage simultaneously. The difference between puppet and man is deliberately blurred, as in the case of Kitano's marionettes. The pleasures and passions of life are illuminated by the mysterious light of legend; the beauty of the world they behold increases in proportion to its finitude: with its ineluctable passage, time marks life's options. The poetry of existence may not be marred by its end. In fact, this is exactly what lends it infinite dimension. Nothing could be more uneventful than watching the slow progress of the film's couple in their exquisitely fashioned costumes, forever tied to each other with a compulsory red cord. The characters of the two other stories look at their otherworldly apparition with awe. The couple offers an exemplary model for meeting approaching death.

Interaction here is at once real and imaginary. This sense of loose bonds lends the elegiac story a peculiar aura. Although the film has a deliberate timelessness about it, we feel the sadness of lost opportunity that speaks of the nature of today's urban solitude as well.

Mosaics

It is well known that the realization of merely rational objectives, cause and effect relations, and formulaic systems are not the only tools of storytelling—not even if in practice these methods are highly treasured and prescribed in some canonized manuals on scriptwriting.

However, when contemplating film's relation to temporality in memorable films, we have to pay attention to "deviations." What I really want to know is how, besides the pure logic of plotting, other approaches can be taken to achieve a poetic effect through the "logic of emotions." Instead of facts, the story is always about experience. The concept of polyphony is at work here; it shapes the story with the demands and forces of multiple meanings.

Fragmented narrative always reflects some inner anxiety and endured tension. When this state of unease appears as discontinuity, hesitation, denial, and doubt all enter the story. For instance, in Bellocchio's sadly forgotten masterpiece *Fist in the Pocket* (1965), the boy preparing to kill his mother takes several attempts to commit the crime. Before we arrive at the dithering "dress rehearsal" on the highway, where he toys with the temptation of the abyss and the final act (only hinted at), we follow the boy through numerous scenes where he simply plays for time and tortures various members of his family. Stretched to infinity, these acts become truly chilling and the director spares no detail in showing the tension generated by endless indecision.

Here also, as in the works of many New Wave directors, like Jean-Luc Godard, Agnès Varda, Eric Rohmer, and later Maurice Pialat, continuity is born through the highlighting of "wanton," unnecessary detail. In form and content, these stresses appear at once bizarre and shocking. The simultaneity of parallel events, the intrusion of incidental detail, and the disorder caused by haphazard occurrences all violate the coded logic of the narrative.

In her best known film, *Cleo from 5 to 7* (1961), Varda's approach encompasses an interval of two hours during which she marks off the boundaries of her heroine's life. What reality does she apprehend by the use of such contingent temporality? What order, what caprice does she capture in the images that unfold?

Her procedure introduces us to the heart of the message: time itself is the main protagonist of her films—not just its passage, its fertile construction-deconstruction, but its many facets, its metamorphosis. Time as a moment of strong density, suspended by the sometimes violent twists of life.

Agnès Varda, *Cleo from 5 to 7,* 1961

Varda surrounds us with an abundance of daily events, the vitality of urban life and the vigor of nature. Yet this is but a catalyst, a special filter that ushers us past banal details and leads to the presence of something substantial.

The forest of Parisian streets is the young woman's natural habitat, the place where she lives, strolls, and does her errands. Wherever we encounter her, every detail of her history appears to be part of a whole. When she becomes ill in the bistro, everyday events unfold around her; when she takes a taxi, the radio announcer reports another historical event—the Algerian war—that for a moment eclipses her own destiny. Through this commotion, Varda manages to suggest the inconceivable richness of simultaneous events, the dizzying heterogeneity of things. Continuity is only the sum of the fragments of life to different degrees. So the hero follows a path paved by the unexpected, whose ultimate moment alone is determined. There are no truly privileged moments; our entire experience carries meaning that signifies our relationship to the world. This is what makes the whole structure conform to the modern exigencies of temporal conception: time is "a serpent to be sold off in slices of portions," as Baudelaire would have it.

It seems appropriate to evoke further Baudelaire's remarks. In "the little poems in prose," sections associate "the frightening with the comical, and even tenderness with hate." And indeed, we feel we witness a series of distinct atmospheric scenes, moments of the grotesque or melancholy, as in the free play of *moments musicaux*.

In a relatively early example from the late sixties, Ken Loach's first work, *Kes* (1969), a documentary-improvisational story-mosaic, takes a leisurely look at scenes of family life, school, and, finally, a sudden passion, the taming of a wild falcon and its destruction motivated by vengeance. However, the inner tension of the protagonist, a skinny, premature adolescent, permeates the story despite this unusual treatment. Besides offering an incisive definition of the setting, the physical details of minute observation and the nervous energy of gesture fuel the story imperceptibly. The series of distinct short scenes gradually gather substance through a presentation focusing on tense movements shifting unexpectedly. The boy's clothes and his bearing, grimaces, and profound emotional attachment to his only friend translate into the methodical and slow depiction of an entire way of life—the barrenness of a small and bleak mining town in 1960s England.

The film applies two asymmetrical rhythmic principles: the repetitive, cold routine of tedium, fatigue, and everyday monotony (school, domineering teachers, a pointless soccer game not without willful cruelty, a loveless home) and the protagonist's endless flight from his tormenting pursuers. The rhythm established by a tireless handheld camera conveys the pulse of inner passions and outside pressures.

Loach's directorial style overwhelms with its autonomy and patient attention to authenticating detail that leaves time for improvisation as well. His observations have density and the power of novelty. There is never a routine movement, never a predictable reaction, whether we look at the form or content of a gesture. Despite the mosaic-like structuring, the absence of all artificial solutions creates a forceful momentum and a current of alternating ebb and flow. People parade all their grotesque deformities before the camera, and not for the sake of entertainment; the unique and peculiar nature of each individual's clothing, mimicry, and tone of voice is revealed under the director's merciless gaze. Loach's lucid and insightful approach creates tragedy devoid of all sentimentality, and we are led to this dark abyss as we follow the boy's destiny.

The American prodigy Harmony Korine's *Gummo* (1997) and *Julien Donkey Boy* (1999) are the most recent examples of this method. *Gummo* could be set up as a flawless model of improvisation. The film is reminiscent of a series of doodles in a notepad about two gawky kids, Solomon and Tummler, who ride around on their bikes, take potshots at cats, and sniff glue from plastic bags as they run wild somewhere in Tennessee. In the aftermath of a devastating hurricane, there is complete chaos all around and no one pays attention to the kids. Besides killing cats, killing time is their most urgent task. When Solomon's mother performs an endless step-dance routine in her ex-husband's clacking patent-leather shoes and threatens to kill her son with a pointed gun unless he smiles, we start to understand what is at stake here.

Still, the spectacle is powerful: there is no moment or gag without the dazzling scene of jumbled debris. What is the point here? In a consumer society in the thrall of objects there is no bigger thrill than more and more objects—and behold, now it all lies before our eyes in a heap of utter uselessness. But this is no longer a mere snub at obsessive acquisition and accumulation. This is the postgame stage where no logical meaning can be attached to utter chaos. So the story itself becomes a stream of unrelated episodes—some good, some mediocre—all bearing the stamp of eccentricity: a parade of a small, shivering boy wearing a bunny cap; a dwarf; obese matrons; pretty young women who attach wired pads to their breasts to make them grow; Mongoloid whores; and albino braves. It is the stuff of pure existence, vegetative subsistence subjected to the lens of the camera, which files by, occasionally accompanied by an almost poetic narrative.

"I wasn't interested in making a film," says Korine. "Instead, I wanted to create an object that documents a kind of behavior. I wanted to show images rather than some kind of comprehensive vision."[1] It is not surprising then that his choice fell on shocking, warped, if not nauseating settings that land characters in crazy situations and wild scenes. This is Korine's "answer" to the lack of a story and, instead of the usual manipulation of plot, his way of working with a raw mass.

Whether we look at *Chungking Express* (1994) or *Fallen Angels* (1995), the films of the Hong Kong–based filmmaker Wong Kar-wai relate the strange experiences of isolated characters who are simply killing time or are in quest of more unhappy pursuits. Loafing around, fragmentation, and the lack of an unfolding story are all deliberate choices as the film follows the bleak lives of the lonely inhabitants of a large city. Here, observation plays a far more fundamental role than any coherent storyline. The characters are caught in an aimless drift and their actions hang on a thin thread governed by accidental events of sometimes significant, sometimes minor consequences.

Wong Kar-wai gives a specific interpretation to his dramatic scenes. When he sets off his characters, he is not interested in regular development rising to a climax and promising a state of equilibrium with its expected lessons. He presents explosive life situations and traces the tension of their unpredictable oscillation with the intensity and variety of perception. Each moment represents a new quality, a foray, an eruption in the making, all granted an equal standing. In their lonely quest for happiness, his heroes, who cannot be said to struggle with much imagination, are doomed to (ordinary) suffering by the very nature of their existence.

This approach fundamentally defines the story's building blocks: the sequence of instinctive acts is ruled by the logic of obstinate relapses. The roles are commanding. The situations are of little consequence; whether they raise hell or languish in exhaustion, characters find themselves in aimless frustration.

In *Days of Being Wild* (1987), the boy's days are spent lying around, drinking, womanizing, or brawling. The springs of ambition remain hidden. In *Chunking Express* and *Fallen Angels,* too, all the characters are engaged in their idiosyncratic obsessions: the hit man murders, the retarded dumb boy hopes to satisfy the first person crossing his path, an abandoned junior police officer calls young girls on the phone (incessantly and without success), a young woman wearing a blond wig screams hysterically because no one notices her despite her distinctive headgear. The lives of these characters are governed by the compulsory performance of weird or ordinary obsessions. Instead of the usual experience of flow, here we must settle for constant shifts and the self-sufficiency of distinct episodes.

In *Days of Being Wild,* the first real encounter with the salesgirl in the snack bar has a poetic intimacy shown through spells of silence and constant distancing. The scene unfolds in long, fixed takes and extreme close-ups. The director highlights just a few notes. What do we learn about the girl with the shimmering hair and supple body, and particularly about the boy always seen from behind? Not much. Only that they move around in some kind of magnetic field—each image is choreographed with infinite patience. We see the face of a clock and witness the memorable singularity of passing minutes with each movement of the clock's hand. For this is an isolated moment in time, theirs alone, a suspended, unending moment. A culmination with a special weight, and not only in the lives of the protagonists; the clock keeps returning, pops up here and there unexpectedly during the bifurcations of the narrative, allowing the viewer to experience the sense of sorrow over a pregnant moment that must be lost forever.

However, in the case of Wong Kar-wai the evocation of a nostalgic atmosphere is not that simple. There is some bold "surfeit," an unabashed accent in the presentation. I'm thinking of the "insolent" sentimentality of the music, which brings back the most explicitly melancholic retro numbers (Zappa's songs played on a jukebox in a bar, "I Have Been in You" or "You Are Always in My Heart"). The sweet tunes and soothing melodies painfully convey the characters' most intimate feelings, but the intense correspondence all but turns against itself. Instead, the music becomes a subtle reference, a tender and ironic commentary, while it clearly remains deeply relevant for the two protagonists. But the director takes the elucidating reference a step further: in the most fervent moment he cuts the music and drags both the protagonists and the viewer back to reality and its banalities.

Epic Narration

Frequently, epic narration makes use of freer forms of episodic development where fateful events work through a compact structure as minor chapters, illustrating the protagonist's character from various angles. If justification for period films lies in the power of original interpretation, then it must be demonstrated in formal solutions as well.

The audacity of Stanley Kubrick's *Barry Lyndon* (1975) lies in the creation of a prosaic version of a historic saga, based on the classical novel by Thackeray. In weaving his story, Kubrick replaced life with empty rituals, the mechanical actions of conventional habits. Instead of keeping to a tight storyline, one episode follows the other; they story consists more of self-contained vignettes than a development of continuous drama.

One telling example reveals the power of the method. It is a love scene, the first encounter between the young and very handsome Barry Lyndon and his much less pretty niece. She is clearly attracted to him and defiantly initiates a game according to which he has to find the velvet ribbon hidden in her cleavage. The young man is timid if not reluctant, but she is insistent and forces him to play the game. With trembling hands and frequent flinching, he finally has to touch her, which leads to the inevitable kiss. Kubrick describes in long, minute details all the gestures, mimicry, and moods of this ambiguous encounter. The scene is endlessly slow and drawn out, as we have to follow all the invisible interior components of the erotic ambience. But precisely through this seemingly unjustified duration we understand the hero's character more than if we were shown so many duels and clashes on the domestic and real battlefield.

The slow treatment of the truly modest event is basically disproportionate. However, in Kubrick's vision it plays a crucial role and deserves our attention. Also, technically, the use of slow reversed zooms enlarges the field of vision and brings us even closer to the experience of the characters.

Narration plays an important role as well. It changes from the first person to the third; and also, foretelling the hero's tale, the author advances, with unassailable and conscious strategy, an ironic stance that creates detachment. The commentary sets the events within the confines of fatality, never without the wryness of an ambiguous rhetoric.

Classical, popular, "sweet" romantic music accompanies the rich events. Schubert and Handel cannot be taken literally for what they represent. Here again is a paradox; the mocking tone of interpretation interferes.

Since this story does not depend upon surprise, it is not the "what" but the "how" that sustains our interest. While foregoing surprise, the film creates suspense, in other words, prolonged time and rhythm that are deliberately held back.

Orchestration

When weighing the merits and drawbacks of fast or slow narration, we actually want to see whether a happy balance has been achieved through the use of varied solutions, whether these serve the creation of an expressive flow. The problem is that in the expressive language of film the articulation of movement takes place on many levels. It is primarily human action and the characters' everyday existence that comes to life on the screen, but the shifting scenes of the natural environment and objects, the dynamics of light and shadow, the importance of color, music, and other elements contribute to a more complex combination.

Here I would only refer to Fassbinder's ambitious work, *Berlin Alexanderplatz* (1980). In an interview, the director attributes to the main character, the former delivery man, pimp, killer, and thief Biberkopf, "a subconscious . . . coupled with staggering imagination and the ability to suffer that raise him above the most notable characters in world literature." The director tried to tell the story "only as part of an apparently inscrutable mythology," following the structure and inspiration of the novel that was deeply affected by the "rattle of elevated trains, the sounds of a metropolis . . . its peculiar rhythms and constant rush back and forth."[2] Eventually, the film found its authentic form in the application of collage. Fassbinder was primarily preoccupied by an interior world raging just beneath the surface, which he presented as an imprint of the "psychosis" of urban existence. "To live in the city," Fassbinder says, "means that your attention is constantly shifting as it dis-

Rainer Werner Fassbinder, *Berlin Alexanderplatz,* 1980

tinguishes among sounds, images and movement. And thus, the tools of selected narrative particles shift accordingly, not unlike the attention of the city dweller, without either the inhabitant or the narrative losing its position as a focal point."[3]

The film is characterized by disconnected sequences, rhapsodic emotional and mood shifts, a rift between the interior and the exterior worlds, between reality and appearance. "Collage" is an apt descriptive term here because, in addition to fragmentation, it refers to an organizing principle where the component parts of distinct particles, sounds, images, and movements are thrown together in a heap that eventually jell into a structured whole. In many respects this is an impossible film, which works through a bold poetic quality as Fassbinder depicts the "screaming murder headlines fit for tabloids" and the tackiness of dime novels together with the delicate sensitivity of the "awakened mind." He explores life's repulsive and teeming vortex with a slow and deliberate attention.

* * *

Time, duration may be defined as the asymmetric vibration of quality and quantity. Lingering cannot be explained by rational causes. Exhaustion and recovery, idleness, slackening and agitation are all ubiquitous impulses to maintain the adequate pace of "progress." This is what the Japanese filmmaker Kitano refers to when he talks about the relativity of time, when, along with showing the simultaneity of disparate lives, he draws attention to the distinct breathing and rhythm of his characters. Just like in music, he says, transition from one moment to the next is the most essential; it is what defines the spirit of a work.[4]

As we have seen, in this multilayered structure the visual force, the choreography of movement and the "straight" or deliberately "parenthetical" use of music define rhythm in equal measure. In more recent films (by Kubrick, Kaurismaki, or Wong Kar-wai) we often delight in the provocative presence of musical interpretation and its paradoxical reversal, which casts the work in the peculiar light of ambiguity. We are dealing with an orchestra where the play and presence of instruments create harmony or its absence, a form of indispensable dissonance.

There is an inverse relationship between unity, fullness, and psychologically perceived content. The denser the content the shorter its apparent duration, while a scene stripped of content appears to last forever. Even if meticulous in the extreme, details that truly engage also fascinate us. This makes us forget the long hours spent before the projection screen as we are drawn in by the subtle play of microscopic layers.

Tsai Ming-liang, *The Hole,* 1998

4   Detours

The Contingent and the "Accidental"
The Workings of Imagination: Fantasy
Insidious Memories
Dreams and Daydreaming
Flash Forward

There is no perceptible development without insertion, without the introduction of "foreign" material. The narrative flow assumes the multiplicity of component parts: the status quo is disturbed by a new quality that obviously exists in a different temporal dimension. In other words, speed accentuates its own rhythm through detours and deceleration. Obstacles are thrown into the smooth current of rational, logical, or even emotional continuity and their accumulation brings the abundance and opening of new opportunities.

The Contingent and the "Accidental"

What is polyphony, discussed above, if not this very multiplicity of components? The horizontal march of the present is bisected vertically by unexpected events, foreign textures, and fresh intensity, which open a gap that allows free excursions and creates a strategy for becoming engaged and immersed in extraneous detail. As Bachelard says: only plurality is capable of creating temporal duration; homogeneous development never carries the promise of progress.[1] The evolution of plurality is as polymorphous as the elaboration of a melody. Causality itself is born only through discontinuity. Cause and effect have tissues of different quality and the web of causes is also often tangled, knotted.

It is well known that prominent modernists frequently applied detours. Is it not this narrative style and structure in Michelangelo Antonioni's elegant films that we enjoy so much? His film *L'Avventura (The Adventure)* is not about the eruption of a dramatic episode into ordinary life (the disappearance of one of the main characters) but a series of contingent, incidental, frivolous escapades and digressions. *Ad-venire,* as the Latins say, is the root for *avventura* in modern Italian: something unknown that is bound to come. In Antonioni's great films, the viewer is seized by the effortless freedom of perception that ignores the canonized rules of storytelling and observes and documents nonessential, minor incidents with a detached gaze. In *La notte,* the camera watches Jeanne Moreau's pensive curiosity, with the same wonder that she expresses as she runs her fingers along wall cracks, the competition of excited boys when they shoot off their firecrackers, or the scene in *Red Desert* where Monica Vitti meets striking workers and takes a hungry bite from a man's sandwich, and later marvels at a boat slipping past a seashore cabin—all *significant* digressions with meanings as important as any major scene. Similarly, one of the most magical episodes in Fellini's *Amarcord* is when, in a mythic fog, the startled small boy enveloped in his cloak and hood unexpectedly encounters an ox that disappears into nothingness as suddenly as it has materialized. What we see is "extraneous matter," useless, with no connection to the subject of the film, but it is precisely this aside, the gaze turned away from more central occurrences (such as the grandfather in *Amarcord* getting lost in front of his own house) that creates a meaningful, rich aura. We slow down, almost coming to a standstill, as it were, allowing time to experience awe, suspenseful expectation, and even anxiety.

It may also be useful to look at a more contemporary example, the Coen brothers' *Fargo*. Here we see a series of deliberate and playfully cunning digressions that create a blend of relativizing irony, insight, and the more conventional horror story. Before the bloodiest, most engrossing scenes there is always time to "make a stop," to pause, to suspend time before the gory scenes, which blow over in a few seconds. The main character, the criminal head of the family, is somewhat slow-witted, always missing the beat. Or consider the hired hostage-takers and assassins, who perform their jobs at an extremely leisurely pace. When they get some whores, they are in no rush and go through the motions with mechanical indolence. Thus these "ancillary" scenes, when the characters simply sit around in bars or stare at the television, become the most chilling source of deadpan humor. In this context it is self-evident that law enforcement organizations conduct criminal investigations with patience, and without much sign of excitement. Our heroine, the pregnant female police officer, is slowed in her movement by her bulging belly. And, while she displays compelling mental prowess as all her observations and gestures hit the target, during her visit to the crime scene she has time to chat with her former classmate and listen to his litany of sob stories. In other scenes as well, she has the energy and curiosity to discuss the weather, family stories, kids, and so on. Nobody is in a rush. On the contrary, leisureliness thus becomes a principle of style and an excellent tool of comedy. The clever inversion of clichés sends a mocking message. The larger the gap between the presented horror and the attitude of those involved, the more striking the absurdity of it all. The deliberate and leisurely retention of tempo is the key to this treatment.

Digressions or detours may have different natures. They can be more or less organic in the way they "intrude" into the narrative, being an unexpected distraction in the flow of the events. Of course, this may not be motivated by caprice or mere whim. A sudden departure or turn from standard time/space relations must be supported by specific internal or external inspiration. Both motivations, the direct challenge presented by the ongoing actions or a personal impulse demanding its own expression, that is, an interruption, create a new rhythm of attention that requires its own duration in time.

Needless to say, the two phenomena cannot be set up against each other dogmatically. In most cases the progress of a character is deflected from its original, "standard" path and drifts into alien territory with the surfacing of a new, tangible factor (such as an object, the unexpected appearance of a person, a change in the natural environment). Or, not entirely free from these external influences, the protagonist is forced to turn inward. For instance, at the urging of suddenly surging memories and associations a story can take an unexpected turn, and the protagonist is led to a path of action whose direction is not immediately revealed. Consequently, the shifting storyline and its ramifications restructure the continuity of the entire plot.

At the first level of departure, the treatment of the character's inner state of mind is not essential. It is enough if we are shown the peculiarity, the unfamiliar quality of a life situation, and even unseen we immediately perceive the potential consequences of such weirdness.

In Ingmar Bergman's *Silence* (1963), a boy wandering through the corridors of a hotel encounters a dwarf. We are not surprised when we see him following the dwarf, driven by his curiosity. Then in a remote hotel suite, he meets a dozen dwarves, members of a circus troupe. As we watch with the boy and spend some time in their company, we enjoy their fun and games and their amusing world. From the point of the story's logic, is this detour necessary at all? Obviously not. The exotic sights and antics of these figures are in stark contrast to the gloomy and tense atmosphere in which the drama unfolds. Yet, Bergman is not sparing of lengthy, self-contained details, depicting their activities. The scene seems to remain an independent unit, as if detached from the story, and Bergman doesn't force his camera to maintain the point of view of the child. Is the episode a counterpoint, a metaphor, or simply a hyperbole? It can be interpreted in a number of ways. One thing is certain, however: the digression takes us to another plane and Bergman is not loath to open a crack in the film's otherwise firmly structured timeframe.

The truth is that while the arbitrariness of the episode is undeniable, we still sense a subtle correlation. For so-called ramifications are usually introduced when at critical junctions accumulated tension demands a transition, an open space to create new order. In this instance it is the boy's unbearable loneliness and boredom that cries out for some kind of miracle. His attention could be drawn by anything. For instance, he cannot help but watch in rapt attention as the old waiter has his dinner. However, the dwarf scene goes beyond that as it develops into a full episode and Bergman's freestyle narrative treatment affords sensitive "phrasing." The camera's somnambulistic glide as it follows the boy's ramble through the corridors sensuously builds up the legitimacy of the subsequent scenes. In this context the dwarf scene is also about the boy (but not exclusively, not aggressively) and in this ambivalence the meaning of the insert gains substance. It becomes yet another layer that underscores the entire film's nightmarish tonality.

In Aki Kaurismaki's sarcastic films, which apparently follow a more ordered structure, the flow is frequently interrupted by unexpected violence that brutally ruptures the quietly unfolding narrative. These digressions seem to be more like *deviations,* which turn the path toward another track. Already in *Ariel* (1988), in one of the early scenes the protagonist "accidentally' collides with the members of a gang that robbed him, and naturally he is the one who gets in trouble and is thrown in jail, which immediately steers the story on a different track. The bifurcation occurs at the height of instability, when everything seems to work against him, or rather when there is but a glimmer of hope for something better. Consequently, the decisive change caused by the chance encounter, the new direction his destiny takes, is radical. And yet, instead of switching to a higher gear, the narrative flow maintains its measured, steady though winding progress.

In *Man without a Past* (2002), the consequences of suddenly arising violence take a similar turn. The protagonist, who suffers from amnesia, unwittingly becomes a witness to a bank robbery as he tries to open a bank account. The experience sets off a course of events: he becomes a hostage, receives threats, lands in the police station, and suffers through a lengthy ordeal in the courts with numerous hilarious twists and turns, followed by another accidental encounter that hands him an odd chore. The succession of all these complicated developments is about the function of random adventures. These have no organic connection to the protagonist's ordinary life, but reveal more and more sang-froid and indifference on the part of our hero—it demonstrates his genuine character through mere chance, through his passivity. Thus with all its autonomy the digression, while it appears to emerge from nowhere and for moments introduces even new characters willy-nilly, becomes an integral part of the story.

The other form of deviation or pause could be described as an *insert,* whose greatest master is undoubtedly the Japanese director Yasujiro Ozu. His films are replete with solutions that treat enigmatic situations and objects, with no direct reference to the main theme, yet create the impression of an organic whole. Whether working with a steady camera or a tracking shot, he invariably evokes a searching, contemplative mood suggesting a sense of unity. In *Early Spring* (1956) and *End of Summer* (1961) he first guides the viewer through the simple layout of a house and living quarters, or the atmosphere of a beach seen through the lens of a stationary camera, as if he wished to present a musical intonation for these films without loading details with the weighty luggage of metaphor.

But he provides the finest and most endearing gesture in his film, *An Autumn Afternoon* (1962). The modest story, recounting the efforts of a widowed father to marry off his daughter, is constantly interrupted by inserts: images of interior and exterior spatial markers, the narrow streets of Tokyo, new residential blocks, the flashing neon lights of recently Americanized bars, or the rhythm of opening and closing doors flickering by. These insertions are not for the simple purpose of setting up a scene or serving the usual role of introducing dramatis personae. The images become the expression of a broader ironic vision, placing phenomena in a sometimes boundless, sometimes historic perspective. Is this the way we live, Ozu wonders, in this slowly swelling current that tastes of and adapts to the dictates of the latest fashion, where old customs are eroded imperceptibly, insidiously by what is "modern." Smokestacks painted in vibrant colors, whiskey that gradually replaces sake, the vacuum cleaner and the refrigerator as the epitome of all our dreams, the clacking of high-heeled shoes to the rhythm of American bar music: a thousand sundry details and objects weave the story's texture with frequent and persistent interruptions. All are presented with the quiet contemplation of tender attention granted in equal measure to each fragment.

In the finalé, the old man's real or imaginary visit to his married daughter's room exudes the same poetic wisdom, as if the camera wished to bid farewell to each object, taking leave of from an entire way of life suffused with so much passion. However, these images establish their autonomy and liberate themselves from the original story. This is what lends them a deep sense of melancholy. What strikes us as unusual is that, while minor scenes are "not motivated," that is, their presence is not justified by any causal necessity, they are far from arbitrary. These insightful characterizations that deliberately avoid human presence appear to serve no other purpose than to measure time and its relentless passage. In these scenes we experience the stillness of meditation, as they become symbols of the ephemeral. Their "emptiness" is the message, as contemplation explores nothingness itself with a groping and tender serenity.

One cannot leave this subject without mentioning the great omission of the film, arguably one of the most exquisite ellipses in the entire history of filmmaking. Ozu simply fails to bring to the screen the central figure of the narrative, the proposed husband. We are led to understand that the marriage arranged by the families eventually takes place and as the person of the bridegroom is of the least interest in this case, we are not burdened with this detail. It is all the more fitting that we watch traditional ritual as the bride, assisted by three women, prepares to leave the house in her stunning kimono and headdress, to abandon her parents' home forever in the company of two awkward fiber trunks. This gaping hole, this obvious void in the middle of a narrative told in such rich detail, illustrates Ozu's magnificent and bold sensibility as he finds the balance between the essential and the incidental, and decides when to linger and when to place a stress.

Interestingly enough, ellipsis can be a wonderful trigger to "jump" to new or amazing paths, bringing about freshness and astonishment, satisfying the spectator's hunger for enjoying surprise.

The Workings of Imagination: Fantasy

Tsai Ming-liang's acclaimed and stridently stylized *The Hole* (1998) evokes an exalted, eerie quality generated by frequently recurring detours. The film's narrative unfolds amidst an unceasing and apocalyptic rush of water. This unstoppable deluge must be endured, though it is more unyielding than the epic floods of the Bible, and it comes to dominate all other aspects of life, bringing forth a new, all-pervasive form of existence. In a stunning inspiration, Ming-liang expresses his heroine's rebellion against her miserable physical condition through the wildest contrast to her tawdry dreamland. With the wild swirl of classic, though stale, musical numbers and blaring hit songs, he demolishes the wall of catastrophic emptiness by invoking the corny yet wonderful and effective world of imagination and dreams. Suddenly—in the midst of peeling and rotting wallpaper, in a setting of opening and closing elevator doors, various cables and befouled hallways—our frail and soaked heroine acts out and becomes one with the rich panoply of cabaret props as she enjoys the charms of the beguiling music. She bursts into song, imitating her idols, kicks up her legs, and sways her hips as she dances, dressed up in flimsy sequined gowns, finally letting go for a few seconds. Obviously, all this splendid performance remains in the realm of make-believe, for in reality she must hold a green plastic bowl over her head to protect her drenched body while she pees. However, the final scene in this fool's paradise leads to new heights. The boy living upstairs lifts the girl up through the gaping *hole* between the two apartments, the last opening for human contact, and she, in her gorgeous red dress, is swept up in a most tender dance into the arms of her prince, who is dressed in a white tuxedo.

The contrast between the two life qualities could not be wider. The musical interludes, loud and playful, remain ironic "cadences" only to raise the pitch of desire under this blinding spell.

Of course, imagination does not always lead to the realm of desires. The bleakness of ordinary days is not relieved by the soothing escape of daydreaming alone. The pathologies of nightmares, phobias, and paranoid delusions are perhaps more common when protagonists come face to face with terror and lose their equilibrium reading real or misinterpreted signals.

Roman Polanski is wont to operate with this terrifying, nightmarish material when his characters suffer from hallucinatory sounds and visions (*Repulsion*, 1965). However, his excellent film *The Tenant*

(1976) is the most telling example of playing with horror and sarcasm. The outcast, a fumbling minor clerk, played by Polanski himself, rents an apartment whose previous tenant committed suicide by jumping from the window. Besides an all-encompassing sense of dread, the chilling story and the setting gradually take power over him; through a bizarre process the clerk comes to identify with the unknown former tenant. Gradually, the inherited belongings start to exercise an irresistible pull. The clerk not only imagines himself stepping into his predecessor's place, but is forced to change his personality as well: he starts to paint his nails, puts on her dresses, and eventually resorts to a wig and makeup to take over her role. He falls in a vertiginous spiral of imagination and is pulled deeper and deeper by a death wish and the desire to repeat the final gesture. He meets his destiny: he steps out of the same window and dies on the building's recently rebuilt glass roof.

However, Polanski would not be himself if he were satisfied with this straightforward plot. The absurdly grotesque scene and its overtones are at least as essential as the unfolding events. He piles up a host of signals and deliberately ambiguous markers before the impossible denouement. But these will still not satisfy his need for mordant humor. As the first plunge is haplessly bungled, the scene is repeated, lending the twisted story its morbid sense of humor. Deliberately and methodically each obligatory cliché of the genre is lined up, as if placed in parentheses: knocks at the door, terrifying darkness, the sound of unidentified steps, the "fortuitous" accidents and experiments in search of death, and so on. His immediate environment, whether imagined or real, is depicted in a highly stylized caricature. The nasty-looking neighbors are hostile, spy on him, and make mysterious denunciations. Paranoid fear and confusion turn him into a "femme fatale": the enjoyment of his new role and the simultaneous vision of that frivolous window drive him to the wildest hallucinations. He fights phantoms, suffers injuries, and feels threatened. However, when he finally makes the first suicidal attempt, his imagination is filled with the image of a huge theater auditorium, an appropriate setting for the final act. Here, the contrast—between the "tragic" salto mortale of the pathetic little man wearing a dress and a wig and the once hostile environment that welcomes him with a thunderous applause of adulation for the first time in his life—is even more striking. But this too is just fantasy, because he does not manage to kill himself. Eventually, resorting to the most bizarre solution, Polanski climbs to the floor through a beautifully filmed stairway to end his life in the most trivial and ridiculous way on the second attempt.

Among the contemporary filmmakers of ambiguity David Lynch is the most outstanding and enigmatic. In his *Mullholland Drive* (2001), the deliberately misleading clues and nightmarish, playful, and disturbing elements blend is such a weird way that even by the ending we are not sure what the real core of the film is supposed to be. Originally planned as a twelve-part TV miniseries, the final piece is one potential version of the realized fragments. Lynch, being an inveterate gambler, has chosen to maintain the puzzling aspect of each episode: are these real or fantasy scenes, dreams or imagination? Are we victims of the heroine's amnesia, or are we just submitted to an unknown gap, due to the missing parts? We can never know which "card" is part of trickstering and to what extent the irregularity is essential for the play. The constant changes of the points of view (whose gaze, whose angle do we follow?) lead inevitably to a half-serious, ironic, topsy-turvy melodrama, in which the only permanence is the anguishing horror. For Lynch this horror is the malicious (or just playful?) adventure of smashing to pieces the much too rational universe. Contradictions are there for themselves, the terrifying meets with the naïve and tender, the evil with the ridiculous. Therefore there is room for everything: from the pornographic to the pathological, from the mocking kitsch to the fantastically theatrical. Lynch's storytelling is like a children's game: cruel, monstrous, and marvelous in a virtuosic way.

Mullholland Drive is an actual location in Los Angeles where truly anything can happen, since crime and violence are natural occurrences there. The mysterious darkness, the even more mysterious lights, the fast-running cars may hide ghastly secrets. We are taken on this roller coaster ride, pushed by abrupt rhythmical extremes from the vertiginous to the hauntingly slow, to experience the menacing ambience of the overgrown metropolis.

Insidious Memories

"Cinema is secret games, souvenirs and dreams," Bergman says. "A lit face, suddenly violent—a hand reaching in a gesture, an open space at dusk and some people sitting around eating apple biscuits. . . . This lit face, this hand reaching in a gesture that seems to convey magic, the old women at their places and the few words without meaning: they are caught in my net like glittering fish."[2] Memories, bizarre details that colonize the mind and create their peculiar, seemingly unrelated lives may become the indispensable components of any authentic narration; even if their presence disturbs and defines the rhythm and entire direction of the film.

"There is some mysterious connection between slowness and memory, haste and forgetting," Kundera says. "In existential mathematics the relationship is expressed in a set of simple equations: the rate of slow progress is in direct proportion to the intensity of recollection, the rate of speed with the intensity of oblivion. Giving definite shape to content is not simply a matter of aesthetics, but of memory as well. For, whatever lacks form also remains inaccessible to memory."[3]

To evoke a great film: we can find telling examples to support these thoughts. Marker says in the narration of *La Jetée* (1962): "Nothing distinguishes memory from other moments: they become recognized only later through their injuries."

The remarks quoted above serve as points of departure for my argument: only traces, imprint-fragments, if not wounds and scars, can say anything about the past. The experience that left its mark is fragmentary and incomplete by definition, lodged in the mind in a distorted form and affected by our prevailing emotional state. And yet, it is precisely this fragmented and transmuted recollection that lends form and meaning to the past.

When it comes to evoking the past, one may take a closer look at the two classic examples of the history of cinema, Alain Resnais's *Hiroshima, mon amour* (1959) and Chris Marker's *La Jetée* (1962). While these well-known films are often cited as examples of nonlinear storytelling, analytical essays rarely treat their aspect central to my topic. Both films have a lot to say about the complex and tormented work of remembering. But that is not all. They also demonstrate how chance stimuli (where and when a memory is stirred), external challenges (associations tied to a concrete object or event), and, finally, the overlapping web of personal, traumatic wounds'reveal with palpable accuracy the intricate nature of the process. I must reemphasize that we are not talking about conjuring the spirits, but instead considering a treatment of the entire *process*. And this is what makes both films exemplary.

The apparently unmotivated, mysterious surfacing of memory-images, and their gradual, usually deferred elucidation is *Hiroshima*'s most astounding aspect. In this context, treatment must take an elliptical form. One can never forget the first association of rhyming images disturbing the elegiac mood of the present: the superimposed hands of two different men. This is the flashing "response" exchanged between the Japanese man's hand lying in bed and another hand, that of another man, a German soldier, as we realize much later. With inimitable precision, Resnais illustrates that memories return only under appropriate circumstances, a singular constellation, and it is this distinct moment that lends meaning and duration to their emergence.

The intimacy between the two lovers is rendered with tact

and lyricism. Emanuelle Riva gets up and looks back at the sleeping man from the balcony door when suddenly a shadow flickers
across her face. Then, for a moment lasting less than a second,
a strange, fragmentary image shatters the scene. This image replaces the hand of the man lying in bed with an image that shows
an upturned palm. The brief reference in the dialogue to a memory from the war occurs only about twenty minutes later. "Was
your lover during the war French?" "No, he was not French," the
woman responds, as the silhouette of a soldier emerges on the
opaque windowpane. The two scenes are linked by music, as Riva
continues. "Yes, it was in Nevers."

This is followed by a more detailed but far from chronologi-
cally arranged series of images, showing a young girl riding a bicycle in bright sunshine, then at dusk on a forest path between
trees. Her date with a German soldier is followed with tracking
shots; then, after a short fade-out, we see a distant view of a wide
field before returning to the present, when the story is continued
by facts related in snippets of conversation.

Throughout, the film operates with this finely tuned structure:
a series of interruptions, detours, counterpoint, anticipated rev-
elations, and withheld information commingle, while the story
unfolding in the present moves forward at a snail's pace, making
the pain of discovery and self-reflection all the more apparent.
The device offers the viewer freedom of choice and acts as a tool
in the search for emotional identification. As Resnais says, "To
make room for the free play of imagination around, behind and
even inside the image, while the screen can work its own magic
. . . to provoke a shift of perspective in the viewer, a slight and
remote change."[4]

The horror of the memory of war, its open wound and the
brutality that followed, is given dramatic effect precisely by the
intimacy and slow development of the enfolding relationship.
The impassive flow of the river, the mysterious play of lights, and

the lyricism of music work with the power of contrast as, carefully gazing through the café window, we witness the absurdity of it all. The presence of the past is so overpowering that it primes the imagination of the Japanese man and the French woman for total personal identification. This is how Hiroshima and Nevers are allowed to merge, the surface of the quietly surging water nearby (a river in Japan) and the distant Loire into a single, inseparable unity.

In contrast to this lyrical confluence of present/past/future, Resnais's other, less recognized work *Muriel* (1963) depicts yet another aspect of retracing memory. We see agitated, fragmented, and incomplete flashes that strike unexpectedly and invade the day's routines. However, these unprocessed bits of memory are always doomed to be broken up and rejected. Each character tries to carry on a "normal" life under the weight of bruising and repressed memories, while the past buried alive is in constant ferment, ripping up the texture of the present. The film is a series of interruptions as it follows the exhausted protagonists groping in an undefined temporal space: the overwhelming burden of two wars, for the older characters the traumas of World War II, for the young man the haunting memory of complicity in murder during the Algerian war—all lead to a violent crisis of conscience. The narrative's neurotic rhythm, often inscrutable references, unexpected outbursts, and the rush of imagined or real events broken to shards maintain the work's tension.

Marker's famous film also shakes us with the unsettling experience of fragmentation. In *La Jetée* (1961) there is no logic demonstrating cause and effect relationships. The recovery of a buried past is a daunting task without the promise of early rewards.

And here we need to introduce a note of explanation. There is a world of difference between spontaneous recollection and the act of remembering. If the first is unintentional and is due to the function of an all but aggressive subconscious mind, the other is

Chris Marker, *La Jetée,* 1962

a deliberate attempt to recapture the past, which, however, is far from guaranteeing the accuracy of the recalled image. Repression has worked and continues to work in both cases, resulting in fragmentation, partial truths, and inevitable distortions.

In short, *La Jetée* is about the obsessive nature of reminiscence. "The film is the story of a man marked by childhood memory. The shocking experience takes aggressive hold and its meaning is only revealed much later, a few years before the start of the Third World War on the Orly airport's vast runway."[5] As an invocation of a large epic work intimating fateful adventures to come, the film is set on its course with these words. It portends grievous troubles without offering a key to the mystery.

The story of *La Jetée* is admittedly about Time: since, according to the science fiction setting, the boundaries of space have been confined, the goal is to send an emissary through time and evoke the past and the future to rescue the present.

The journey into the past unfolds slowly and haltingly, with the lyricism of a yearning love. Our hero must expend enormous effort to conjure up an encounter with the "other," the "obscure object of his desire." The repeated attempts simultaneously illustrate the labor of reminiscing—to recapture memory traces—but also accurately describe the drama of human rapprochement and attempts at making contact. Are these memory traces or mere magic, the viewer wonders, as another effort appears on the screen.

The film suggests that the struggle, the effort to leave the confines of time and space is a fight for survival. Man's self-liberation amounts to waging war against time, an attempted break from the prison of time, and each transcendental victory of imagination, love, or learning is ephemeral by definition. We cannot escape time's advance toward death even if the images of consciousness, piled up in the museum of accumulated knowledge and experience, appear as witnesses of a paradoxical victory over time. This recognition, at once a realization of our limitations and an active process, is an incessant effort to attack the infinite boundaries to the very end. *La Jetée* covers both aspects of the struggle.

Marker depicts a poignantly authentic journey (time travel), perhaps the most relevant for the topic under discussion. Stops along the road modify the course without apparent motive or reason. Even if we accept that the work of remembering is the result of deliberate operation, man has absolutely no power to define or influence its development. The latent forces of desire and inhibition are at work here. Obeying unknown impulses, obstacles constantly undermine the potential for evocation by demanding space for a host of random details. The emergence or sudden vanishing of recalled images is not motivated by rational or at least manifestly cause-and-effect relationships. Thus in the adventure of remembering, not only the "when," but also the "what" of conjured memories appear to be wholly arbitrary. From the point of narration this leads to a fluctuation of breaks, timorous endeavors, and resumed efforts that follow an erratic order.

In the course of his imaginary journey, the protagonist finds himself in some fascinating moments of times past. One discovers a gradual progression in this archaeological discovery. The first image is an almost idyllic landscape with grazing animals, then suddenly we are in a "real," modest bedroom from the prewar years, with light entering through the window and an unmade bed. And even more: "real" children, "real" pigeons, "real" cats, and a cemetery with "real" tombstones appear. Then the mysterious airport, the Jetee, is seen, but differently—at this time completely empty. Later, suddenly, a young woman appears, but another one—not the one pursued. Then more landscape and ruins, when finally the real woman is found whom he had seen back then and whose imprinted memory became the focal point of the entire undertaking. Yet all effort to hold on to her presence, following her in various situations (in a car, with indifference), is in vain; the figure will not surrender again. The series of unfamiliar, trivial image fragments continues: statues, torsos—like in a museum. Whose museum? Could it be the stone collection of his memories? The series of images in this film of reminiscence is an exceptional representation of the dynamics of imagination. Its rules are revealed in the repeated attempts at "trial and error." How many experiments are needed to hit the focal point, the target? There is no definite, direct strike without search and failure.

Let us recall that the journey is primarily not motivated by personal desire but external bidding. Our hero, a man "blessed with exceptional sensibilities" and marked by an indelible memory, is destined to become the emissary of time. Scientists can merely launch him into time, as it were, while he, endowed with the faculty of a creative mind, may return with a bounty.

However, repeated attempts to set off on the journey, painful and requiring extreme concentration, are never guaranteed a successful outcome. The road is full of deceptive digressions. In the strange world where he lands he is overwhelmed by an inconceivable abundance: his vision is attracted by a panoply of objects, glass and plastic wonders. We enter a different time zone. The experience turns out to be anything but a pleasant excursion. At times he collapses, cannot go on. As if overwhelmed by a different time wave, he needs a shot of energy to resume the race.

Marker illustrates the real intricacy of time. The film demonstrates the complexity of temporal perception by letting the intrinsically silent images of the past move together with the sounds of another time, that of the actual present: the fragmented, whispered instructions and commands of the experimenters can be heard now and then. We wander simultaneously in two distinct time zones. All this becomes extremely important because it suggests that the act of remembering is fundamentally surreal: it never gains material substance, never becomes tangible reality, and inevitably leads to suffering, while its meager results must be paid for by our hero. For, in this case, remembering takes place under duress that only raises the stake of the enterprise. And this is where Marker creates the multiple layers referred to above: the ephemeral nature of the traumatically personal (recaptured intimacy in its original form and place) and later the externally guided return/reliving (then departure). The external intervention is violent, and the subsequent loss and final demise are inevitable.

The film is exquisitely subtle in its structure and tempo as it brings the tragic adventure to light. We share the emotional tension of love in the rhythm, the increased fragmentation and the flickering of gradually shorter and shorter images (we must not forget that Marker applies a unique form, the continuous flow of stills and "frozen shots" in this unique foto-roman), but also, in a reversal, in extreme slow motion as we follow the pair on their leisurely visit to a museum of natural history, in the last moments of their relationship, playing for time, powerless. Their meandering through the corridors of the museum and among its artifacts is painfully protracted. With good reason however: their happiness and the anguish of a presumably unintended farewell demands a different cadence.

Borges's famous metaphysical short story, *The Circular Ruins,* comes to mind. It speaks of nothing less than the suffocating power of a dream: creating an entire world without having full control over our creations. As in a play of the imagination, human figures and actions are the children of dreams or memory—they do and do not exist. But once they assume flesh and blood and escape, like the genie from the bottle, they start to live their own life and we have little control over their future. Our powerlessness in the face of this mystery is the only solid, stubborn truth. The closing circle illustrates the fatal limitation of our knowledge and the relativity of freedom: the dreamer turns out to be dreamed, the pursuer is pursued. As it is expressed in Borges's classical closure: "With relief, with humiliation, with terror, he realized that he, too, was but appearance, that another man was dreaming him."[6]

Marker also talks about time's simultaneous limitations and flexibility. While time is finite for mortals, it may be stretched and reshaped, its borders skillfully dodged. Imagination and memory may deceive the laws of time's linear passage, canceling the absolute hold of the principles of before and after, past and future. However, this game has its constraints. According to the metaphor of *La Jetée,* imagination may take off from the runway, but what it manages to accumulate in the recesses of deep consciousness becomes similar to the artifacts displayed in museums: imprints, torsos, and fragments. We realize that the ruins are surrounded by walls with no exit from this enclosed space.

Memory is a land of contrasts, Marker says. The series of recalled images suspended in time becomes stationary and moving at once, as if the images continued their march simultaneously. In addition to the immediate metaphor offered by the film's title, *La Jetée* relies on the expressive power of another image as well: the recurring vision of ruins, torsos, and the frozen, lifeless collection of a museum. If the first evokes the sensation of Icarus's adventure, the attempt to conquer time and space, the ruins bespeak of time's victory over the creations of man, they reveal their path of destruction. The contrast and unresolved conflict of the two major themes summarizes the film's essence. The time allotted to us can be expanded and we can outwit its boundaries with the help of memory and imagination. And it is precisely this journey through malleable space that lends time its human dimension.

If there is a film in which memory, fantasy, and dreams are blended into one homogeneous whole, Tarkovsky's *Mirror* is the best example. It is, of course, justified by the admitted autobiographical inspiration, according to which the author-hero evokes in a half-dreaming, half-sober state the currents of childhood traumas, mysterious memory-fragments and moments of strong reminiscences as they have been stored in his mind. A nostalgic river of recurring and blurred images, snatches of poetic-picturesque turns of mind, natural phenomena and real actions flows before our eyes. Scars and solitude, the sorrow of an incomprehensible abandonment, color the darkish, deep-brown images, foreboding wind and rain. Something is always broken, rolls away, is ravaged by fire then suddenly burns out. The young mother in the center is constantly running, escaping, and disturbed of remorse, hurt and irritated, as if searching for some solace in an unfathomable power. The kid, appearing at two different ages, three and nine or so, apparently identifies entirely with her.

The process doesn't know any order. Time is indivisible. Distant and further past events align with black and white war footage. Among the coherent or incoherent encounters and separations there is no recognizable rationale or associative connection.

The intensity of the stream resembles only a kind of musical development. Indeed, this development characterizes mostly the nature of dreams: the alternation of irregular changes between different places and times, jumps from mysterious locations to unknown faces, labyrinthic corridors, and mystical forests soaked in rain. There is no way, and of course no intention either, to put together the contradictory or rhyming details: they are much more the manifold enlightening of a grievous state of mind, the play of the crystal nature of memory-time, using the expression of Deleuze.

If Chris Marker and Alain Resnais stressed the painful work of remembering, and therefore alluded to the capricious gradualism of the process, for Tarkovsky any analytical approach to the "dream work" wouldn't even occur. One undivided throbbing block maintains the duality of mourning and melancholy, for the two are inseparable to him. Each moment tells of the same thing: the suffering of bereavement and the melancholy of perishing, with the tone of inconsolable complaint, magnificently framing the experience into a mesmerizing artful form. The dimensions of time coalesce, longer or more ephemeral events mix rhapsodically: the gathering of a dropped bag's content, or a substantial argument about a child's destiny doesn't differ in any way, either in weight or in duration. Visiting an unknown woman; the silence of endless waiting; a frequent dialogue with a mirror; or the ritualistic washing and combing of the heroine's beautiful hair remain highlights of the film, characterized by the merciless precision and sharpness of memory images. And yet, the overwhelming feel is the unity of the film, for it has an unusually rich texture, ambience, and saturation with infinite amount of fragments. The music by Bach and Pergolesi is more than solemn, it is part of the sensuous, emotion-filled aura of the movie.

Tarkovsky builds up his work vertically. The layers are not spread out in time but in the depth of one single moment. The sometimes applied slow-motion emphasizes the same mystery: this is the time of the anguishing unknown, the suddenly falling and stopping rain, the abrupt interruption of an almost endless run.

The mirror is more than a simple metaphor, which once magically received everything to reflect it. The mirror is reality, too, which often served as a partner for dialogues, a witness that constrains to relive the scars maybe not fully cicatrified in order to bring to life the buried past.

Dreams and Daydreaming

Of course, memories and dreams belong to two different realms, although their interplay and correspondences are at least as significant as their differences. For both are fed by real stimuli and it is only the quality of the generated image and the chain of succession that show distinct characteristics.

Since the classic observations of Henri Bergson, Susanne Langer, and Jean Epstein, much has been said about the relationship of film and dreams. All analysts have recognized that in both cases images are transformed and tend to create symbolic meaning. Moreover, film and dreams alike are characterized by significant distortion and great sensual power that generate an unusual level of intensity. Langer observes that "the dreamer is always at the center of the dream . . . always there, so that his relation is equidistant from all events."[7] This observation is relevant for film as far as it lends the story's immediacy the power of direct authenticity.

As we turn to undisputed classics, Bergman and Fellini must take their place center stage. From *Wild Strawberries* (1957), *Persona* (1966), and *Cries and Whispers* (1973) to the self-confessional *8½*, it is obvious that these films are the incisively accurate representations of Freud's interpretation of dreams.

In these works we meet with the disquieting reality of dreams whose anguish differs from the pain conjured up by repressed memory-based imagination. As our heroes struggle with a peculiar form of unreality, tragedy spares them, even if the experience brings suffering, and their story becomes burdened with a sense of futility and humiliation.

In *Wild Strawberries,* the old man's dreams are textbook examples of seemingly bewildering Freudian anxiety dreams with strong references to the present, offering a dramatic illustration of inner conflicts. The story is not just about an old man (prominent in his profession, about to receive an award) being scolded by one of the teachers of his youth, but rather about the apparently random, fatal, and humiliating punishment meted out in a string of unmerciful blows. In Bergman's creative vision, all detail evokes death and the aura of a dreadful end: the clock without hands, the coach without its wheels, the coffin, light and shadow, the echoless silence. Their accumulated effect creates a correspondence among ostensibly diverging fragments. When a nail is driven through a hand, the brutal act is interpreted as an explicit sign of a hoped-for or deserved dreaded punishment. The symbol appears not only at the thematic level but also as part of the structure in the fluid rush and lapses of oneiric and violent transitions.

Wild Strawberries' other much-cited dreamlike conjuring of the past is the portrayal of the old man's return to the site of his earlier traumas and sins, establishing an inseparable bond between past and present. When the seventy-year-old actor Sjostrom appears unseen at a family get-together and witnesses his wife's unfaithfulness with the consciousness of an old man, we learn more about the disturbing and barely acknowledged laws of repression than we would from any verbal confession or a familiar visual presentation of flashback. The organic fusion of the two time planes is most revealing in its simplicity.

The opening image of *8½* is also an enigmatic, most telling dreamscape, where the director/protagonist struggles with his phantoms and demons. Hapless, he tries to escape from a dark tunnel in a traffic jam, surrounded by an army of creepy, infuriating characters, femme fatales and repulsive men, all threatening, overbearing creatures that he breathlessly tries to escape. The whole scene is oppressive and endlessly protracted, made only more chilling by the soundless rush of images, only occasionally disturbed by his desperate knocking on the window pane. But Fellini's fantasy cannot stop here. With a sudden jump, he yanks us from this suffocating darkness to celestial heights where—inexplicably and hilariously—he starts flying and catches sight of a riding man, his producer, who pulls him aggressively down to earth. We are to follow him, plunging through the air, in his large black hat and floating black coat.

The sudden change is staggering. Yet the panting of our protagonist in his hotel room on sweat-soaked pillows, as he reaches out his hand for help, suggests that this incongruous detail is an integral part of the previous scene, obeying the rules of disjointed dreams. On the border of sleep and awakening he apparently gets closer to his everyday worries and anxieties.

In connection to the use of dreams in film, we must note at least two traditional approaches: the insertion takes place either with or without a clear signal, a stressed punctuation. In the early history of film, neglecting warning signs was inconceivable: music, lap dissolves with close-ups, subtitles, and so on served as signposts to a transition. Today, these devices appear outdated. However, their omission brings new elements to create a fresh and exciting quality by erasing the line between the two worlds of reality and dreams. While the essence of the oneiric material differs from everyday empiricism, the question is precisely how psychologically revealing this alien body could be, despite its unlikely and yet betraying form.

Think of the shocking dream fragment when the image of the

director's presumably dead parents appears in front of an eerily long white cemetery wall and, amid a torrent of accusations and warnings, our protagonist is kissed on the mouth by the mother entering the scene in a veiled hat. Is this oedipal symbolism, childhood memory, or desire that disturbs awakening consciousness with its raw physicality? The phenomenon is manifold and it is precisely its elusiveness that marks the story of our hero.

The entire film thus becomes an entangled patchwork of reality and make-believe. Ravaged consciousness is dragged back and forth between the here-and-now and fantasy, daydreaming and a most lucid consciousness. All devastating, joyous, oneiric, and grotesque options are treated uniformly as concrete physical reality on the screen. This unusual homogeneity lends the film its unique character. *8½*, Fellini says, "(is) something between a muddled visit to a psychiatrist and an examination of a distorted conscience with Limbo as the setting." [8] The smoothness of transitions, the camera's floating buoyancy as it moves with such ease through time and space, the extreme contrast of black and white, similar to the peculiar counter-movement of the camera and the characters, all act to reinforce the film's vertiginous, dreamlike aspect. The spa scene, the procession of gorgeous women in white hats down an endless flight of stairs, preparations for and the proceedings of a meeting with the cardinal—the images waft by in the weightless space of fairyland. Wagner's music and the mysterious whispering voices, although creating different effects, lift the film to the same sublime level. We witness a series of wonders—in flesh and blood. And not only in the oft-quoted closing scene (white-dressed figures dancing in a circle, where the protagonist directs the festivity as a child), but constantly all through the film. The choreography of the fleeting images of childhood and the harem scene, with its once-beguiling women, plays on infinite possibilities with disarming humor and charm. However, this requires an inner serenity with an intimate knowledge of time's rhythm—the musical essence of a freely surging narrative.

If we are on the subject of the inexhaustible reserve of dreaming fantasy, we cannot go on without mentioning Fellini's *Amarcord*, a film that operates all through with this unique, freely roaming technique. Through unfolding scenes of the ecstatic, enraptured wait for REX the magic-ship, the teenage boys' swaying dance under softly falling snowflakes, or, back in the foggy landscape, the sudden disappearance of the old grandfather, the film tracks joyful passages of plenitude and undulating time. Practically all the scenes function as digressions. Some are hilarious, such as the boys' sinful "self-stimulation" in the rocking car or the prank to embarrass the teacher with the huge breasts; some are erotic, such as the mesmerized stare at Gradisca's red cap and swaying hips; and other scenes are sadly humiliating, as when the father is ridiculed with castor oil. Each episode leads in a different, distant direction with an abandon that only recognizes inner time, the prerogative of the magician alone.

"I am deeply attracted to everything that offers man a more generous scale, in fact anything with more mystery and anguish; in any case, something that is neither soothing nor comforting. I prefer vast space whose edges are lost in the haze to small, well-lit structures held captive within massive walls."[9]

Fellini conjures up phantoms, his own mythical memories with the poetic extension of entranced freedom. His unfettered imagination sails to the vertiginous depths of dreams. *And the Ship Sails On* is the title of one of his films. And indeed, the fierce and the grotesque, the tragic and the tender all float together with the natural abandon and blessed acceptance of risk, of rise and fall.

Flash Forward

Detour/digression has another, less frequently applied form: the projection, hinting of minor details that will jell only much later, if at all. Compared to the flashback, the flashforward is more rarely used, although it may yield remarkable results. In Francis Ford Coppola's *The Conversation* (1974), the paranoid private eye, played by Gene Hackman, surrounds himself with a few odd objects in his cheerless apartment. Among them is a saxophone whose special function is revealed only toward the end of the film, when, after the protagonist makes the hysterical connection between his persecution and his inability to do anything about it, he turns his back to the real world and starts to play the instrument in the middle of his completely trashed apartment. Up to that point the occasionally seen trivial object was ignored as a useless prop, but its presentation was necessary for its subsequent dramatic "promotion," when it emerged as the symbol of his revolt and a frenzied and lonely protest.

Jane Campion's *Sweetie* starts with shots of a mysterious garden, the close-up of a tree trunk and fallen leaves. We have little understanding of the sequence's full meaning and instead are simply affected emotionally as we surrender to the story, which is otherwise delivered in a deliberately unaffected style. The garden and the tree return several times in the film, although with less symbolic force. Again, we realize their significance only toward the end of the film, as they become the witnesses and agents of our protagonist's destruction. Projection does not serve a rational purpose; instead, it is used to provide suitable emotional intonation.

Wong Kar-wai makes an even more mysterious use of the all but hypnotic tool of projection. In *Days of Being Wild* (1991) we experience the ravings of the drifting protagonist amid longings to escape and barbarous destruction, hopelessly in search of a miraculous genesis (the unknown mother). But let us take a look at the film's opening scene. The camera hovers in a leisurely way along and above a lush, green-blue jungle scene—a mesmerizing, enigmatic sequence of images. The whole scene has a sublime, softly sensuous, yet surreal quality. It operates with a strong dreamlike affect. This is reinforced by the nostalgic music whose painful lyricism, instead of giving some pointers, only makes us lose our way. Where are we? In what space and whose time reference? All remains beyond the reach of reason. The image only returns toward the end of the film, perhaps as the last glance of the dying protagonist, providing some kind of clue to this exquisitely poetic metaphor. However, the scene is granted but a fleeting moment, and the secret is brushed only by a slight release of tension. The story's dimensions pointing beyond the film's protagonists remain undisturbed.

In this sense the standard looping or framing structure is of little consequence, because in his approach the essence lies in the juxtaposition of various internal/external temporal/spatial zones, the overlapping and collision of two distinct temporal orders. For the first sequence does not anticipate, according to the principles of linearity, something to come but rather evokes, or reminds us of, another *present* and *future* to prepare the viewer for a palpable sense of reality. As the film projects the future, it brings into focus the realm of simultaneous possibilities, demonstrating their tangible immediacy.

Wong Kar-wai also applies this mysterious forward leap in *Happy Together* (1997) with even more stylization. In a scene starting out in black and white in a barren room, suddenly the full-color image of a romantically radiant landscape is projected: the scene is shattered by a huge, torrential waterfall without bothering to provide a modicum of relational context. The spectacle is shocking and devoid of information, standing there like a strange attractor all on its own, only to manipulate subsequent events unseen. The cascading water roars and hypnotizes, disrupting all logical time and space relations. Obviously, it rouses interest and makes one wonder, generating expectations for later interpretation. Of course, we sense that the scene is relevant for the protagonists, to their vague desires, perhaps; however, when the image returns later and gains concrete substance, when one of the protagonists finally succeeds in reaching this wonder of nature, nothing is the same any longer.

As the symbolic object of desire, this blissful landscape is no longer a distant, secret fascination. The first dreamy view shown from an unfathomable high angle presents a more prosaic sight. Despite the realization of a longed-for encounter, the visit ends up as a forlorn event. The experience is suffused with the sense of fulfillment and loss, while the key motif, we finally understand, has followed the story throughout, albeit with an ironic smirk. Now we come to recognize the malicious sneer behind the frequent repeats. The image recurs as the cheapest kitsch during their get-togethers in the form of a gaudy, painted waterfall on a lampshade, following them around in all their shared quarters.

The sequence of images is not governed by the logic of events or motivated directly by emotions. Bits of the story float around in suspension driven along by their sensuous, enigmatic, and evocative energy. Wong Kar-wai does not offer an explanation; he is not afraid to sidestep the main channel of the narrative, and is wont to insert extraneous material that leaves the viewer time to grasp correlation. He works with visceral, freely surging associations. His world is made round by its multiplicity and the mysteries of anticipation.

The two puzzling examples described above are evidently past all rational and depth psychology. Instead, their transcendence speaks about the existential rootedness of man in his broader surroundings and a relationship between man and the world that extends beyond individual being. While our protagonists suffer or make love, the film suggests there is a truly autonomous world, ignorant of their existence, whose significance by definition is much larger than any private experience. This is why the director has the courage to apply digression so freely through repetitions, sparing no time or space in the overall composition of the film. The wonder of the green-blue jungle and the Igauzu waterfall exist on their own, in and of themselves. They are there, concurrently, even when no one thinks of them; sovereign and majestic entities in a shared universe. And this is also why they deserve the lengthy treatment they receive.

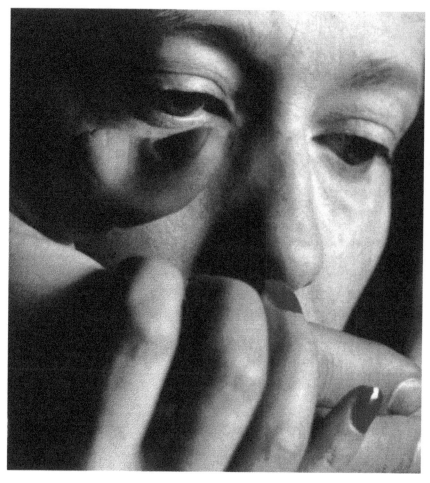

Alain Cavalier, *Libera me,* 1993

5 Seeing in Time: *Quasi una pausa*

The Human Face
The Face of Things
The Landscape
Silence

"Art does not reproduce what is visible, but makes things visible," says Paul Klee in his celebrated *Creative Confession*. Imagination, condensation, and interpretation demand the greatest accuracy from the creator and the viewer alike. In film, one must be aware of this perspective, which is capable of meaningful concentration and organic expression. While objects and natural forms carry enormous integrity, Klee says, "every development is based on movement . . . for space is also a temporal concept."[1]

Klee speaks about a multitude of latent, "temporal" truths obscured by traditional rationalism. Art has the responsibility to bring them to life and reveal their complex functions, since we are looking not merely at the form but also with the intent to understand the functions of these truths. The essential question is how to present the world of compelling objects invigorated by man's creative gaze.

In respect to our immediate environment, this dynamic approach is extremely productive when reproduced on film. There is a curious equivalence on the screen with regards to the human and the physical environment and the significance of landscape, objects, and faces. Klee names this unity "an enrichment of the orchestra of multiple forms, in a limitless fashion of potentials and conjunctions."[2] We need to pay attention to often neglected particularities, which speak about the essence of the unfolding drama: the continued existence and change of things. This inherent temporality affects the fluctuation of the narrative. Fast development and halts alternate, and the more we need to linger on minute details, the more the slow down, stop, or pause is meaningful and necessary.

Thus it is interesting to examine from the point of storytelling how careful regard shapes our all-too-ordinary routines and what, beyond the attraction of mere spectacle, the "face of things" can tell us. For each thing, whether breathing or inert, dwells simultaneously in the past and the future.

The conscious articulation of time, its elevation to the position of an independent and active player, is the crucial issue here. The "what" we see is emphasized through the duration, the "how long" we focus on it. Some of the greatest thinkers of modernism, like Deleuze, paid particular attention to this problem. In his famous work, *Time Image,* Deleuze analyzes how perception relies on elliptical, drifting, and fundamentally weak relationships that transform the narrative, and he concludes that intensity lies in the gaze of the protagonists. They, and through them the viewers, invest objects with meaning, emotional content, and the need to understand the world opening before them.

Ephemeral interests, memories, and emotions enliven everyday perception. Even dead moments and empty spaces become vibrant and replete with meaning. Then, in films, the result, even if it moves with the leisurely pace of a ballad, says much about the heroes. The much maligned stroll and aimless ambling are far from metaphors for a non-event; instead, they render time visible in all its nakedness.

Through objects, they lend signification and give dimensionality a perceptible shape. The complexity of an image's temporality, the dichotomy of the granular image is described by Deleuze as "time crystals," which express the ephemeral here and now—right in front of us—while capturing the preserved, virtual parts of the past as well. All tangible objects and sights are pregnant with the past. Deleuze believes visual culture demands that images be cleaned of encrusted clichés. The apparent void must be challenged—stripped of its surfeit of platitudes and faced in all its immensity. The time image speaks to us directly, Deleuze maintains, for movement, instead of being motivated by reason, is driven by inner impulses. This is what he calls "the intensity of gaze." Movement is not measured by time; on the contrary, time is measured by movement, he concludes.

Welles, Cassavetes, Bresson, and Bergman, to mention but a few great names that come to mind, make the conscious effort to strip away all decorative stylistic elements and hold up the essence of dramatic tension by focusing the camera's attention on the object at hand. This, however, works only through the careful development of an inner content that requires duration, such as in music. The order of succession is never mechanical. It is precisely the polyphonic nature, the brave and meaningful integration of "extraneous" elements, which lends lively undulations. The unfolding renders implacable time visible through replacements (in which things "stand for something else and more," as the saying goes), in order to make perceptible time's burden. Sensible artists articulate emotions, feelings, joy and pain, mood, and ambiance with the force of temporally accentuated vision, first of all by bringing the human face to center stage.

The Human Face

Bergman's *Persona* (1966) opens with Liv Ullmann's huge close-up, enlarged to fill the entire screen and hovering mysteriously out of focus, while a young boy standing in the foreground tries to touch the apparition with an outstretched hand. In this terrifyingly disproportionate relationship of the face (larger than the boy) and the longing gesture to caress, all the mysteries and inevitable traps of cinematic representation are palpably present. For indeed, we as spectators do nothing else than the boy: we wish to sense and feel that distant and elusive other, forever present and absent at the same time. For there is something incomprehensible and un-acceptable about the fact that a figure stands before our eyes in all its physical reality, yet it lacks all corporeality. If we touched the phantom it would disappear, leaving nothing but flickering light, a dance of fleeting shadows projected on the screen.

Indeed, the enlarged human face is one of film's first wonders and it has not lost its hold on us to this day. Separated from the body, isolated from all contexts, like Dreyer's Falconetti in *Jeanne d'Arc* (1928), the face has come to epitomize the depth of human suffering. An emblem, a shocking dramatic stage, is conjured by Godard in his *Vivre sa vie* (1962) when he matches that face with Anna Karina's crying close-up. We are to share her grief, her instinctive physical reaction to the overpowering proximity of an-other body. Since this goes beyond mere portrayal or a character study, the fully exposed face and its powerful presentation carry transcendent, iconic meaning. Is the face a mirror of the soul? Or rather is the face the metaphysical summary of human pain and anxiety?

Cassavetes's perhaps most dramatic film has the title *Faces* (1968). From the first minute it is clear that the film's essence lies in this peculiar concentration. The complicated story featuring a host of characters relies primarily on the power of physiognomy and mimicry. Besides the heroine Gena Rowlands's temptingly enigmatic face, showing her loneliness, forced playfulness, and various disguises, the film brings unusually close several other characters appearing for a few seconds, such as the far from attractive Seymour Cassel, or a parade of aging men's bristly faces, which personify a peculiar mix of inner tension and brutality steeped in violence. These intrusive faces betray not a hint of serenity or a moment of relief. Eyes shimmer, quivering with devastation, lost balance, injury, and full-blown aggression. The camera follows the duel, defeat, and retreat of faces with cold detachment. Approaching head on or from a revealing angle, the camera penetrates almost to the level of animal instinct. False eyelashes, deliberately tussled hair, clumsy boasting, or defiant humiliation become exposed through these extremes of sensuality. Genuine tears and raging outbursts all speak of these characters' fallibility and impotent nakedness. If we have ever seen a camera filming a vivisection that does not recoil from pain and even torture, the example of *Faces* proves that the broken mirror of the soul, the face is the most defenseless victim of the camera's relentless search for truth.

Not surprisingly, Cassavetes never had many supporters and followers in his lifetime. His obduracy went beyond the acceptable and caused unease; instead of looking for the "beautiful," he recorded tormented, disintegrated, and even ugly faces fallen to pieces under the weight of struggle. His camera liberated his heroes with faces distorted by stress from the mask of the acceptable, *comme il faut* look.

But let us look at another film, Barbara Loden's excellent but undeservedly forgotten *Wanda* (1970). In this deceptively simple work, the heroine is adrift with nothing to do, almost arrogant in her indifference, although, despite all apparent insignificance, her fate, the power and vitality of her expression (the author of the film plays the lead role), engage the viewer and allow for the discovery of the character's unique qualities throughout the film. True enough, she shows little interest in her husband and children and cares little if she loses them. She sets out on an adventure without enthusiasm. However, the haphazard events of her empty existence, dragging herself from one casual partner to the next, toss her farther off course than she would like or one would expect. She may become the sole accomplice and ally of a crusty and surly criminal, yet she preserves or rather recognizes in herself an uncommon resilience. In this world she is doomed to nothingness, making empty circles until a dangerous operation sweeps her along. She goes along not only to meet violent demands that go beyond her obvious humiliation, but she also plays an accessory to crime all the way to the unexpected, devastating loss. Events inexorably move from bad to worse, yet this does not lead to the steady degradation of the heroine's inner world. Just the opposite; she becomes more complex as, paradoxically, from infantile apathy she moves to commitment and eventually becomes capable of experiencing trauma. The drama illustrates that, despite the destructive forces of various adventures, she can be deeply affected by the crisis. The road to crime and the human story that leads to catharsis are not identical and do not overlap in the narrative arc.

The complexity of Barbara Loden's face builds up a multitude of layers: it watches intently, comprehends, protests, expects, demands, and is capable of suffering. The leaden face of the principal character, initially shown with tacky hairpins, by the end of the film reappears in long-held shots as deeply moving and heartrending. Walter Benjamin's words are most appropriate here: "The image is a thing where, in an enlightening and unique constellation, a Point in Time meets with the Present. In other words, the image is the dialectic of standstill."[3]

It is no accident that, besides the sensual and erotic pull of great stars, we can be deeply moved by amateur actors as well. Stavros (played by a young nonprofessional actor) in Elia Kazan's America, America (1963) strives to adapt to the New World with an enigmatic, hopeful, yet always equivocal smile. The overwhelming power of his close-ups is more than characterization; they represent the summary of a destiny that justifies the filmmaker's bold use of the expression. The boy's smile is active, in fact a typical form of reaction in the service of a specific strategy. The shifting consistency of the smile is remarkable, a form of symbolic marker for each new life situation. Kazan attributed much to his Anatolian origins, particularly what he called in his autobiography his desire to deeply understand the emigrant's capacity to adjust. He named this phenomenon "the Anatolian smile," which he recognized and disliked in his father (or also in himself?), calling it "the smile that hides resentment."

Thinking of nonprofessional actors, we feel an almost personal connection to Vittorio De Sica's disheveled, unshaven, poster-hanging bicycle thief, in his shabby hat; to the mischievous young boy when he cannot hide his eyes filled with tears; the pockmarked face of the epileptic thief; or the seductive smile of Fellini's lascivious Saraghina in *8½* as she looks defiantly at potential clients. The gaze of Kiarostami's village lovers in *Through the Olive Trees*, the anxious effort of the distraught small boy looking in vain for his friend's house . . . all these memorable close-ups become the most telling physical traces of profound human destinies. We see unparalleled, exceptional faces, instead of faces corresponding to the dictates of uniform showbiz fads or cheap sex-appeal.

Already in *Thérèse* (1986) and particularly in *Libera me* (1993), Alain Cavalier goes back almost to the traditions of ascetic resignation developed in the silent era. His amateur characters operate with the most direct, instinctive gestures of physiognomy and mimicry, the "root and branch" of their uniqueness, and the unmatched personal marks left by stupor and sweat. All hackneyed ideas, abstract notions, or fashionable concepts of beauty are done away with. Instead, bizarre traits, forms, twitching nerves, a silhouette of a nose, and a tic around the mouth stand for inimitable irregularity. This is why in these mythologies the face becomes the medium of minimalism. Everything takes place there. In this limited yet endlessly expanded paradoxical space we reach the exceptional and excruciating depths of intensity.

Of course, the mystery of the face in close-up has been explored innumerable times, demonstrating the power of this unique invention of cinematography. For my purpose here it is relevant insofar as it has come to shape the narrative and become its grossly oversized component, as it were. In other words, the face becomes the stage of turbulence, either in the form of outburst or as an emphatically restrained mode of tension.

Balazs writes in his famous book, *Visible Man,* how the vibrant presence of the face renders unseen, inner content. Its mobility creates polyphony, or as Balazs says, the "harmony" of emotions, and simultaneously reveals their contrasting layers as it is not subject to the linearity of writing. The extraordinary mobility (temporal articulation) is matched with the effectiveness of the close-up (spatial articulation). The face bespeaks of the wonder of intensity and intimacy, the revelation of some magical aura that, in addition to the sensuousness of physical proximity, brings a novel means of psychological identification to the screen. The enlarged face filling the full screen is more than a mere face—it encompasses all. The face thus becomes the stage of the entire drama, hence its magic.

Balazs sees the aesthetic of the film in "involvement" in the literal sense, in its peerless sensuality, and he is not the only one for whom the close-up represents an unmatched artistic principle. "My first conscious memory of film was a close-up," says Eisenstein.[4] And we could continue with similar quotes from Jean Epstein, Murnau, and Sternberg, through Buñuel and Godard.

It is perfectly clear, however, that for Dreyer, Bresson, Bergman, Tarkovsky, and Cavalier (to mention some of the most spiritual filmmakers), beyond its physical reality, the human face represents a deeply felt epiphany. I refer here to Levinas's enlightening description when he defines the values of the face hidden behind its nakedness, vulnerability and beauty.

The face is a language preceding the word, a genuine language
stripped of all barriers . . . that invites a response . . . a language
of the inaudible, the unspeakable. An open book, written work!
An order that speaks to man's individuality . . . singularity and
transcendence. The epiphany of the face is ethical . . . it assumes
the transcendence of the expression.[5]

Cavalier says, "Once I am interested in the face, nothing else
matters. All that comes from somewhere else is nothing more
than sponging off the extraordinary energies of film generated
and filled constantly by the face."[6] With attention and silence, the
motionless camera searches for the ineffable in the human face
shown in a close-up. Bresson, who rejected the commercialized
typology of the actor, speaks for "the model, enclosed in his mysterious appearance he has brought home to him all of him, that
was outside. It is here, behind this forehead and face."[7]

Since the human face is subject to constant change, this, in
turn, is the result of an interaction steeped in time. "A face is like
a blank sheet that cries out for a design," writes the American art
psychologist James Elkins:

As I look at a face I also sense a desire to somehow complete it,
by seeing it as intensely as I can . . . a face is something that is
incomplete, a work in progress that stands in continuous need
of being seen or touched or written upon. And maybe that is
the fundamental reason for our fascination with faces: like the
personalities they express and the ideas they communicate,
faces need to be used because they are not finished images.[8]

In this context, one cannot omit Ingmar Bergman's latest
movie *Saraband* (2003), which doesn't simply repeat or continue
his former obsessions and themes (realized in *Scenes from a Marriage*) but through its truly original structure centers more than
any other film on his protagonists' facial expressions.

The musical form of the saraband is a specific treatment of
rhythm and tone, "a slow measured treat," to use the technical

description. Even the central core, the Bach Cello Saraband, involves intricate contrapuntal lines, in which "the multiple stops rob time from the best and lend . . . gravity to the movement."[9] In the film the melodic line, carried out in distinct ten movements, often give way to dissonant two-part harmony, creating violent and painful scenes. Tenderness, subtlety, even humor are not excluded from the fabric of anger, cruelty, and selfishness. This is precisely Bergman's bold interpretation with which he dares to disguise human frailty, wild passions, and the nakedness of suddenly shifting, contradictory emotional emotions. And all these complex impulses appear on the stage of the human face.

The bony visage of the lead, played by Erland Josephson, betrays his bitterness and narcissism, already bereft of the security of self-confidence. All his emotions are substantially revealed on his face: his supercilious dignity, his humiliating deafness, and finally his ultimate weakness and whimpering anxiety as he begs to get into his ex-wife (Liv Ullmann) Marianne's bed. We see to what extent the old man's character is cursed with hatred and indifference, evil stubbornness, and pettiness. In what other manner could these intricate feelings come to the fore if not through Bergman's excessive concentration on the characters' faces?

We live it through, carried along with these excesses, moving with the tormented rhythm of the unfolding states of mind. Since nothing is fully complete, we bear the previously accumulated experience further within ourselves. Incompleteness refers to the adventure of creating pulsing in time; we look at things with the mobilizing energy of memories, dreams, and illusions, converse with the visible world, and we respond to the truly penetrating gaze of objects.

The Face of Things

Naturally, classic films did not only exploit and enjoy the power of the human visage. Filmmakers discovered similar qualities and

Luis Buñuel, *Viridiana,* 1961

unique cinematographic treasures in the "obscene sensuality" of objects (Epstein), investing objects with vitality and an emotional charge. The viewer experienced these magic effects through the unlimited expansion of dimensions.

Of course, the use of the close-up introduces a peculiar event in the narrative flow: it creates a caesura, an enlargement, and a moment of singular attention. A brief pause in the rush of images. A loud cry and breathtaking silence all at once. A definite reduction of pace to confront, enchant, or create anxiety depending on the mood or psychological requirement of the moment.

Quasi una pausa. This is what composers say when the phrase is stretched to its limit and, instead of a further melodic development, they divert attention to the emotional content, the importance of "experiencing" the moment.

To refer to the most classic examples, like Eisenstein's baby carriage bouncing downhill, or the *pars pro toto* of the pince-nez in *Potemkin;* Chaplin's globe in the *Great Dictator;* Renoir's rocking swing and elegiacally gliding boat in *Partie de Campagne;* James Dean's toy figure in the opening sequence of *Rebel without a Cause;* Hitchcock's nightmarish hotel with the embalmed mother in *Psycho;* Bresson's reductive discipline where each event is limited to a specifically chosen detail. In these works the face and the object serve as equally dramatic stages. The camera documents the pickpocket's professional skills (in Bresson's film of the same name) by showing the varied features of the wallets and purses he deals with; in *A Man Escaped,* Bresson's camera shows the prisoner's endless struggle with a single tin spoon.

These objects belong to the protagonists and are often standins for their actions and gestures as some permanent (abbreviated) yet powerful attribute. Let us look at a more recent example: in Hal Hartley's *Trust* (1991), the rebellious, bitter hero plays with a hand grenade all through the film. The object is meant to symbolize his rage and determination. In the end, in a climatic final act, the threatening presence of the grenade does lead to an explosion, though not in a simplistically foreseeable physical sense.

Agnès Varda's highly successful film *The Gleaners and I* (2000) concentrates almost exclusively on the exceptional role of objects. Shrewd junk collectors or waste-dump diggers are hunting and looking for the rejected, abandoned, or forgotten jumble in a promising adventure. Fortunately we don't see any spectacular horror or misery. Her landscape is anything but a mournful cemetery. On the contrary: to all appearances it functions as the evidence of survival. In her vision the objects speak about the power of successfully recycled things. The crippled refrigerators can be repaired or even turned into china cabinets! The chairs with broken legs and torn couches could be fixed and tamed, made to look as if they are from better material than plastic. Also, Varda places herself without hesitation into the gleaners' families. We have to share the artist's pleasure as she marvels at the sight of mauve cabbages, a Van der Weyden painting, or the huge trucks evoking her childhood amazement as they glide away. We see her joy when she finds a godsent naive painting or a truly useless clock without its hands, constructed out of two porcelain cats. These fascinating, lucid, and ludicrous objects are a feast for the filmmaker's and our eyes, creating a portrait not only about the gleaners but also about the "glaneuse."

Nothing offers a more precise and captivating representation of the nature of human desire than the dizzying scenes in Vittorio De Sica's *Miracle in Milan* (1951), where the residents of a shantytown, on recognizing Toto's magic powers, ask him to produce the "obscure" objects of their desire. And what do we find in the horn of plenty? A bunch of useless and glittering things displaying the signs of wealth: furs and top hats, glamorous evening dresses, and jingling glass chandeliers. Then comes the slightly less reasonable demand for cash itself, millions and hundreds of millions, then billions and uncountable trillions. The dreams escape their moorings and the flood of objects inundates the entire miserable settlement. These objects of luxury are seen as the opposite of poverty and deprivation. Hoarding and the orgy of objects speak simultaneously of their futility and the people's insatiable nature of hunger.

In other instances, in certain scenes we sense the hidden, indirect symbolism of objects. For instance, let us take Tsai Mingliang's fish tanks, which recur in every interior in each of his films. With repeated scenes of pouring monsoon rain and water gushing from all directions, the ubiquitous presence of these fish tanks seems bizarre and unnecessary. Fish of various types and sizes, in their illuminated glass prisons, swim in silence and without apparent purpose. They are neither attractive nor repulsive; they avoid each other and stay their course. Their vegetative state is never disturbed by storms or entanglements; they change direction effortlessly with inexplicable ease: literally, they breathe and live like fish in water. Apparently, they enjoy life and exist undisturbed in their universe. Whether the aquarium is large or small, it always occupies the same ignored spot of the apartment as the permanently turned on yet never watched television set blinking in some corner. Two odd complementary vessels framing motion, indispensable yet neglected fixtures of every household. Having been placed there, they exist in a void with no essential function to perform. Instead, they are additional objects of an eerie uniformity, tools of leveling. Their uniqueness is absorbed and underlined by the same emptiness, the void, and the ubiquitous hole that shapes the choreography of main characters. We could say that they are accentuated elements of the flow, embodiments of the director's basic narrative principle to suggest the streaming of his characters' lives.

In one of Alain Cavalier's last films, *La rencontre* (1996), radical reduction operates without human characters. It presents the viewer only with the life of objects dear to absent humans. And indeed, these close-ups show their most hidden faces from angles never perceived before: two "embracing" spectacles, a pair of shoes under the magnifying glass, the life of an insect on the windowsill. All everyday, trivial objects are seen from a vantage point that lends them a curious glow. In *Libera me* (1993), the image of a badly ripped book cover signifies brutality, and the close-up of a torn photograph stands for the "wound" caused by a gesture. Details say more about the violence of oppression than does the presentation of blows themselves. In the hands of jailers or trampled on the ground, the battered passports, the last vestiges of identity, become emblematic signs. The accepted symbolic energy of enlarged fragments works against the sweeping current like a barrier in a stream; it demands attention, hints at correlation, and refers to accumulated time.

Fragmentation is the primary tool of stripping down to the essentials, "indispensable if we wish to avoid the sin of representation," writes Bresson in *Notes on the Cinematographer.* "Things and people must be seen in their distinct fragments. Details must be isolated . . . instead of addition, one creates meaning through reduction."[10]

Walter Benjamin writes on the same subject as follows:

> The close ups of the things around us, by focusing on hidden details of familiar objects, by exploring commonplace milieus under the ingenious guidance of the camera, the film, on the one hand, extends our comprehension of the necessities which rule our lives; on the other hand, it manages to assure us of an immense and unexpected field of action; with the close up, space expands, with slow motion, movement is extended. . . . An unconsciously penetrated space is substituted for a space consciously explored by man. [11]

The Landscape

Finally, we must say a few words about the role played by the landscape and the natural environment. Despite the long history of abuse perpetrated in this area (gratuitously beautiful scenery, cheap kitschy postcards), a large number of outstanding examples illustrate how effectively the narrative is served by the choice of landscape and the manner of its representation. In some cases these depictions may attain the rank of dramatis personae. It is all but self-evident that in Kiarostami's *Life and Nothing More* (1991), the muted presentation of a scene after the big earthquake, the astonishing simplicity of the fusion of ruins and the surrounding landscape says something fundamentally new and thought-provoking about human behavior. The ravaged and wounded land is revealed in all its vulnerability and nakedness as the protagonist drives through in his car. What we need to understand we may learn only through this sprawling and calm presentation: the co-existence of the pain of survival and innate vitality, the taste of everyday existence, the taste of cherries.

Almost forty years ago we looked bewildered at the Japanese Hiroshi Teshigahara's *Woman of the Dunes* (1964), a film based on a novel by Kobo Abe. The all-engulfing sand that must be resisted ceaselessly without the hope of ever overcoming it clearly grows to have a symbolic value, while it affects us in its most visceral reality. It reveals a thousand faces as it attacks, inundates, suffocates, and drifts incessantly. When the wind starts to blow, it not only penetrates each corner, but seeps under the skin of living creatures. No doubt, this grim natural phenomenon is the story's genuine leading protagonist whose power embodies the black-and-white film's ominous force. The sea of sand appears as a black hole that absorbs all light and surrounding life. And by the time it forces the hero to surrender in the end, we have already comprehended and sensed the supernatural in nature. It is about the struggle of man and the external world where individual existence is eclipsed by the inscrutable laws of the universe. To use Pasolini's appropriate definition with its raw directness, the "barbaric metaphor" penetrates under our skin to deliver its added meaning.

In his latest work *Dolls,* Takeshi Kitano makes a deliberate progress through the seasons to create a nonrealistic, poetic tone with fairyland vistas and the shifting colors of spring, summer, fall, and winter. "What is most appealing for me in Japanese landscape representation," he says in an interview, "is the relationship between beauty and death. The Japanese worship of the cherry blossom is tied to the idea of their imminent demise, their ephemeral existence. In fact, the intense red color of maple leaves is also a signal of approaching death. And snow is seen as a shroud that conceals life." The meaning of this sense of transcendence does not need to be explained further. Beauty is not in and of itself and definitely not decorative, but rather it is the companion of man's ultimate adventure, of death. This is the reason its colors tend toward the extreme to leave behind all natural quality. Or think about the meaning of the title of his widely acclaimed film *Hana-bi* (Fireworks). "*Hana* means 'flower,' something exquisite and transient, and *bi* stands for 'fire,' symbolizing violence and death," he says.[12]

Tsai Ming-liang uses rain and the motif of water in a number of his films to express the symbolic meaning of the hole. In a curious paradox, this pouring rain, this infernal, interminable inundation becomes the representation of the void that surrounds his protagonists. The cascading water, the torrential and relentless rain, as well as the riot of running faucets and leaking pipes stand for the wider meaning of an all-embracing experience. Water bubbling, pelting, swirling in the background or in full view overflows everything. From above or surging from sinks and flood-drains it becomes the pathogenic substance of the "human condition."

Tsai Ming-liang insists on returning over and over again to the themes of rain and flooding waters to contemplate their import in his protagonists' lives. There is no natural "measure" in its application. The dreadful physical presence of this theme is overwhelming, not just terribly sensuous but also long, infinite. In *Vive L'Amour, The River,* and finally in *The Hole,* the coursing water continues to cascade and crash into toilets and bathtubs, showing apocalyptic devastation, a truly unstoppable deluge. In this way the orchestration of the polyphonic medium with its disproportionate choices reveals in the most expressive form the all-encompassing vision of the film.

Great directors repaint and redraw the natural landscape. They have the ability to reshape the external world to suit the material and spiritual needs of their vision and style. Starting with Marcel Carne's fog-shrouded quays, to the Paris of the New Wave directors, through Fellini's Rome, and Tanner's and Wenders's Lisbon, the scenery not only has its own life; it has a soul and character distinctly unique and immediately recognizable once touched by these directors. And this is why these films demand so much time. Their function obviously goes far beyond mere geographic orientation, contingency, or accurate description—their self-sustained atmosphere and duration belong to the story's essence.

Angelopoulos's Greece, this rainy, bleak, and stony landscape, has little in common with the average traveler's experience. His consistent vision changes so little that even in his lesser known work, such as *The Beekeeper,* where the hero played by Mastroianni crosses the country north to south in his lonely quest, the tone and aura of the landscape barely changes as we progress from cold to warm regions. As a projection of the inner world, the environment shows no light and warmth; amid barren shrubs and desiccated forests, in an abandoned, uninviting, and unresponsive milieu, the hero must perish alone.

A determined philosophical and pictorial sensitivity elevates Kim Ki-duk's *Spring, Summer, Fall, Winter . . . and Spring* to the level of a highly spiritual and severely reduced work. The potentials of human destiny are substantially demonstrated in the "eternal" circle of the seasons. One single, utterly elaborate and artful location carries the charge to evoke through the slightest and subtlest nuances the changes in nature, as the water and snow, the color of leaves, the sky and the trees follow the metamorphosis of lives: hatred and violence, attachment and friendship. Kim Ki-duk's particular talent brings equally close the earthy natural and the religious Zen experience. Customary natural beauty has no room here: the rigor of the composition reminds the viewer of a more solemn and abstract content.

Similarly the Hungarian director Miklós Jancsó's *puszta* (prairie), with its endless void and barrenness, reflects the director's inner experience and intended message. In his films *Round Up* (1965) and *The Reds and Whites* (1967), which stirred much interest at the time, his searching, prowling camera takes in huge vistas as he depicts a windswept and bleak landscape. Even if in his later *Red Psalm* the vision became crowded and restless, this has little effect on his treatment of the wide-open dimensions of space. The huge scale and wide horizon defined rhythm with a clearly recognizable emotional charge. In all the films, the *temps mort* of long takes emphasizes slowly advancing and threatening time. The scenes carry the burden of history expressed by visual and temporal forces supplementing each other.

These films are notable for their unusual treatment of proportion: in a powerful and indifferent natural setting the individual is diminished in stature. In their scale and duration, takes with a propensity for long shots represent this correlation as well. The effect is not unlike in the classic Westerns, where the lonely hero follows his stern destiny through a vast, open, vulnerable space. The more awe-inspiring and endless the often foreboding or majestic landscape, the more poignant is the movement of the pursuing or pursued mortal through that space. A preference for large format lends the work large breadth as well.

We must also talk about the significance of the representation of the urban landscape. Of course, it was not French New Wave directors who discovered the metropolis for cinema, and primarily Paris with its narrow cobblestone streets, grand boulevards, and suddenly exploding car traffic. Italian neorealism offered up the irresistible beauties and desolation of postwar Rome, Milan, and a host of other enchanting Italian cities. The novelty of postwar representation lay in the courage of showing the city in a direct, documentary style after an era of artificial or cursory studio treatments.

Form the point of my topic, the ever larger role given to the city and the street is the most important, for what is crucial here is not so much the demand for equal status with the main characters of the story but rather the experience of an all-powerful, authentic environment without which the unfolding drama would lose credibility. And here again, what matters is the integration of the less than beautiful, or rather the emphatically ugly, desolate, wasted, rundown, and vacated that came to serve as the context and background of variously lost lives. Let's think of the rather famous "manifestos" and trend of urbanists from the late sixties and early seventies, like the claims of Ettore Sottsass, for instance, who said that the "uncute" forms of postindustrial society provide a type of resistance to commodity fetishism, thus to display them goes beyond the prosaic details of reality. They unveil the "psycho-erotic self-indulgence concerning possession," he said.[13] Fassbinder might be among the great examples who recurrently focused on these aspects of contemporary life.

And finally, after the more familiar cities and landscapes of Europe, over the past few decades we have acquired a more intimate knowledge of the not so "exotic" quarters of Hong Kong, Tokyo, Taipei, or Mumbai/Bombay. Sadly, by now there is little defining or authentic in the uniformity of skyscrapers and shantytowns, the undistinguished features of highways and overpasses, or the atmosphere of speeding commuter trains. Housing projects or suburbia, supermarkets or screaming ambulances—does anyone know with any certainty what country we are in? The truth is, more often than not we are lost.

It appears that instead of diversification, we often witness the leveling of the visual field. And this is what makes the search for the original and accurate all the more essential in the context of increasingly uniform visual treatment. For our sense of expressive temporality, the conscientious description and evocation of a distinct milieu, particularly in its twenty-first—century variety that lies ahead of us, is indispensable.

This is why the few farsighted and sensitive creators who have presented us with uniquely penetrating details deserve all our respect, such as Tsai Ming-liang, Wong Kar-wai, and Agnès Varda, or, to return to the master of the simple and accurate rendering of a Japanese way of life, Ozu. According to the Japanese scholar Tadao Sato: "In the domestic dramas which Ozu created, his constant quest was to refine the beauty of the Japanese daily lifestyle, which involved people sitting on the tatami. Ozu made an absolute priority to position characters so that they mirrored each other and maintained a steady and agreeable conversational pace. He portrayed them . . . according to their Japanese custom of sitting on tatami floors. . . . Therefore he didn't just lower his camera, he experimented with ways of heightening the beauty of the frame in which seated characters remained immobile . . . never rushing his story along."[14] This all sounds simple, yet the accuracy of the insight is enlightening. Context, daily habits, and space-time perception converged to build up Ozu's inimitable style.

It is a peculiar experience to see, after a few decades, the sensible homage to Ozu by Hou Hsiao-hsien in his new film, *Café Lumière.* While in the work of Ozu we are to discover the slow transformation of the traditional Japanese lifestyle, imbued by his nostalgic-ironical gaze, Hou's films present the hybrid face of today's Tokyo as the most natural evidence. The design of the intricate railroad lines crossing all over the city, over packed metro stations with millions of indifferent people, fill the frame. Although traces of the past, such as narrow old streets with small houses, are still present, they are portrayed without emotion, almost lifelessly. The ancient buildings stand sometimes between the high-rises, but they have lost their charm and intimacy. Naked, ungainly cables and bulky wires represent the indispensable need and presence of electricity, with no attempt to hide the hurried, unequal catching up to a twenty-first-century technological victory. They coexist, these elements of the small and the big, the provincial and the metropolitan, both in dressing and behavior.

One more betraying observation: Hou Hsiao-hsien, not unlike some of his Japanese contemporaries, avoids deliberately the emphasis of the human face. It is the consequence of his reserved, guarded presentation. Relying on long takes, the big dramatic effects are far removed from his field of interest. The patient, meditating view of space is in harmony with the restrained calm of his time perception: the new quotidian lifestyle is shown in a quiet modest fashion.

I think that the more a specific texture of the landscape becomes an integral part of the narration, the more it may bring closer to the spectator a truly diversified, vivid rhythm that does not refuse patience but gives to time a telling attention, contributing in this way to the creation of a self-contained universe of the work.

Silence

"In our fictional stories I see the privileged opportunity to lend shape to our formless and essentially *silent* [my emphasis] temporal experience,"[15] says Ricœur. Often, the logic of emotions does not reach the stage of verbalization. And yet, silence is not a unique feature of the nonevent and the void.

There is a natural correlation between the dignity of a slow pace and silence. Spiritual attention doesn't tolerate loudness. Again, profound stillness gives birth to a remarkable power of intensity. Bergman, Bresson, Tarkovsky, and Angelopoulos provide the most telling examples of salutary reserve. Not only is there little dialogue, but silence always occupies center stage in their films. Even in this category we find a uniquely outstanding example in Alain Cavalier's *Libera me* that dooms itself to total silence.

In this film about the century's cruel practices of oppression giving free rein to torture and efforts of resistance, not one word is uttered. Cavalier's parable lifts the drama to the level of universal phenomena. After so much horrific and cynical abuse, the scandal of humiliation and torment left the director bereft of language. He declined to trivialize the unspeakable. "What does the lack of speech signify," Cavalier rightfully wonders in his notes on the film. "How can one avoid the trap of mannerism? One may only film moments that exclude language. It is about ethical and aesthetic behavior." In his option for silence, he looks for the purity and naked essence of spiritual and physical representation, consciously creating a specific temporal composition. Through the fate of his characters he follows the shifts of direct experience in some form of *largo desolato,* where "the solitary person generates energy by refusing to speak."[16] And this is how the screen becomes the locus of time suspended by silence. A silent scream. Empty void on the surface, and explosion underneath. As gesture and the voice speak in so many shades of meaning, they avoid the most common disease—clever comments, rhetorical pronouncements. The more accurate and detailed the presentation, the more haunting the wordless, relentless action. And the viewer is not spared either. With rare concentration, he must sit through and watch the unbearable.

Cavalier's example is exceptional and extreme, for the concept of silence does not necessarily mean the film must be devoid of a single word spoken by the characters. Instead, it usually means that the viewer must follow situations where profound silence is the most adequate form of expression while, at the same time, it is only temporary, because it is only the given moment that does not allow or require verbal definition.

With regards to *La grande illusion* (1937), Jean Renoir relates that for the end of the movie he wrote a dramatic parting scene between Jean Gabin and Dalio as they leave together through the deep snow. However, the actors were unable to perform the scene with the brilliant dialogue. Apparently, the overly emotion-filled "big" scene did not fit into the mood of the film's style. That is when the idea occurred that the bitter pangs of farewell, suggesting inconclusiveness and fragmentation, should be depicted by silence and the humming of a silly little song, "Il était un petit navire." Loud heat got replaced by soft, almost wry complicity, enacted in a quiet fashion.

In *8½* Claudia (Cardinale) makes several appearances with

her shimmering whiteness and gentle smile. She does not say a word, and it is her floating presence and encouraging smile that speak to Guido. Whenever she returns, she is all tenderness and radiance, hinting at some future promise without a word spoken. When at the end of the film Mastroianni "conjures" her once more from his dreams, his imagination, or possibly his tentative plans, she says and repeats several times a short sentence as a final judgment, in warning. Listening to Guido's haplessness and complaints, she says simply: "Because you cannot love, you do not know how to love." This simple remark is given all the more weight as it follows a long period of expectation and silence as she, shrouded in silence, has already doomed the maestro to loneliness in a glowing and limpid light.

The function of lyrical silence is obviously profound. When we think of films defined by loneliness, elegiac sorrow, or hopelessness, it is self-evident that silence will create a more tender and poetic aura. To cite another extreme example, Kitano's *Scene at the Sea* (1991) tells the story of two deaf-mute youths, although silence is not simply the function of their physical handicap. For quite some time we barely notice that the lack of dialogue can be attributed to this fact. Instead we witness the simple and elemental attachment between the two characters and realize that their strong reliance on each other rests on their physical proximity, attention, and mutual devotion, even as a misunderstanding leads to a fit of jealousy. The gestures, mimicry, tears, or any other playful tools of communication reveal no sign of affectation or aberration. They understand each other without and beyond rational speech. And thus, their love progresses at a modest pace through profound feelings to its tragic end.

It is also clear that in the absence of human speech, all sound and clattering acquires more relevance than usual. The main theme is taken over by all the auditory complements of walking, movements, and noises of the natural environment to evoke, instead of the burden of deafness, the dimension of an alternate reality.

In this context the insistent and characteristic taciturnity of entirely different genres, like thrillers and whodunits, is most intriguing; in the most tense moments telltale speech must be banned. There, excitement at its peak signifies that in the slow, muffled silence of action every tiny movement is calculated to lead to a successful conclusion. Real suspense suffers no exchange, especially no interpretive commentary. And in this eager concentration only protracted time and patient stalking can create a powerful effect.

Fred Zinnemann's *High Noon* (1952) depicts the lonely sheriff's (Gary Cooper) tense and heroic struggle against bandits and a less-than-cooperative small community. The sheriff's noble simplicity and moral stance exclude all explanatory patterns. His courage is defined by action and confrontation with all its attendant risks. And while some rules of the Western would demand fast-paced action, Zinnemann has the good sense to recognize that aloofness and discipline lend more dignity, represented by the world of silence. Therefore the film demands attention not only with its reserve, but also with its long, nerve-racking moments of silence when, indeed, the stake is life or death, and the director has the courage to hold out seemingly forever before offering a release. Silence and withheld motion attend to every detail; piano and decrescendo go together, enhancing not only rhythm but the entire texture of the film.

War movies are wont to use this strategy of building tension where the necessity of action and anticipation rises above everything else, while deafening noises, cannon blasts, and the crackling of bullets remind the viewer of the far from harmless horror of the game.

As for rhythm, the constant back and forth between staccato and glissando is intriguing; this is perhaps the only method to demonstrate the weight of the balancing act between life and death, the risk of unforeseeable forces. Similarly, hiding, fleeing, and the moments before clashes logically operate with retention, for the longer the release is held, the more adrenaline accumulates in viewer and character alike.

* * *

Finally, my examples about the human face or the features of landscapes and objects or silence itself all illustrate the curious correlation between visual power and duration, space and the perceived length of time. True, the desire to achieve something more besides mere communication or the elemental requirement of coherence, to allow the work to mediate a real sense of adventure through focused attention, requires a firm strategy. In outstanding productions the landscape, faces, well-chosen sets with the force of character are as much dramatis personae as the narrative's struggling flesh-and-blood characters. They "act" with and for them. Moments of silence have the same effect; they create the high peaks of tension and the pauses of rest in order to achieve unity out of diversity.

Seeing in time means nothing less than creating a whole in space and time alike; devoting profound attention and time to phenomena that usually remain unobserved. It comprises both aspects of my interest in rhythm: providing great moments of halt, a break for eruption or for subtle, hidden emotions.

Yasujiro Ozu, *Early Spring,* 1956

6 Repetitions or Reprise

The Weight of Permanence
The Comedy of the Mechanism
The Same yet Different
"What If" and "As If"
Tema con variazione

The Weight of Permanence

Repetition is another means of interruption by digression, slowing up the action of a film. It would be easy to dismiss it offhand, claiming that reprise, showing something that has already been seen before, is mere redundancy. And yet, this form of emphasis is all the more relevant as it represents just as essential an element of articulation as ellipsis and allusion. Repetition elicits viewer participation from just the opposite direction—via the negative force of omission.

The frequent insertion of certain elements in the flow of Ozu's images is one of the most intriguing examples. He applied the technique with such consistency that one must take note of its refined play, the subtle significance of uniformity and variegation. In fact, instead of repetition, reprise is rather about "retake" in Kierkegaard's sense of the word (for this is the original meaning of the word, in Danish, according to him, as is also evident in French, "when something new is added").[1] What we see is the relived banalities of everyday life: the endless routine of family visits, manly drinking, and slightly vulgar jokes. And the less information these images carry, the more obvious the compulsory, rigid nature of these rites. But what purpose do they serve when they are so patently insignificant? Kierkegaard defines retake as a paradox, "The dialectic of repetition is easy, for that which is repeated has been—otherwise it wouldn't be repeated—but the very fact that it has been makes the repetition into something new."[2] Thus the repeated versions simultaneously offer the experience of the same yet something else. Kierkegaard speaks about creative retake as "renewal," the most accurate expression of the power of reapplication. The gained intensity doesn't simply refer to some spatial movement but to the temporal as well. It is a productive anticipation leading to fulfillment, a "metamorphosis"—"time has performed its duty" and thus it "increases power." Kierkegaard continues:

> In art as well, the individual cannot be serious enough; from time to time he needs to return to some sort of primary state . . . and approach it with an affective tonality. . . . The one opting for reprise is alive. He does not rush along like an adolescent in pursuit of butterflies, and standing on tiptoes does not cast a glance at the wonders of the world . . . and does not chain himself to the spinning wheel of memory like an old woman. He is content to proceed on his way—thanks to reprise.[3]

The role played by reprise is not unlike that of *tema con variazione* in music. Variation represents the pleasure offered by a constant dichotomy: the simultaneous play of joyful recognition (a sense of security offered by the familiar) and the novelty of slight shifting (the unknown). As in Ozu's films: scenes of the customary gathering of his characters, their innocent fun and games, the moderate or excessive bouts of drinking sake are all familiar yet always somewhat different. On the second encounter or somewhat later one recognizes previously seen takes. Yet we also become conscious of interruption and the lapse of time, as well as some form of increase born in the transition (transcendence).

Ozu's Japanese critics, primarily Shiguehiko Hasumi in his imaginative study of the director's work, attribute great importance to scenes of meals, dressing and changing, the show of living quarters, and the weather in the creation of an authentic aura in his films. Hasumi, for instance, describes in great detail the compulsory and elaborate routines around the dining table at family gatherings. He follows with unfailing precision the gradual transformation in Ozu's films of Japanese eating habits as they move from traditional roots to the adoption of European meat and fruit dishes, well past tofu and the canonized fare of classical Japanese cuisine. In Hasumi's presentation this becomes a metaphor for the historic and social changes of the postwar era, just as in modern clothing he perceives the cautious withdrawal from formal traditions under the pressure of Western influence. Besides the realism of illustration, it is the regular introduction of symbols that lends Ozu's storytelling such a unique character. Obviously, fashion, costumes, hairdos, customs, and other accessories of daily life, such as cars, interiors or furnishings, gadgets, and other accessories leave their characteristic stamp on each film. However, Ozu keeps returning with apparent love and devotion to these details precisely because for him the real fabric and tonal qualities of life are more important than any further development of the plot. This also explains why he makes references to continuity and sequences even in the titles of his films: *Late Spring, An Autumn Afternoon, Early Summer,* and so on all evoke strong atmospheres; or consider *The Flavor of Green Tea over Rice;* and assonances in titles such as *An Inn in Tokyo, Tokyo Story, Tokyo Twilight,* and *Woman of Tokyo.* The associations remind us of subtle variations; the *tema con variazione* is applied as a consistent aesthetic principle.

When the viewer is confronted with the return of certain objects or environmental landmarks, with the suspension of the narrative the director evokes an overwhelming sense of permanence.

Clothing hung on the balcony to dry, an awkward little neon light modestly signaling the excitement of modern life, or the modest furnishings of humble homes do not bespeak the living conditions of the protagonists alone. Instead, their frequent appearance serves the function of accretion: with their quiet persistence things continue to return and to be present to mark the confines of their existence. Independent of them all, life "exists and insists on carrying on." We seem to have lost the thread of the story but not quite; the opening gesture widens the horizon before destinies. The ephemeral nature of the protagonists' troubles and their survival in the face of suffering start to claim the viewer's attention. With the application of insertions mentioned above, regular digressions from the storyline, and the unusually low camera angles, the director minimizes personal tragedy and offers the freedom of contemplation in its stead. Rejecting great emotional scenes and spectacular conflicts, Ozu emphasizes the mysterious equality between objects and humans. Many critics describe his style as transcendent because, instead of the mutability of emotions, he concentrates on the permanent nature of phenomena, on instances that, in the context of his culture, are experienced as eternal.

This is all the more interesting because other, equally perceptive critics emphasize just the opposite. For instance, the Iranian-born Yousef Ishaghpour wrote a long essay on Ozu, *Les formes de l'impermanence.* As already suggested in the title, all conclusions of the study speak of the lack of permanence. In his opinion, Ozu's wisdom lies in the recognition that life follows a transient path: the individual, his happiness, and his memories are all ephemeral without constancy, for existence is predicated on sacrifice. Ishaghpour speaks about an Eastern morality that, above all else, lives by the self-evident acceptance of fate. The daily routines of family life, marriage, birth and death are fundamentals that, to use Hegel's terminology, belong to the category of mourning. These are the rituals of mortality, even in their simplest, most mundane manifestations.

Ishaghpour's conclusion appears all the more arguable because what else could the courage and patience of repetition aim for than the presentation of order shaped by tradition and the permanence of things. What is the chronicle of the ordinary lives of ordinary people if not the demonstration of the persistence of habits, emphasized by the measured use of tempo and rhythm? Ozu steers clear of all bombast, all dramatization. In building up scenes, he keeps an all but equal distance from his heroes and their environment, neither too far nor too close. And his returning gaze, the steady equilibrium of the camera's gaze, highlights the ceremony's humble solemnity.

Instead, the paradox lies in the fact that while no one has ever looked at things and shaped a story with more simplicity than Ozu, we know no other directors who made films more sure-handedly, in such transparent and immediately recognizable style. For his complexity becomes ripe for meditation precisely as he avoids strident and rapid extremes. When a director leaves time for the slightest stirrings of time's passage, seeks out the intimacy of frontality, follows long scenes and interludes with patience and discovers as much content as one would find in any action-packed sequence, he creates complexity by definition—all minute observations communicate the organic micro-dynamism of existence.

Parting, solitude, death, and acquiescence in the inevitability of their alternating rhythm touch the viewer to the core. They create an aura that envelops or rather permeates the entire oeuvre. For, with the precise definition of visual depth and shadow, the sensibility of a consistently used objective (a 50mm lens), time is conjured in space, even in empty space. What is more powerful: melancholy or modest happiness? Ozu does not distinguish between the two states, and as he enchants the viewer with his gentle progress and repetitions, he presents his quiet wisdom as a gift.

Ozu is obviously not the only director to make use of the method of pulsating repetition. Since we are already in Japan, we cannot forget about Kaneto Shindô of the same generation and his internationally acclaimed *Island* (1960). Using unparalleled reduction and the unflagging obstinacy of repetition, the film is about the harsh discipline of a strenuous life fighting the "naked island." Without dialogue, the film achieves shocking dramatic impact relying on the subtle variations by Hikaru Hayashi's music alone. With all the suffering of strain, perseverance, and sweat, the ultimate concentration locked in repetition and reprise releases extraordinary human warmth and emotional depth. The invention for a single voice thus becomes polyphonic through accretion, a form known in music as well (think of Ravel's "Bolero"), where repetition carries all that has been accumulated before.

Clearly, intensity grows with the conscious emphasis on reduction. For instance, Bresson, known for his extreme puritanism, prefers to work with a few themes that he further compresses and applies with great frequency. He not only attributes immense significance to physical gestures but also prefers to approach the metaphysical through the tangible. *The Pickpocket* (1959) and *Le Procès de Jeanne d'Arc* (1962) illustrate the relentless nature of destiny through countless identical shots and the repetition of sets and situations. Rhythmic marches, knocking footsteps, the constant return of identical, tightly framed opening/closing doors—all are tools of an ascetic presentation. With these alone Bresson manages to create a lasting image of the demystification of the universe and a human vulnerability that is not without majesty. Again, in *Au hasard, Balthazar* (1966), with bold directness he conjures life's constant swing between good and evil through the vicissitudes of a small donkey. Love and humiliation, jealousy and revenge, and the sudden, capricious shifts of emotions are driven home with the incessant repetition of a drumbeat. The drama is built on enlarged details, repeated gestures, and an infinitely pared down language. Through endless repetition, the viewer is led to recognize a set of laws. While the viewer may follow events in another location and at different times, he is forced to return to and remember as much what is constant and in synchrony as any new development. "Build your film on white, on silence and the stationary," Bresson writes in his *Notes*,[4] and he continues, "Don't run after poetry, it penetrates unaided through the joins (ellipses)."[5] One is allowed to, in fact one should, leave room for accents (imagination is stimulated by recognition), which allows the elimination of clichés and etches on the memory what may carry the essential point—all a matter of style, Bresson believes.

In more contemporary films we can often find deliberately applied interruptions in a repetitive way, which try in a Brechtian mode to remind us of a more general idea, hidden connections beyond the story itself, formally emphasizing the deeper sense of the fable.

Fatih Akın's successful Turkish-German film *Head-On* (2004), though it abundantly relies on the power of rock and punk, drugs and violence, tells the story of the new generation of the *gastarbeiter* (guestworkers) in a very original structure. The restless, frantic movie suddenly dares to change tone and mood in a startlingly repetitive fashion: it evokes an old-fashioned show, featuring songs with sentimental melodies presented by an elderly, somewhat heavyset star, accompanied by a large orchestra, with all the musicians in smoking jackets. Seven times, indeed seven times we have to stop the rushing story and come back to the same odd setting: a red carpet, a postcard-like décor, and in the background the glittering blue Bosporus. We are listening to the same nostalgic, heart-rending Turkish tunes. What is their role here? Of course any emotional identification could not be suggested either with the young protagonists, or the author himself. Yet, they are here, inextinguishably, like a stupid old dream; willing—or unwilling—they return, viscerally present as traces from the past, even if they deserve all the doubtful qualification and quotation marks that color them. Thus, the collision of the two, the new and the old cultures, the assimilated German and the half-forgotten ancestor meet, also calling attention to an ambiguous, weird pride. We come from Westernized roots as well, not just the barbarian; the elegant costumes are not that much different from the style the German bourgeoisie used to boast, although in both places they became obsolete.

The director's stubborn reprise of these totally out of place "inserts" expresses his sober, bitter comment, stepping out from the narrative, as Brecht allowed himself many times in his famous plays. Their extraneous character is not just alien but becomes a mocking, keen acknowledgment of the ambiguity of the emigrant existence.

The Comedy of the Mechanism

One of the most successful and recently rediscovered masters of reprise is Jacques Tati, who, in all his work, used precisely this method as the foundation of his comic language.

Initially Tati created a ubiquitous character based on his own quixotic figure, embodying his peculiar bearing and movements. Whether on vacation, in the role of the absent-minded uncle, or as the fumbling client of *Play Time*'s elegant futuristic offices, Monsieur Hulot always remains himself, Monsieur Tati-Hulot. His standard gestures, his height, and his angular gait balanced with his bent back, hat, and nod of the head have become comedy's stock-in-trade. Did he repeat himself? With stubborn resolve. Did he borrow from himself? Time and time again. Did he take his hero down the same alley? Of course he did. Apparently he was little concerned with the narrative flow. In fact, he was more intrigued by a peculiar retention as he approached a specific scene three or four times only to squeeze the last drop of juice from a joke.

One could say that this type of repetition is typical of all comic forms, even burlesque, for we have known since Bergson that laughing is fundamentally born in the wake of the insistent application of mechanical responses, as we recognize the power of events over man's blundering efforts. Buster Keaton has no better follower than Tati. Endlessly repeated patterns and uninhibited, innovative accents become the source of irresistible humor. As in the works of his pre-

Jacques Tati, *Play Time,* 1967

decessors, each gesture is original (sui generis) and different from what would be dictated by will or common practice. Both Keaton and Tati give the impression that they are total failures, but the second time around they beat the odds. Their temporary defeat actually demonstrates that, thanks to the characters' unflappable persistence, their setback may just as well be seen as a victory. Along with his doggedness, the hero proves his exceptional talent.

For instance, Tati regularly plays on the contrast of the inflexibility and unusual suppleness of the body. His gags, to quote Havel, "do nothing less than stretch to the absurd the contrast between one set of logic and another. This has nothing to do with rejecting tradition—just the opposite: it is fully exploited as his gags draw their energy from it."[6] Ahead of his time, in *Play Time* (made in 1967!) Tati recognizes the paradoxes in the tempo and physical conditions of modern urban life. While life has accelerated beyond all necessity, and the literal transparency (everything is made of glass) of comfort and the environment has become the only ideal, the consequences are quite the opposite: progress leads to gridlock and traffic jams and a permanent state of disorientation. Instead of easy access, our hero constantly runs into walls, doors, windows, and furniture. In *Monsieur Hulot Goes on Vacation,* Monsieur Tati-Hulot is always running late. This is why he has to make repeated attempts to get on the road with his old jalopy, to become strikingly successful playing ping pong or tennis, or finding out how to enter the dining room. He must make several efforts to reach his goal: he struggles with doors and the rules of etiquette. In *Mon Oncle* he greets people no less than sixty times in the film, including the radio announcer and the hat on the rack. Clearly, the series of "redundant" gestures provide character description. Polite behavior is motivated by the need to comply; through excess, however, the effort becomes a hilarious comment on an ill-adjusted character.

Returning to *Play Time,* here repetition does not only involve human action. All the buildings and environmental landmarks become familiar as one encounters a sameness everywhere. So much so that tourists arriving at the Paris airport are disoriented on finding the same airport they had left behind. And the hotel can be barely distinguished from the surrounding buildings.

"Is there no action in *Play Time?*" Tati asks this question in an interview given to *Cahiers du cinéma.* "There are people, prisoners of modern architecture sentenced by architects to move forever in straight lines . . . never in a circle or semi-circle . . . everything is built according to the logic of labyrinthine angles of office-buildings where everyone is forced to turn the corner and return along the same path . . . . In these stores and exhibition halls, you are not allowed to take small detours. . . . Even when dancing, people move along straight lines. And if at the end we encounter a merry go round, it never stops. Eventually, my people accept to live among these circumstances and objects."[7]

The criticism of uniformity by Tati means that the limited options and environmental conditions of modern life are rendered pathetic through frequent repetitions. Accordingly, the story develops at a slow pace, which thus becomes the expression of the absurd; the herd mentality becomes the moral of the wry-funny story where the individual is constantly forced to ape others and start all over again.

Where Tati mocks the external signs of modern existence with his camera, in *Calendar* (1993) the Canadian-Armenian Atom Egoyan in his playful-ironic style embarks on the analysis of a single emotional state.

The plot is purposely sparse: sitting in his apartment, a photographer (played by Egoyan himself) recalls the events of a visit to Armenia when he, his wife, and a guide toured the country to photograph historic monuments for a calendar. However, the wife remains in the distant land, and he suspects that she has developed an intimate relationship with the guide. The protagonist covers all the stations of looking for attractive company. Imbued with jealousy and remembering, his field of action is deliberately limited, while for his greater amusement he applies highly sophisticated communication tools.

This mundane/dramatic situation is suitable for analyzing. On the one hand there is the selective nature of memory and its barely perceptible processes, as well as longing, the attempts of imagination, and substitution. At the same time the director tries to avoid the appearance of excessive pathos. Thus, the unfolding events are deliberately awkward, oddly grotesque, as the hero is constantly interrupted in his pursuits by a stream of visitors. He invites twelve women, always under the same circumstances, for a simple offer of dessert and a glass of wine. We see the same table, the same shot with the bottle of wine and the repeat of the same clumsy scene: suddenly, the guests interrupt the strained conversation to make puzzling calls to their sweethearts, always in different languages. They carry on their passionate/flustered chatter in German, Russian, Arabic, Greek, Hebrew, Spanish, and who knows what other tongues. When the last conversation is finished, we realize that we have seen scenes performed on demand.

There is no need to explain that the play with symmetry, funny repetitions, and the magic number twelve that follows the twelve months of the year serve as vigorous principles of articulation. Twelve landmark churches, twelve telephone calls, and twelve guests weave a rather busy texture, rich in ingredients. Of course the structure places the entire story between parentheses, elevating all events to the level of the hypothetical.

This is a daring approach, deliberately mocking narrative convention. With flagrant redundancies and intentional prevarications, the narrative rises to such absurd levels as to lend this far from major but all the more zesty and entertaining work renewed energy. Egoyan resorts to endless repetitions and variations to illustrate the multiple layers of a highly ambivalent state of affairs. And with that he boldly challenges film's customary rising rhythm.

The Same yet Different

Film history's unparalleled masterpiece, Kurosawa's *Rashômon* (1950), offered a radically new insight into the complexity of film narrative. The story told from four different perspectives undertook much more than a simple meditation on the relative nature of truth. Instead, the film underscored the relevance of subjective truths and the fact that perforce each participant and witness interprets events differently; the point is made that no single right version can be constructed.

Our vision and interpretation of phenomena always pass through a distorting medium, and the facts revealed one after the other in the film are projections of so many prisms that bounce off each other and distort reality. Kurosawa's greatness lies in the fact that, in rejecting a universal notion of time, he examines superimposed moments in time and the inner truth of a single event that shifts with each new point of view. The enigma is not only the alpha and omega of multiplicity but also the realization that the reintegration of shattered reality always results in a new perception of reality. Thus complexity gains a deeper significance: ambiguity and the surfeit of options posit further openness, and a coherent closure remains elusive.

What is most relevant for my present argument is the consummate and illuminating precision of stylistic realization. Past the wisdom of its proposition, the creation of unique textures and their subtle contradiction contributes to the haunting expressiveness of a sensual presentation. The composition is contrapuntal, which further deepens the unique integrity of recalled realities as well as emphasizing their problematic nature. With the subtle yet significant discrepancies in the testimonies, besides building intensity, the film accepts a slackening of the narrative flow.

The huge gate and the pouring rain, the prison yard where the interrogation takes place, and the forest are worlds apart. With their solidity the first two are in stark contrast with the lively animation of the forest. On the other hand, light and darkness create another order. While the "invocation" of the rain-soaked gate is oppressively sinister, the sun-scorched prison yard is equally dreary. And the forest, shot through with light where wild movement and at times nerve-racking stillness cast deep shadows, becomes a mysterious jungle. Finally, the play of the camera represents yet another layer of interpretation: following the almost prancing steps of the lumberjack, it gradually comes to a sudden, shocking halt to record the fierce and merciless rush of the struggle.

While in these scenes the camera follows a complex choreography as it circles, swoops down, glides, soars, and threatens, in the prison yard it settles at the judge's eye-level and exploits the unnerving vision offered by the depth of the image.

Thus, rhythm is rendered artfully meaningful: rising or declining, slow and fast, light and dark, the dissonance of syncopation and suddenly bursting harmonies illuminate internal realities—these are devices that transform emotions into motion. With their musical and tonal mastery they emphasize the gaping chasm between the various testimonies, giving voice to the singularity of human experience. Obviously, the mad rush would have no such strong resonance without stillness and slow motion—the two extreme states presume and complement each other.

We shall return to an analysis of the closing scenes later when we have the opportunity to ponder endgame variations.

"What If" and "As If"

Reprise, the invitation to enticing, magical play, is an obsession for the Polish director Kieslowski. Here, I will discuss only two of his film realizations, *Blind Chance* (1981) and *The Double Life of Véronique* (1991).

Clearly, pondering the role of chance is an irresistible challenge to all experimenting artists. We often wonder, "What if?" How would a minor, insignificant factor have shifted and altered the course of events? What determined the eventual outcome, and would other alternatives be just as plausible?

In *Blind Chance* we see three variations on a theme set in a rather intriguing framework: the first, let us call it the primal story, runs sixty minutes, the second runs thirty minutes, and the third runs twenty minutes. While this arc gives a balanced proportion, its rhythm also suggests an underlying meaning.

What is the logic of these gradually diminishing variations, one may wonder? Kieslowski examines the possible turns of a young man's fate in Poland in the historically turbulent years of the 1970s, when the lack of democracy creates constant uncertainty and, due to the whims of external forces, no one is in control of his own destiny. One has no mastery over the present or the future.

From a formal viewpoint, Kieslowski chose a minimal theme for his variations: Is the young hero going to make or miss the train, and what are the consequences of either eventuality.

The protagonist of the film is an average person, neither better nor worse than any of the others of his generation. Subjected to harsh sociopolitical forces, a victim of pervasive autocracy, his freedom of movement is highly confined. His destiny is essentially predetermined—he may propose, while the powers-that-be dispose.

The facts of his life are sadly ominous. The loss of his parents makes him vulnerable at an early age, and his attachment to a surrogate father—who, after years in prison on trumped-up charges offers alcohol as the only solution—holds little promise for the future. As soon as the young man joins the political arena his actions take an ill-omened turn—he is doomed to suffer moral and emotional defeat. The factual variation: boarding the train in the first "movement" ends in total failure.

The second variation could be the exploration of an alternative path; here, missing the train leads to an even more tragic turn of events. While in this case he opts for courageous political resistance, his everyday life is made even more miserable. Prison and friendship fail to bring real salvation, and he remains desperately lonely.

Finally, the last scenario appears to offer the best hope. This time he seems close to attaining a "normal" emotional and professional position. However, after he takes leave of his idyllic family on his first trip abroad, the plane explodes and his life ends in an absurd accident.

A harsh lesson indeed, but Kieslowski needed to take stock of these alternatives to ponder the relationship between man and his social environment. And his conclusion, particularly in that specific moment of history, was not less gloomy than the former variations. It offers the recognition that far from dumb luck, the accidental is rather the all but inherent attribute of an unjust social order. "In the social sphere," the director says, "we are ruled by contingencies. The film demonstrates how political power shapes personal destiny, and describes forces that in one way or another become abhorrent."[8]

Kieslowski's structural method deliberately follows a musical model. The texture of the film is woven with returning themes and densely applied patterns. While the film reflects the drudgery of daily routines, the short segment of a life it presents gains substance as the logic behind so many accidents slowly emerges through recurring events. And even as the story is overshadowed by disillusion, the director maintains a vibrant sensibility demonstrated by his pleasure in dwelling on details. "I enjoy observing fragments of life and I love films that explore the tiny segments of life without explaining how things started or how they will end."[9] In other words, the accident for him is the mystery that seeks out and accepts profound questions.

The Double Life of Véronique is an unusual and rather lonely experiment in using repetition. Of course, there are many similarities between the Polish Weronika and French Véronique but the director is primarily interested in the nature of intuition: what is that almost magical quality of déjà vu that evokes the sense of familiarity, of something that had already happened in the past, whether it concerns a location or a person. Véronique and Weronika are double personalities and, even as they live parallel lives following their own destinies, in some sense they are related as if they were variations of each other.

Kieslowski gives the viewer complete freedom of interpretation. While he suggests certain solutions, these never work as a cipher. Enigma is an integral part of the story. Their complementary nature, similar or identical affinities (for music, for instance), create a bond between the two young women. In fact, we get the feeling they are oddly drawn to each other.

But this is also part of the mystery and the peculiar adventure that requires no justification: He relates the same story twice, differently, as if the similarities between the two destinies simultaneously may or may not be significant, maintaining an intriguing ambiguity.

The prologue to the film before the credits gives an odd hint of the mystery to come: we see the starry sky and a little girl who watches. "This is not fog—these are stars, millions of stars," a voice says in Polish. Then we see the same girl as she holds a leaf in her hand and hear the voice, this time in French: "It is springtime."

Neither statement carries real information; instead, they set an emotional tone. They refer to unknown events that precede the story seen on the screen and they suggest that the two girls are actually the same person. Later, however, the similar and/or identical natures return only by way of subtle allusions and fragmentary, obscure reminders. Be that as it may, Kieslowski's ambition to work in the conditional mode is rather intriguing. A sense of "as if," "perhaps," "who knows" lurks just beneath the surface of the story all the way through. This "as if" quality lends the story a weightless, unanchored quality. Ignoring cause and effect relationships, the rational core is altered by a more poetic, leisurely game.

Kieslowski's attraction to variations appears to be highly consistent. Working with two, three, and in fact ten alternatives in *Decalogue* clearly demonstrates his restiveness and insatiability in the face of a single option. Far from representing the arbitrary and superficial, his variations offer various options for defining law, freedom, and an interpretation of reality. Not only in content, but also in a formal sense, variations always return to the same starting point and take different turns only as they follow the diverging paths of slight transformations. Ignoring predictable and closed situations, Kieslowski always opts for evolving developments and thus avoids the trap of potentially oversimplified formulas. In a statement he has admitted that he was so intensely aware of the endless potential in contrasts, encounters, and digressions that during the production of *The Double Life of Véronique* he envisioned seventeen (!) final versions. The weight given to his constantly recurring, elegantly handled themes underlines this sense as well. Some characters appear in different contexts and wander from one film to the next, so besides the pleasures of surprise and recognition, the viewer also has the chance to experience a more complex sense of continuity.

Of course Kieslowski is not the only director to think of series or alternative choices. To try out different turning points and outcomes seems to be rather seductive.

Tema con variazione

The German Tom Tykwer played with the skill of a *jongleur* in deliberately choosing three variations in his successful film *Run Lola Run* (1998).Not only did he assimilate with apparent pleasure the new discoveries of mixed media—animation, video, black/white flashback, colored time-lapse, special effects and narration—but the game with the idea of "what if" seduced him, as well. It is as if he wanted to illustrate the vertigo of chaos theory: each variation offers a different outcome of random chance caused by fortuitous external occurrences. Lola may die if she arrives too late to save his criminal friend; it can be his lover who becomes the victim; finally both may escape with the "dough" found twice thanks to their drug dealing, if . . . if incalculable obstacles, car accidents, family dramas, or a last-minute hit in the casino do not enter into the ongoing run.

With the rushing, never stopping, stormy running of the incredibly inventive and indefatigable heroine, the director seems to demonstrate that each step is unpredictable and chance is the only dominant factor in our existence. Her uncommon tenacity for self-sacrifice is in vain, because it is not human will or decision that matters but the arbitrary incidental events of life that may collide with the original goal. It is obvious that the impact of popular video games, the countless potential available, is the inspiration of this story-experiment, as if the director wanted to illustrate the enigmatic consequences of the "butterfly effect." Anyhow, if we have examples of constant turbulences, without a moment of flow, this film might be a great model to think about its unusual impact.

As to the attraction of the magic power of series and numbers, Rohmer and Greenaway are undeniably in the foreground. Rohmer in his film series *Six Contes Moraux* and *Comédies et Proverbes,* or Greenaway in *Drowning by Numbers,* take pleasure in the embrace of stressed formal (numeric) articulation, not unlike some modern painters like Monet and Matisse who, besides the self-evident distinction of quality, recaptured the playfulness of quantity as well. In some cases (but obviously not as a rule) the plural does represent more than the singular. A new meaning arises from its very emphatic, displayed repetition, highly sensitive to the creative changeability and activity of time.

In subtle variations we also enjoy the pleasure of continuity, searching in rapt attention for the significance of the slightest shift, for the surfacing of a new perspective, a different emphasis.

"Que fait le temps?" Bergson asked with justification. What does time's pulsation signify as it confronts us with its constant rhythms, transformations, and quotations? And we cannot ignore Freud's discovery when he spoke about the *journey* of memories and memory traces, the way they are traveling with us, creating new configurations through repetition. There is a direct link between perception and consciousness: memory, association, and desire have a direct impact on current events. Memory demands repetition and the reinterpretation of the past. Our story does not dwell simply in the past, Lacan notes as well. "The story belongs to the past as far as it becomes history in the present—and it becomes history in the present because we have experienced it in the past."[10]

Life's dynamism is defined and sustained by desire. It generates activity where the three temporal ecstasies (the exits from the present, that is, the past and the future) and a shift from a state of stagnation toward the future intersect. There is a movement in the direction of something else, toward a new horizon. The resulting disparity between the same and the different lends human time its genuine, truly pulsating dimension.

And in this context, the weight of *times,* the sum of diverse times becomes perceptible again. The surfeit is due not only to the simultaneity of recollections and memory traces but also to the paradoxical reverberations of successive events. We conduct our lives over and over again following similar yet always slightly different procedures. Time does not pass independently of us, but rather the *passage* is subject to constant shifting, condensation, transformation, suppression, and return. As memories catch up with us and assume new shapes, we move among the present, the past, and the future.

It is also important to note that by its very nature perception itself is not all-embracing; it is a form of involvement, yet not a fully experienced impression. This is why we must recover forgotten and buried memories and rekindle their obscured meaning through repetition/recollection. The encounter mobilizes new memory traces and drives us toward new experience.

When building a narrative structure, reprise and retake must be allowed to bring their rich potential into play, lending authenticity to the dynamics of human existence.

Theo Angelopoulos, *The Weeping Meadow,* 1985

7 Odysseys

Space Solitude
In the Labyrinth of the Zone
The Maze of History
Timeless Time
The Arc of the Passions

Space Solitude

There are genres and approaches in film where the works reach for a larger framework, beyond attempts at realism or verisimilitude. These films measure our place and future in the world in cosmic dimensions. Stanley Kubrick's *2001: A Space Odyssey* (1968) belongs to this category and remains one of the most successful films to date.

The film tackles a vast and mysterious subject: a cosmic adventure that raises philosophical questions about the origins and purpose of life. The space-time dimensions of human civilization are challenged by another existence, beyond human "standards" of intelligence, and the encounter will inevitably lead to unsolvable mysteries. Because the extraterrestrial being, or cosmic force, represented in the form of a black monolith, appears both as a threat and as a sign of hope for humanity. Kubrick sets up the story beyond the disaster of a future world in which the power of robots prevails over humans, without offering any intrinsic value. Therefore the pervasive melancholy, emphasized not only with the end of the journey, conjuring up the restart of life from dawn, but by the variegated romantic music, as well. "Such cosmic intelligence . . . would be as far removed from man as we are from the ants," says Kubrick, in an interview. "They could be an instantaneous telepathic communication throughout the universe; they might have achieved total mastery over matter; in their ultimate form, they might exist as a disembodied immortal consciousness."[1]

Kubrick departs from the famous Arthur Clarke novel (though they collaborated on the script) in order to give voice and form to his personal, more complex vision, including his doubt-charged mythical inclinations. The title's allusion to the Homeric odyssey comprises the characteristic duality of Kubrick's sphere of thoughts: the perennial, poetic values of mythology and the ironic, uncertain outcome of the big journey. In the first sequence, titled "The Dawn of Man," Richard Strauss's *Thus Spake Zarathustra,* evoking Nietzsche, suggests the idea of eternal return, but one that is not exempt from the grotesque and the scarily bizarre.

I don't want to enter into a full analysis of this rich and irregular movie. What matters here is the perception of time in Kubrick's film, the specific way he handles the presence of time, its human–nonhuman measure, beyond the unparalleled handling of space and spectacle.

The paradox of *2001* resides precisely in the fact that everything appears in its most ordinary, simple form. While the mystical Black Monolith becomes the embodiment of an all-embracing intelligence, as a threatening or maybe liberating symbol of mankind's entire evolution over millions of years, the central protagonists of the film follow their life as normal, mundane beings. The space traveling itself happens amid truly banal, routine activities: gymnastics, calisthenics, eating from plastic trays. Conversations take place within a glacial, faceless environment, familiar in any chain hotel. The perfectly sophisticated machines, the seamlessly functioning weightless toilets, the supervisory computers reveal much about the results of the radiant development of technology, yet there is no indication of the slightest enrichment of any emotional refinement. The endless path from the ape to the man, and further to the "superman," to the murderous hostility between human beings and the machine, but also among the scientists themselves, lead us back to the beginning, the place from where we started the whole journey. There we find the mystery of the unknown, the secrets of the silent space. However, the odyssey is still not utterly dramatic: it moves ahead in a more epic way, step by step. And the circle doesn't stop. When the old human arrives at the end, passing away becomes suddenly a miraculous rebirth. What was dead comes to life immediately in the form of a fetus, gazing at the world in a way that suggests a new, circulating planet.

Kubrick is most successful in evoking the exceptional mission with startling effects. His method lies in perpetuating an extremely slow pace and using the hypnotic power of mechanical motion. He works with endless patience. The exploration proceeds step by step, forcing the viewer to make close observations. Every visual detail and discovery is achieved through painfully slow recognition and breathtaking progress. Each subsequent insight into life's routines or the mystery machine is gained through the detachment of annoying, smooth gliding. When something out of the ordinary happens (such as weightlessness or walking upside down), or when the barren, coldly minimalist, and mechanized interior offers little spectacle, the effect is always the same: the viewer waits with bated breath as he tries to get his bearings. However, no relief is granted, for Kubrick constantly seeks new formulations and visual effects to surprise and awe.

Moreover, we are not given enough information for spatial orientation, for normal coordinates do not apply. The ingenuity of the visual aspect in science fiction is that nothing appears the same as it is here on earth—not the doors, surfaces, colors, or distances. Kubrick loves endless corridors that go on infinitely, and he also depicts the disquieting experience of a flat horizon. The effect is vertiginous, because we suspect that dangers lurk in these endless vistas. The space appears to be much too fragile. When it shifts and turns in on itself, another element of playfulness and surprise is introduced. Let us not forget that the four chapters of the film, marking stages over four million years, strive to suggest the full history of the universe, without predicting the return of closure, letting us guess the final outcome.

The spaceships and their interior are bizarre and surreal. Along with their clever functionality, some surprising design elements constantly warn of their otherworldly associations. We do not easily grasp their hidden potentials and the nature of their genius. All becomes clear only gradually, through meticulous exposition.

In other words, Kubrick is brazenly slow in telling the story, using deliberately little action and narrative turning points; he is extremely sparing with information, postponing for long intervals definition or revelation as well; and, most importantly, he also adds to the viewer's inescapable sense of insecurity by employing the nature of dilatory physical motion itself. As a result, the work unfolds as a silky, dreamlike chimera, without spasms or loud accents.

Kubrick's approach is also linked with a truly unexpected and unseemly element: the world of music. Much has already been written on the "incongruity" of Johann Strauss's "Blue Danube" waltz in the film, but as we later listen to Khachaturian's or even Ligeti's romantic melodies we get a better sense of Kubrick's intention: old-fashioned emotionalism and perfect automation are combined for an odd encounter. These disparate elements form a sarcastic complement that launches the entire adventure into a region of elusiveness well beyond everyday experience.

Ambiguity is the real voice of Kubrick. Starting with a harsh, animalesque barbarism, arriving at a more sophisticated, technicalized barbarism, Kubrick questions the meaning of evolution and does not find too much glory in it. Yet, Kubrick's sense of death doesn't encompass a simplistic ending, but, rather, he evokes through his surreal, fantastic presentation a kind of eternal circulation, transcending the merely human perspective.

This is the cultural heritage of the European/North American/British author, putting himself between quotation marks, self-doubting and self-mocking—yet resigned to his fate. Kubrick raises space adventure to majestic heights only to mock the superhuman and grotesque features of the enterprise, while he also lends the venture a unique splendor.

Kubrick is sardonic, a romantic-ironic believer. As he approches the enigmatic end of the film, he releases the viewer with a gift of emphatically ravishing beauty. The universe's limitless wealth beyond all human imagination and the dazzling swirl of colors confront us above all with their unfathomable quality, with the sparkling variety of shades, shapes, volumes, and forms—the heretofore slow motion erupts into a turbulent spectacle. Here his poetry breaks off from his skeptical message, evoking an existing and lasting value; even if the galaxy surpasses the human measure, nature and the cosmos live, within infinite spaces and times.

Kubrick's *2001* is one of the earliest examples of a genre that gained wide popularity in subsequent years. However, no other filmmaker has since recognized so profoundly the alien and metaphysical essence of the enterprise and made the film's exceptional rhythm the basis of his visual language.

Kubrick's *The Shining* (1980) displays a radically different approach. And yet, the self lost in isolation and the metaphor of the labyrinth finds a pronounced, unusual form in this work as well. In its inimitable style, the film depicts a long journey. However, instead of leading to a well-defined destination, the journey leads inward to encroaching madness and the loss of control. The looming darkness of the end points to the dissolution of ordinary human standards, yet the accurately designed arc casts a dark shadow that becomes threatening and bloodcurdling.

The Shining creates the most paradoxical form of the horror film genre: except for an omen that bodes ill at the opening, almost nothing significant happens in the first half of the film. Then we follow the stations of a slow, gradual descent into madness that culminates in the final, drawn-out scenes of a deadly chase.

The essence lies in the unusual, yet so Kubrick-like, treatment of space. Here, the director gives free rein to his almost perverse talent when he literally plays around with the infinite as he meanders through an inscrutable, endless labyrinth looking for an elusive exit. This palpable motif is shown at the beginning and the end of the film, but the real point is the hypnotic and endless combination of thrilling tracking shots that maintain and steadily increase the tension, without mercy but always with a superior sense of proportion.

Of course, Kubrick is the most conscious master-editor of rhythmic variation. Menacing, repressed passions that suddenly explode hurl his protagonist on a self-destructive course of action. Cutting all ties, Jack Nicholson goes after his victims in a wild rampage, rushing through huge empty spaces and endless corridors, breaking down all obstacles inside, such as walls and doors, and then running outside through a winter wilderness. Falling in a fit of madness, he runs into the labyrinth, armed with lethal weapons. In *The Shining,* each image and each scene operates with the crushing force of oversized dimensions. Characters wandering through cavernous rooms and a child riding his bike in endless circles induce dreadful apprehension. Whether through measured movements—such as the wife's tentative attempts at appeasement, or the repeated shots of the child shown from behind wandering the maze of corridors—Kubrick exploits tempo and rhythm, the artful contrast of extreme slowness and the sudden shift to its opposite. The two distinct time dimensions build a suspenseful aura precisely through their juxtaposition. We experience hot and cold chills, shivers, and a constant sense of dread, expecting more horrors to come.

The oversized proportions demand alert attention from the viewer. The eye must cover areas that, from a narrative point, appear deliberately "superfluous," redundant, and a waste of time. And yet, it all works with an elemental force: the charged view transcends the story.

Then comes the "walk-through," the steady expansion of kinetic energy that also leads in the direction of ritenuto. The viewer must follow the characters through the immense and excruciatingly long space, perceive the constantly recurring theme of the child riding his bicycle. Framing is essential here. We always see the child from the rear, emphasizing the nearly abstract quality of his movement: what matters is not the human being himself but his journey, the uninterrupted road with its startling twists and turns. On and on it goes, through space and time, far beyond our need for any further information.

And finally, a third component is the accompaniment of the peculiar rhythm of the camera's mechanical motion. Tracking movement is always slow, generating fear and anxiety. We proceed in a crawl that evokes ominous premonitions. The effect is baleful and the scary, slowly advancing horror is almost palpable.

The contrasts are stretched further with the effects of sound. Obviously, the complex counterpoint between massive space and movement therein calls for deep silence that suddenly bursts into wild screaming. If the thriller has a template, Kubrick makes full use of the genre's best traditions. The techniques of creating delayed suspense are generally known, but Kubrick applies them to the extreme, irreverently.

The method, if you like, is based on psychological motivation for it speaks about the destructive and unpredictable consequences of glacial solitude and isolation. However, while the film makes full use of exhilaration generated by speed, eventually its profound originality lies in deliberate retention. The spectator is tried and viscerally engaged through the lengthy anticipation

In the Labyrinth of the Zone

Of all the great leisurely authors, Tarkovsky is undoubtedly one of the most distinguished. His mesmerizing reticence and quiet demeanor create a *majestuoso* solemnity. The all but weightless movement of his protagonists and patient camera are meant to sculpt time itself, "to express infinity by stopping the flow of time," as he says. The paradox of his achievement lies in seizing the passage of time in its timelessness or, to put it more precisely, in its inner time, that is, directing the gaze past the banality of the story to a metaphysical reality. His films, *Andrey Rublyov, The Mirror,* and especially *Stalker,* work as single, homogenous currents whose rhythm is shaped not by caesura but by an endless serenity and rapt attention. For time, as the negation of the purely physical action, acts as a reinterpretation of the burden of existence, and thus its perceptible deferral points to an interior journey. Events do not simply take place in the external world, but rather in profoundly experienced spirituality. "There was a time when the future was the continuation of the present. Change appeared over the edge of the horizon. By today, the present and the future have been fused . . . there is no more time, no more future," the writer-hero of *Stalker* states.

With Tarkovsky, all time experience is measured against the end of time—thus the unusual breadth of his oeuvre. His eschatology attempts nothing less than to conjure infinity itself.

As for the formal ideal, perhaps surprisingly at first glance, Tarkovsky follows the example of Eisenstein and draws inspiration from haiku. The traditional Japanese verse is characterized primarily by its succinctness, while Tarkovsky is never sparing on length. However, it is his dense visual language and unexpected juxtapositions that fire the imagination, just as they do in haiku. His poetic language is built on "apt and precise observation" and startling transitions; the core of experience beyond ordinary physical dimension.

"What attracts me in haiku," Tarkovsky says, "is its observation of life—pure, subtle, and one with its subjects."

As it passes by	The dew has fallen
The moon barely touches	on all the spikes of blackthorn
Fishhooks in the waves	There hang little drops

"This is pure observation," Tarkovsky says. "The observation of a phenomenon passing through time."[2]

Tarkovsky is deeply preoccupied with the illustration of the laws of time and "the aesthetic structure of facts as they change through time." Then he reaches the concept central to his method: rhythm is the most effective and dominant component of the moving image, "expressing the passage of time within the frame." The emphasis is on "within the frame." The breath and the heartbeat of time is either pulsating in the visible image or it does not exist at all. Other components, such as editing, visual effects, sound, and the actors' performance, are all secondary—all that is alive is manifested by the rhythm of the image, which is

> filled with time, and organizes the unified, living structure inherent in the film: and the time that pulsates through the blood vessels of the film, making it alive, is of varying rhythmic pressure. . . . What you see in the frame is not limited to visual depiction, but is a pointer to something stretching out beyond the frame and to infinity . . . beyond the edges of the frame, lives within time if time lives within it; this two-way process is a determining factor of cinema.[3]

He called this modeling "sculpting time": "to take the various time-pressures, which we could designate, metaphorically as brook, spate, river, waterfall, and ocean—joining them together engenders that unique rhythmic design which is the author's sense of time."[4]

Both ambitions are crucial: the search for diversity and eternity he refers to so often. Tarkovsky's concept of time becomes unique through the simultaneous use of the two extremes. He attempts to give shape to the variability inherent in pulsation and the incomplete (uncompletable) nature of the flow of time.

It is enough to invoke the unforgettable opening scene in *Rublyov,* which summarizes Tarkovsky's entire ars poetica. Images of flying, the rising and crashing of the balloon made of rags, becomes the metaphor for mystical faith and dark prophecy, the tragic soaring of human and artistic imagination. His dreamer attempts the impossible when he prepares to jump from the top of the belfry and levitates for a long time over a heaving landscape below. We sense the danger, the looming failure, yet anxiously hope against hope for the success of the improbable undertaking. However, Icarus's adventure had to end in failure. The hero had the imagination and ingenuity to create the magic device, and the courage to face great risk—all in vain. For a few moments of pure bliss he triumphs: "I'm flying, I'm flying!" he howls in exaltation before he falls to the ground and is crushed to death.

The opening sequence, like the entire picture, takes hold of the viewer and, despite the painful fiasco, we are swept up by the majesty of the whole enterprise. Here we must again quote Tarkovsky's uniquely sensitive and poised approach: "We spent a long time," he says, "working out how to destroy the plastic symbol on which the episode was built, and reached the conclusion that the root of the trouble was in the wings. And in order to dispel the Icarus overtones we decided on an air balloon. This was a clumsy object put together from skins, ropes and rags, and we felt it rid the episode of spurious rhetoric and turned it into a unique happening."⁵

This rare instance of courage deserves all our respect. Avoiding the hazards of trite symbolism, recognizing the "incongruent" nature of filmmaking (one of Tarkovsky's favorite expressions)— this is the source of the originality of his artistic imagination. Just as later in the film, *Rublyov,* his paradoxical career unfolding with many twists and turns in the face of all odds, all forms of oppression, suffering, and bloody struggle, finds his own truth and dignified authority. Similarly Tarkovsky, working with monumental measures, with simple yet all-encompassing narrative tempo and rhythm, creates his own language and grammar.

Stalker, made more than ten years later, is no less tragic in its tone. *Stalker* could be seen as a science fiction film, for the labyrinth of the "zone" is not of this world and our protagonists leave their prosaic lives in search of some unnamable, highly classified secret. Thus their adventure, the exploration of the unknown, acquires a philosophical dimension (not unlike *Rublyov*), lifting the film far above the standards of the genre and encouraging the viewer to interpret its unusual handling of time from this perspective.

Stalker runs for close to three hours and consists of 142 shots. Those are long takes, of course, where all movement inside tightly cropped images concentrates on the symbolic space and the fragile existence of the struggling heroes. Life in the zone knows no rational progress, only constant toil, fatigue, and anxiety in the face of the uncertain. This explains the almost painful rhythmic segments and the conscious retention of tempi. The aura of spirituality weighs heavily and demands sustained attention—to follow developments to the last detail from a distance located in some broader totality. Our protagonists advance toward the unattainable through an abandoned, overgrown, and rain-soaked landscape or decaying underground caverns. However, the journey does not lead to a safe haven. By the time we return to hum-drum existence, the legendary "secret" is degraded to the level of other moments of transcendence. The mystery of the glass starting to move without apparent cause, the magic power of the young girl representing the future, unfold with chilling slowness. While there is constant reference to illumination and epiphany, the director keeps his focus on the "search as a process." Instead of mere revelation and empty metaphor, Tarkovsky models time and evokes Valery: "History is still not Time, nor is it evolution. . . . Time is a state: the flame in which there lives the salamander of the human soul."[6]

The Maze of History

Angelopoulos is the other great example of a director invoking the mythological world of great epic poetry, thus creating a particular rhythm, appropriate to the undertaking. The coherent fabric of his oeuvre is built up with large forms. The unmistakable style, an obstinacy of perspective and method are revealed in the originality of his treatment of time. His films betray a sensitive, well-articulated musical structure with the revelatory force of a classical tale—the two being all but inseparable from each other.

He set to film a series of Odysseys, the quarrels of troubled wanderers, ill-fated souls with history or the powerful, always making time for people to experience hopeful and frustrated beliefs, desires, and suffering. All efforts are attempts at homecoming while, according to the rules of life, home will never be what it had once been. Time reshapes not only the hero but his world of origin as well. Destiny is the road itself, his films suggest, a mandatory adventure in the grip of time, as in the *Travelling Players, Voyage to Cythera,* and *Landscape in the Mist.* "The rootedness in ancestry," as Angelopoulos puts it, is "not expressed simply by adopting or developing the tale; instead, it works as some kind of subterranean force, as a hidden and deep current." As such, it is not a simple reinterpretation of the Odyssey but takes "the myth of the return of Ulysses as its starting point."[7]

Angelopoulos has abandoned conventional rules in making his three- to four-hour-long movies. Within the boldly extended duration, the protagonists' transfigured destiny is elevated in a majestic aura, as if each step was a question and a threat: a meditation and the object of quiet resignation in the face of the inevitable blow. We appear to progress under duress, and events are colored by melancholy and the anguish of experience. These films work as requiems, as celebrations of a farewell to hope.

"In the beginning was the journey," says the modern Greek poet George Seferis, and we understand how it became Angelopoulos's favorite quote. After the acclaimed *Travelling Players* (1975), a constantly renewed sense of the journey imbues and shapes his films but never as mere spatial displacement or geographical change. Angelopoulos's wanderers explore the drama of passing time, following the tragic rhythm of purpose, passion, and perception. The journey gains deeper meaning, transcending past and present, dreams and imagination. Its scenes become the interior world of his heroes; at once both closed and vulnerably open to absorb the exterior.

Restrained, ceremonious in rhythm, with layered structures, his films express the intricate nature of his characters' quest. Such a narrative arc is deliberately fragmented, admitting the inevitable doubts and leaps of thought, the "non-coherence" of things, as he has phrased it. A kind of *ricercar,* or recapture, as it is called in music, articulates the form that seeks to capture the restless tension of his travelers.

The structure of his masterful presentations brings about a dazzling display. Turbulence and flow vary by turns, as he follows the story of his characters, and incites us to travel with them magically. He unveils the pitfalls of certainty and doubts and calls upon us to live the whole tortuous adventure. We are warned, along with his hero in *Voyage to Cythera,* not to "lose the rhythm" and to accept the returns to the beginnings, the almost unfathomable roots of hopes and force, both physical and emotional.

The emotional journey of his films, including the recent *The Weeping Meadow* (1985), is that of the inevitable progression of grief. It does not take the hero closer to stability and peaceful certainty but rather toward darker regions of loss.

The rhythmic accent, as usual in Angelopoulos's oeuvre, is defined by deliberate restraint. Tension and anguish do not give rise to a fast pace, on the contrary. However, all the historic and emotional changes are abrupt, merciless. While he takes ample time to linger on stretched-out moments, to elaborate their calligraphy, the blows of sudden cruelty intrude with brutal energy.

The Weeping Meadow is the first part of a planned trilogy in which he intends to sum up his country's twentieth-century mythical history. Starting with the exodus of the beginnings, the destiny of his people consists of rootlessness and mourning. This epic traveling, as always in his films, is evoked through emblematic, poetic episodes: wandering on the rainy, stony streets, accompanied by the sorrowful sounds of the melodies of the accordion; bloody animals hanged on the trees; dirty rivers inundating the whole village; and abandoned railway stations signal the stages of the tormented wandering.

The story that encompasses about thirty years of history is at once tormented, following the big commotions of the century, but also profoundly personal and emotion-centered. In reality the fever and the tragic suffering of a "forbidden" secret love affair mold the unfolding events, starting at the age of early youth to the final end caused by the war. Escapes, the threat of homelessness, and vulnerability fill the magnificent frescoes: the passions find their form in artful compositions; pain and joy are equally elevated to a level of visually upsetting, expressive beauty. The inspiration of Antigone and the Odyssey, Angelopoulos's most personal, naturally adopted traditions, color the doomed destinies.

For example, consider the scene featuring an enigmatic dance of the bride on the seashore in her floating white bridal veil, surrounded by a group of black-clad men; a catafalque on the gliding raft, and the obligatory worn suitcases in the hands of people always on the move, wearing their Sunday best, ready to go, whether to funerals or far away. There is no scene without upsetting meaning and composition, be it indoors or outdoors. They all become interior landscapes, expressing the hard fate of the protagonists. Sometimes the more playful or diabolical melodies of the accordion bring a tiny liveliness into the sorrow of the small communities' life, but basically the historical, mythological conflicts shape and interrupt the daily order of the connections.

The basic motif of eternal traveling determines the ambiance and rhythm of the movie. The flow of the film, "like rivers which run to the sea, are related to the traveling, to the exile," Angelopoulos says. The long takes have certainly been his major stylistic feature, but here they undertake a slightly different function, foremost that of blurring the boundaries between lyrical images and objective events. The geometrical layout of the frame is also less stringent. He rarely uses close-ups, since his characters always breathe with their environment, yet the camera is here more personal, more supple, and the composition exhibits a tender rigor (if those two terms can be linked).

The fluidity of the film is created in a highly sophisticated way. Angelopoulos refers to the peculiar mode of shooting used by Kurosawa that he wanted to apply in this film. Willing to use an exaggerated zoom, he moves from 25mm to 250mm lenses, thus calling attention to the shot itself. There is a clear "heating up" in the gesture, pointing at the emotional content, when toward the ending the mourning of Eleni upon the loss of her beloved ones reaches its unbearable peak. We may surely consider it as "turbulence" in a cinematic way. The long takes, like magic tools, hold together the distant spaces and times, in which beauty and melancholy create coherence.

There is nothing more telling than his own confession:

> A film's rhythm is an inner rhythm, therefore a personal sense of time. In my films the rhythm resembles time dilation but in actual fact it is not. The ratio of filmic time to real time is 1:1. The fact that it appears like a time dilation of the sort that in music terms we would call ritenuto or lento allows the viewers, if they let themselves, to savor or breathe time.
>
> In contrast I find that in most of today's film production there is an acceleration that compresses time and abolishes the sense of real time. . . . It is not to let the viewer enter into dialogue with the film. Abolishing so-called "dead time" is abolishing the pauses as they exist in music. Abolishing pauses means eliminating a film's inner music. Films travel with their secret music.[8]

In the "reconstruction" of Eleni, "Ulysses' gaze" draws an imaginary exode and "voyage to Cythera," in which his "travelling players," like shadows of seekers of a better life, pass through the "landscape in the mist."[9]

Timeless Time

Besides these classic masters, the films of the Hungarian director Bela Tarr generated attention in the last few years. His nearly eight-hour-long *Satan's Tango* (1994) and his much shorter and extremely dense *Werkmeister Harmonies* (2000) offer more recent examples of exceptionally measured presentation.

Satan's Tango is the exceedingly restrained conjuring of a single theme, a single moment in time, and a singularly thick atmosphere. The story takes place at a ramshackle farm and, while not

Bela Tarr, *Satan's Tango,* 1994

trying to deny its symbolism, brings its physical reality to almost unbearable closeness. It illustrates with terrifying meticulousness a world of mud, mating animals, decaying houses ready for the wrecking ball, foul-smelling kitchens and smoke-filled pubs. The slow development of the narrative in this miserable environment speaks of trapped human souls. Almost nothing happens to them, yet one senses that everything is determined from above (by faceless authorities) at a distance—helplessness, petty hatred, and mutual distrust dominate the rites of fear, deceit, and vague attempts at escape.

Yet, the social brew is complex and intricately textured. An understanding of the impotence and bitterness of more or less dominant characters requires its own time. They are sunk in a hopeless and bleak mud-existence, as if held by a demonic curse. Like a devastating disease, the farm is eating them alive. A single movement requires a long time, not to mention the reaction and defense needed to arrive at the minimum of consciousness. Tarr's protagonists are not given the sense to comprehend their condition. They creep blindly into the next situation—to fall and sink into the mud again.

Where nothing happens, deadly silence reigns. Only alcohol brings some life—loss of consciousness and violence. Other than that, there are only the routines of a vegetative existence and the withering desire to get away. No matter how, where, with whom. Only to escape as far away as possible. Long, slow scenes of subhuman life, lost hope for any change. Dancing a tango, or the play of a retarded girl with a cat as she tortures the animal to death, lasts forever, until there is total exhaustion, without relief. This is not the work of will, but that of repressed instinct and un-consciousness.

The power of destiny lies in its inevitability: the imperative to follow through, the manifest fatality of things. When the characters are on the move, we follow them on the rain-soaked gravel path, a long stretch of road leading to a frequently mentioned (symbolic) junction. For they have left the normal world behind a long time ago and live in the middle of nowhere, in no man's land. Even an awareness of the end does not help, as there is no present, only the unbearable perpetuity of existence. The metaphor of the opening shot is also the most bruising summary of the film. It is dark, minutes before dawn. Mooing cattle roam aimlessly in the distance mounting each other here and there, then roll in the mud. The slowly panning camera circles and envelops them. The barely changing scene appears stationary, threatening in its monotony and silence. Then we see a window framing a man's dark silhouette, and the dirty patterns of the curtain. As the camera moves back a bit suddenly a woman appears bringing a wash-basin, and she starts squatting above it in order to casually clean herself after a presumably finished intercourse. Her action lasts beyond normal time. And precisely this "disproportion," the unity of length and sharp ellipsis, creates the uncanny ambiance, as if projecting the path of an entire destiny. This is it—and nothing else.

Our characters exist in this open prison, a cage without bars, in the total uniformity of space, subjected to the pressure of motionless or extremely decelerated time. The quality of time is made apparent by a ceaseless rain with stubborn consistency, offering no hope for a break.

And yet, the inclement weather is not the punishment of nature. It is as indifferent as the vegetation itself. When man abandons himself, there is nothing to stem the power of dark rain crashing down. And the result is unmitigated homogeneity of texture: naked branches in the wind, frail and trembling animals, weather-beaten trench coats, threadbare leather jerkins, unshaven faces, and hideous knitted caps drawn over deep-set eyes.

Where are we, and when does all this take place? One hundred or ten years ago, or today? The demoralized school director and the permanently drunk doctor remind us of a fatal anachronism: we stay where we have always been—from the beginning of time until the inscrutable end. With their relentless obsession, the many similar characters and the host of inconsequential narrative threads weave an increasingly tight web. Satan's tango? No. It is all creepily banal and hapless—anything but hellish. Even if it has lost all its taste, color, and impulse, this is far from the opposite of heavenly. It lacks even the majesty of pain and suffering. It is merely a vegetative state where living forms take in and unload, empty and decrease only to slowly fade into this life-forsaken void.

Tarr's descriptive language knows but two extremes: long shots and close-ups, but both are characterized by long duration. The slowly moving, unobtrusive camera makes its presence barely perceptible. The method thus eliminates all descriptive references.

Even among the masters of slow films, Tarr is unique in making the passage of time or its painfully slow-paced movement the essence of his work: this is the existence of human beings deprived of action and events in their allotted time. Therefore not man but time itself becomes the protagonist. And this is why it must play such a prominent role.

If Tarkovsky is solemn, Tarr is the opposite: viscerally naturalistic and tangibly direct. Although he also evokes the sense of the labyrinth, as there is no escape, everything moves in closed space and time, if slithering can be defined as movement. Here too, reduction leads to constant attempts at restarts and the origin of things—all bound to the soil, however, without obvious metaphysical prospects. Man is surrounded by a dead past and a dead future. There is only the present stretching to infinity; once the mind is extinguished there is no memory or ambition. Intention is replaced by distention: the prolongation and inexorable extension of time.

The lack of solemnity does not mean the lack of a ponderous tone: oppressive and grim hopelessness permeates the movement of humans and the camera alike and defines the play of light and shadow. Thus all moments are ominous, emanating a sense of menace and nervous tension.

In *Werkmeister* the director makes a similar use of the inscrutable and chilling aura of objects and the environment. In the opening scene of the film we follow the path of a huge, metal-plated trailer (carrying the whale, the promise of sensational spectacle). As we continue to watch the vehicle rumbling down streets in the dead of night and know less and less about its mission, the more threatening it becomes. The shadow it casts is more unnerving than the clumsy hulk of the trailer itself, while its clatter shatters the tranquility of the night.

Werkmeister is also the development of a single theme, that is, a restart at a level of higher intensity reached through accumulation. Thus the rhythm, while deliberately monotonous, produces the impression of a crescendo. Time moves only vertically, downward in the direction of an ever deeper tension. Or seemingly upward, into the direction of senseless madness, where rational sobriety has long lost its ground. There are scenes in which the protagonists, wild children or drunken adults alike, no longer know any limits. They go on in their unrestrainable impulses until they literally collapse. Nevertheless, the overall nature of the film affects the spectator as evenly oppressive, despite the incidental eruptions.

Valuska, the dimwit, is the smallest unit in this swirling universe. He may observe everything and even execute some orders, but nothing mitigates his utter powerlessness. He may be the carrier of messages; he bounces around among his clients haphazardly, like a small planet set on its course. He comes and goes among other people like a meteorite spinning around larger celestial bodies. This is intimated in the metaphor of the opening scene where, in a dreamlike sequence, he has his drinking buddies dance to the movement of the planets. When the explosive energy of the powerful ones is exhausted, he escapes their orbit and suddenly starts to fall, to crash into the void.

This invisible spiral is the film's main theme and rhythmic foundation. Valuska follows his own path slowly, surrendering to prevailing winds and external impulses. His path is defined by friction and bouncing instead of inner motivation. For the space where he is allowed to operate also defines the limits of his stunted existence. As he meets his destiny he becomes more innocent, lighter and more weightless. Thus, instead of moving at a brisk pace, he simply plods on.

There is one outstanding scene in which the metaphor of the vicious circle becomes fully spectacular. Valuska and his "boss" are required to meet the authorities in order to reinstate order. As they walk next to each other in an increasingly relentless rhythm and tension, the camera focuses on the profile of their faces, very closely, and only after a while do we realize that they are going round and round, circling all around as if under a spell. The growing speed makes it foreboding and disquieting: we have to sense their doom.

In spite of a few sequences when turbulences violently occur, the film's rhythm is built on the principle of retention. What cannot be stopped cannot be accelerated either: each thing moves at its own speed and tempo, including the most brutal violence and foaming rage. The time of inner impulses is past explanation or measuring (the revolt of workers and their destructive passion, the delirium of the officer relishing power deriving from his adored gun). Everything lasts until full exhaustion, while the battle is constantly joined. Drinking, the time of closing, or the flame flickering and dying on the stove are all natural phenomena, just as the depletion of human energies leads inevitably to self-degradation.

Tarr's black-and-white films boldly apply the consistency of stylistic and tonal unity. Thus the worlds they present are whole and homogenous even as they apparently play but on a few "instruments." But, as we know, intensity is never a function of quantity.

The Arc of the Passions

There is another, fundamentally different master of metaphysical secrets, the philosopher poet of video-haiku: Bill Viola. Nothing stands farther from him than Kubrick's sarcasm, Tarkovsky's prophetic pessimism, Angelopoulos's history-craving, or Tarr's naturalist expressionism. Steeped in Oriental philosophy, Viola speaks to us inspired by Zen, Taoism, and Buddhism with the solemnity of utter simplicity. "If we pose a question with proper ceremony," he writes, "the universe will respond." His close to three decades of work have demonstrated that his stark solemnity, concentrated and fervent, can "create an intensity that . . . burns through the retina and may penetrate the surface of the brain . . . to rid itself of clichés."[10]

Viola produces video installations. His works *Fire, Water, Breath* (1997) and *The Messenger* (1997) are perhaps the most

Bill Viola, *Dolorosa,* 2000

transparent and metaphorical in their visual immediacy. The first one literally illustrates the cosmic adventure where man follows his destiny through fire and water, simultaneously harnessing and resisting their power, up until his last breath. We follow two parallel stories he calls *Crossings;* from the depths of two huge projection screens a human figure approaches us at a painfully slow pace. The slow motion emphasizes the drama of the apparently trivial stride. Then the figure comes to a standstill and looms over us enlarged to twice the average human scale. On one side water drops on him from high above, which gradually turns into a torrent until he is completely submerged. On the other side the human figure is simultaneously surrounded by leaping flames rising into a firebrand, which throws sparks that will also engulf him. Then suddenly the storm abates and all the "passions" are extinguished. The space goes dark. Nothing but silence and void. And the whole cycle starts over again in an eerie languor. After this series Viola named his videos "The Arc of Passions."[11]

The metaphor is simple and profound all at once. Crossing

over fire and water—could any human endeavor be more mundane or any desire more direct? In its most physical immediacy, the exercise refers to the metaphysical core of the effort. The paradoxical time frame of the installation is also an effective summary of an idea. In a few fleeting minutes the entire destiny of man unfolds before our eyes: birth, the encounter of elements, the experience of their total power over us and final demise, and then some incomprehensible beyond. Continuity, the indisputable fact of intransigence. The law of constant return. The absolute purity of the event reduced to the bare minimum is awe-inspiring. Birth, maturity, and arrival are slow, while the end comes with blinding speed. And yet, this jarring rhythm hides unexpected harmony. For the cyclical recurrence lends the event a different accent.

Besides the distinct length of duration, the visual effect is equally gripping. The relationship between man and the elements is not burdened by solemn comments. We are witnessing an encounter, not a combat. Man is not small and frail, as represented in so many shallow presentations, and the elements are also more than simply destructive and brutal forces of nature. The two exist in tandem, facing each other or, rather, intertwined, to fill their allotted time. For in *Crossings* it is not only the human figure that disappears, but also the fire goes out and the water recedes. Their existence is not eternal either. Increase and eventual decline are their natural lot as well. Viola's treatment avoids evaluative antinomies. Instead of stressing the opposition of good and evil, Viola presents their equivalence, equal beauty and mysterious order.

The video installation *Messenger* works with similar themes. In a brief parable that runs only a few minutes, a naked man slowly emerges from a body of swirling, churning water. When he finally reaches the surface he opens his eyes and takes a deep breath. The accompanying sound amplifies his breathing to something close to suffocation and howling. Then he sinks back into the depths to start the whole process over again, until he reaches breathlessness. The unity of man and the elements—the relation-ship suggesting both mortality and rebirth in nature—emphasizes the continuous order of existence. Man must simultaneously ex-perience the desire for action and his finite nature, the cyclical law of the process that transcends the singular.

Slow motion and sudden shift of pace are integral to Viola's working method. Cosmological order knows of no temporal sym-metry. "Reality is not logical," Viola says, "and our perceptions are not logical either, only our concepts about them make them appear as such."[12]

In the artist's interpretation the process and human destiny are truly passages, fundamental natural phenomena not unlike the existence of inert matter. In the relatively long duration of densely packed time we must experience the significance of things on our skin, with our eyes and ears. "With time, perception be-comes equal to thought," Viola explains. And impression turns into deeper understanding.

In the past few years, Viola has gone even further in the cre-ative interpretation of time. In his famous 1995 "deconstruction" piece *Greeting,* he unraveled the subject of a sixteenth-century Renaissance painting in exactly ten minutes. The painting itself illustrates the encounter of two women and the ecstatic commu-nication of some secret as they greet each other (perhaps sharing the joy of motherhood). However, the transposition of the original religious mystery into a modern context and the unnatural pro-longation of the adaptation evolve into the expression of some sort of ceremonial thought in Viola's work. Gestures and subtle emotional reactions are rendered deliberately artificial through slow motion to mediate the enigmatic character of a psychologi-cal state.

With the help of high-definition video technology and digital composition, the series of images put to motion at two recent New York exhibitions, *Passions* (2000) and *Going Forth by the*

Day (2002) at the Guggenheim, are simultaneously revelatory and perhaps a bit narcissistically artful at times. In these videos we arrive at a level of slow motion that literally puts our perception to the test, that is, it fundamentally alters the experience itself. The transition between normal and abnormal, and the creation of an unfamiliar movement-dimension is almost shivering.

In *Passions* we see image compositions, diptychs and triptychs running over 15, 20, 30, and 80 minutes, in one case stretched to 120 minutes in extreme slow motion, in an enigmatically exposed and restrained form.

As the faces come to "life" (for in *Passions* we are talking about regular portraits) through their proximity and the detail revealed by close attention, we are forced to follow a series of changes, emotional/physiognomic/psychological transformations. The slightest twitch in a face, the throbbing vein and gaze, are all there in front of us in a form never perceived before, and they can be questioned and comprehended. Precisely because the shifts are barely perceptible, we have to get used to the micro-dimensions of the shifting states never before seen, and our attention becomes incredibly astute and demanding.

Going Forth by the Day's (2002) five huge images, which could be described as cinematic frescoes, occupy a large room kept in complete darkness in the Guggenheim, and this time they narrate a "coherent story" but in a far from traditional format. The different stations of life are projected on four walls and over a doorway, keeping in motion "stories" that have no direct relationship to each other. Again, as in *Greetings,* the inspiration comes from Old Master paintings, this time Giottto's fourteenth-century fresco in Padua and Signorelli's fifteenth-century fresco cycle in the Orvieto Cathedral. Again, the project involves an exploration through the endless extension of real time. And as soon as it is over, the process starts all over again, always at a different moment in time. The first one follows the swirling red of birth without human shape; the second is a metaphor for a walk through the woods, the animation of an aimless ramble. Ordinary people keep walking, short and tall, young and old, dressed in all styles, together or alone, moving always from left to right. We never see the beginning or the end of the forest path, a four- to five-meter-long section of the road. What matters are movement and the homogeneity of the passing figures. All things are naturalistic in their accuracy: the trees, the light, and the normal movement of people filing by. The video lifts the pure, physical fact of "the course of life" to the level of the ordinary.

Another image (the third one) depicts the stations of simple, practical preparations for death, ending with packing and boarding a boat, steps and actions whose symbolism would be hard to deny. Some depart leaving the empty room behind in a small house along the river (the place where the unknown person actually passed away), others decide or are forced to make the crossing embarking on a ferry with a few collected belongings. They start off across the water to the other side, and we are not given the chance to see the features of the other side or the moment of arrival.

The entire installation runs for ninety minutes; one may follow one or the other story, sitting on the ground in the middle, as ones patience and curiosity allows.

These pieces do not develop a coherent narrative in the classical sense, where either the characters or the method of presentation display some signs of unity. The stage is populated by unfamiliar yet clearly defined locations and spatial compositions, and realistic, nonstylized human figures lifted from everyday life. All of them disappear at the end of the episode, when the entire cycle starts all over again. Needless to say, in the course of ninety minutes, simple events are raised to mystical heights again as we try to absorb the meaning of a walk through the forest, a waterfall in a city street, or a peek into the empty silence of an abandoned house. But, as the series is more about the interpretation of time, we look beyond a pervasive monotony to rhythmic changes occurring here and there. The flow, while it appears to be steady, is interrupted by occasional turbulence—an effective way to illustrate the correlation between two different life forms and their mutual dependencies. And yet, it is often difficult to ignore the occasional gaps in intensity and the disruptive mannerism of thought.

In Viola's work, slow motion serves to remind the viewer at every turn of the invisible, that which remains unrecognized, and the missed detail. In other words, he attempts to lead the viewer to enjoy a virtually spiritual presence or proximity. He looks for ways to move the threshold of perception. We watch and anticipate something that lies hidden just behind and below the immediately perceptible.

Aki Kaurismaki, *Man without a Past,* 2002

8 Everyday Rituals

The Rhythm of Monotony
The Detachment of the Deadpan
What Does Boredom Hide?
Ironic Serenity
The Evidence of Existence

The Rhythm of Monotony

The form of film narrative that takes on the representation of the routines, pleasures, or failures of everyday life appears all but paradoxical. The tendency to promote the mundane has unfortunately become a hotbed for redundancies, making room for a flood of petty-mindedness and boring monotony. The wryness and critical edge of some "irregular" filmmakers was needed to return us the disruptive forces of humdrum existence.

In the structure of an exceptionally unorthodox yet most remarkable film, in Michael Haneke's *The Seventh Continent* (1989), this not immediately obvious relationship between the quotidian and the disruption is rather conspicuously shown. Through a strongly highlighted, trivially ordinary, short series of details we get to follow the everyday life of a normal suburban family in a present-day big city. The most mundane episodes of breakfast, clambering out of bed, brushing their teeth, a car wash, school, and a ceremonial lunch and dinner are kept at a length of mere signals; the images flash by quickly one after the other, but in a series of stubborn repetitions. The fleeting scenes are always separated by the interruption of a fade out, avoiding even the appearance of continuity or transformation. Are we proceeding slowly or fast? Since nothing remarkable happens, we can't perceive any development.

Two-thirds of the film is taken up by this stifling ordinariness, by this series of uneventful banal moments, pointing to the direction of leveling. Life is dominated by an undramatic, mechanistic existence that is broken occasionally (three times altogether) by irrepressible fits of emotion: crying and collapsing, but the reasons for these outbursts are concealed. The fits come from nowhere and end suddenly to restore normalcy.

So the structure conspicuously operates on a single level defined by an almost knocking rhythm and an even tempo. The closing movement is suddenly composed in a totally different rhythm, but then the entire machinery breaks down. However, this too remains unexplained: the respectable, hardworking father, the good husband, and successful employee steps out of the circle. With a frenzied determination and consistency he destroys absolutely everything around himself: his objects, his money, his entire house, and finally he drags his whole family with him into this suicidal vortex. The protagonist says, "Ich glaube, wir schaffen es nur, wenn wie systematisch vorgehen" (I believe we can only do this if we are going about it methodically). The death of things and protagonists is complete and irrevocable.

Besides the grave message of this subject, the rhythmic character of the film, the deliberate slowness, and the acceleration of tempo are truly interesting. This heaping up of fragments, so typical of Haneke (his following film bore the title of *71 Fragments of a Chronology of Chance,* 1994), shows, in the words of the director, speaking at a press conference in Cannes in 1989, "my country's emotional glaciation." The calm chronicle of a routine existence erupts into savage, turbulent, and systematic violence. Even though the theme turns toward the abyss, a descending rhythm is accompanied by a sudden acceleration. The emptiness of monotony is replaced by the relentless consistency of a self-destructive murderous sequence carried to the bitter end.

Of course, the example is telling exactly because of its extreme nature. It shows us suggestively that this story of fatal alienation could be told precisely by relying on an unusual rhythm and tempo pattern. The monotony of the more than two-thirds running time switches over to another, relying on short, throbbing actions. The third part consists of fifty-four scenes out of the film's total of eighty-five, but the principle of de-dramatization remains consistent, further emphasizing the stern message of the movie.

In Pasolini's *Accatone* (1961), the story of a loafer who is also a pimp and a thief is told elegantly and with epic simplicity. "They are squalid characters, characters outside of historical consciousness," says Pasolini. "These elements, at play in the psychology of a poor, poverty stricken wretch, a lumpenproletarian, are always in a certain measure 'pure' because they are without consciousness and thus 'essential.'"[1] Pure and essential are for him equal in value since the life of his hero is not determined by the dramatic articulation of psychological or historical consciousness.

This is why he could continue his train of thoughts with this precision: "I simplified to the maximum the objective simplicity of the cinema. And the result ought to have been—and in part was—a sacredness: a technique of sacredness that profoundly affected settings and characters; there is nothing more technically sacred than a *slow* pan."[2] (I think we have the right not to take "sacred" literally. After all, it's clear that he himself uses it in a technical sense, since he associates with it an unassuming tracking and a humble, attentive note-taking.)

The emphasis here is on a persistent rhythm and a lengthy display. Pasolini's writing technique and rhythmic order is consciously built on this apparently neutral plan-sequence (long take), which, contrary to the common practice, doesn't really aim at a continuity of causal dramatic events. It is no accident that he repeats this in one of his articles, by saying that this procedure "is composed of fragments that can be extremely long or infinitesimal . . . understood as possible infinite subjective shots," in which the frontal, long, back-and-forth camera movements create the physical sensation of a *slow,* leveled drifting, and of an organic belonging to the environment. The emotional values are equally distributed.

Indeed, with Pasolini the characters mill about freely, committing crimes, stealing, cheating, and having a good time in this wide-narrow world. They do these things "innocently" because they are done unemphatically. The many supporting characters, the physical reality of the environment, and the background are constantly present. And this is how the inevitable death in the last scene can stay clear of every trace of bombastic outburst, although it does have a poetic aura. It brings us up close to the evidence of a certain kind of existence, while at the same time with a grand gesture it reveals fate's far-reaching elemental force. He makes his interpretation complete with an "incongruent" weaving into his texture the music of Bach's "St. Mathew's Passion." By doing this he simultaneously elevates and blasphemes the fateful tragedy of the story.

This is why it's possible that the film's ending, the brutal death, can take place without any sort of overly dramatic, wild eruption. A gushing out, as a natural continuation, the uninterrupted flow of ordinariness, a part of life, is realized in it. Instead of acceleration, a matter-of-fact portrayal of a certain even rhythm is given. Death is not a "tremendous explosion" as it is so often at the end of films; its occurrence and acknowledgment quietly rise through irregular fissures.

The Detachment of the Deadpan

A different kind of vision comes to the fore in the cases of some young "subversive" directors, who similarly apply the lightness of an antidramatic approach.

With their apparently cool manipulation, directors like Jarmusch and Kaurismaki take the risk of setting before us in transparent space their protagonists wallowing in idleness and sleepy torpor. In the grotesque activity of vacuum cleaning (*Stranger Than Paradise*), or in the haplessness of Japanese tourists in the Elvis Presley Museum (*Mystery Train*), with their vocabulary reduced to five words, we enjoy the subtle mockery and flippant sarcasm. The more mechanical the representation of human desire and activity, the more their emptiness is revealed. We are faced with the mechanical quality of ritual, the weird puppet-like and funny-pathetic behavior of people. The artificial enlargement of the surface of things is set in the center of our attention, suggesting the absurdity of slowly advancing time. Probing the gap that stretches between the magnitude of the goal and the energy expended to reach it, patiently exploring each moment of inertia—these activities are unexpected sources of mirth. This stinging game does not release the viewer from the sidesplitting constraint of self-reflection.

In *Dead Man* (1995), one of Jarmusch's more recent films, languid movement becomes a parody of style. In contrast to the mandatory gallop of Westerns, here all action is turned on its head. The grotesque adventures of the film's characters are the opposite of heroism as they dawdle along in sleepy languor, unperturbed by the occasional gunfights and flying bullets. The reluctant progress of action with its jerky tempo offers excellent opportunities for comedy.

Even the opening sequence of the film surprises and arouses our curiosity: what is the point of the minute documentation of the train ride, focusing on so many strangers? When is all this peace and quiet going to blow? Then, when the first obligatory shots are fired, we begin to suspect what is to come. The young man, with his lackadaisical wandering among buildings, and between/after his slightly bored yet quite pleasant love-making with the prostitute, starts to act according to script prescriptions: if others start to shoot, he must respond in kind and defend himself as best he can. The more he acts out the role dictated by the rules of the game, the more playful his rendering of the character becomes. He is given time to experience and carry through the assigned role.

Jarmusch's stylistic approach is a return to well-rehearsed techniques. He trivializes the grand and the dramatic to disclose the underlying routine and shabby qualities. The sendup deepens his complicity with the viewer—the source of the fun, the pleasure of mirthful recognition.

There is some blasé, wry weariness in Kaurismaki's characters as well, like those who have no more expectations, for whom nothing holds a surprise any longer. As if they were spared by some wistful scorn from further distress, from overheated emotions. Keep cool, no reason to get excited, they say, and this constitutes a most radical refutation of contemporary existence. In his earlier films, *Shadow in Paradise* (1986), *Ariel* (1988), and *The Match Factory Girl* (1989), he operates with the same provocation of de-dramatization, while lending each film a different overtone. On the one hand, he boldly accentuates the harsh rhythm of deliberate levity, of repetition and the relentless layering of events. The episodes are based on the most trivial life situations: images of the repetitive drudgery of garbage men (*Shadow in Paradise*), lay-offs, factory closings, sitting around in bars with the natural apathy of the unemployed (*Ariel*). These scenes roll on, animated by a charge kept at the same reduced voltage. On the other hand, when a stroke victim faints and dies, or a suicide in a restroom is shown as part of the general flow of events and treated as self-evident, the dramatic arc is deliberately ignored amid the banality of daily pottering or petty crime. We move on as if nothing had happened. Events file by with equal indifference on the wispy current of "life's flow."

In *The Match Factory Girl,* buying a red dress gains more importance in the girl's life than the fatal end, the preparation and showing (or rather the deliberate *no-show*) of the poisoning of the parents and guests. The lengthy and detailed presentation as the girl portions rat poison with scientific precision into glasses becomes unbearably creepy, while the consequences of her scheme are left to our imagination. Perhaps for the sake of further provocation, Kaurismaki says: "[The girl] does not commit any crime; no one dies of such a small amount of poison, and at the end the men, whom the viewer may take for police officers, but also for a nephew and an uncle, are showing her photos of a newborn, and could invite her to a picnic in the country. Based on the visual evidence no court could prove that the girl had killed four persons; in this 70-minute film it is the viewer who commits four murders and sends the girl to prison."[3]

Revealing comments, indeed, and even if we do not take them at their face value, they betray a radicalism of approach and allow a glimpse into the subversive irony of rejecting a host of hackneyed ideas, applying the most uncommon courage of ellipsis.

The approach is stressed by clearly apparent formal solutions. As we saw some years ago in Jarmusch's *Stranger Than Paradise,* Kaurismaki is not only wont to use ellipses, but also he often inserts blackouts between certain episodes. Instead of creating continuity, with artificial interruptions he expresses the arbitrary accumulation of events and life's blind monotony. The listless days of dreary work and equally dreary unemployment roll by with drumming regularity, to lead in some cases to an unexpected happy end (*Ariel, Man without a Past*), in others to cruel, all but invisible crime without punishment. Kaurismaki's gesture hides the detachment of irony. Instead of blaming his protagonists, he condemns the insolent power of circumstances. For whether they are kept going by the sheer force of human discipline or the compulsion of keeping busy, the final outcome is beyond their control. The decision lies with dumb luck; thus the director may afford or rather chooses to ignore rhythmic shifts. Fate has nothing to do with our desire or what we deserve, he suggests. We won't get far by rushing, and success has nothing to do with haste. In the face of the wholly indifferent population of a metropolis, all effort is in vain. At times fate gets the better of them and metes out unjust punishment; at times it rewards the hard-working ones, but never along the lines of good or evil. They are governed by capricious, irrational fatalism. This explains Kaurismaki's unique articulation of time, making it the bedrock of his stylistic principle: steady progress kept at an even keel. Come rain or shine, the forces of chance rule over all. His originality comes to life in the seamless unfolding of events, one ceaseless process of causality, and a fateful development of defeat, or sometimes suddenly, an unexpected, miraculous success.

The point of departure is always the definition of a dire social condition. As to the personal one, it is totally accidental. Ariel, for instance, starts with a surprising blessing, a gift. He receives the car keys of a fellow unemployed colleague in order to enjoy a ride in his spectacular white convertible, only to understand that the man just killed himself in the restroom. And yet, that fantastic present immediately brings about further catastrophes. In *The Match Factory Girl,* the protagonist's dead-end, almost slavelike job leads her to a senseless revolt. Kaurismaki enjoys springing surprising developments on his viewers, without bothering to explain to us anything particular about their origin.

Since in Kaurismaki's approach there is no psychology, only exaggerated emphasis on cause-and-effect relationships, he is simply spoofing, mocking their inevitable necessity. Therefore there is a deliberate abstraction through the reduction of any emotional reaction. Whatever happens in the life of the protagonist is only hinted at, in the shortest flash possible. All "substantial," "dramatic" events happen in the ellipsis, bringing about a genuinely mischievous, stunning effect. The shorthand becomes the main source of comedy.

His characters are perfect players. Even their love appears as "emotionless," matter of fact, funny. They act without words; they know everything so deeply well. This is a superb stylistic gimmick, working against the stream. Using all classical narrative patterns, he reverses them, showing them as natural actions with plain ups and downs and in which, decidedly, there is no morality involved. This de-dramatization creates a droll evenness. All sequences are given equal weight and the same (short) duration. The deadpan humor only enhances the effect. While the number of episodes is not necessarily fewer than in classic action films, their sequencing generates a peculiar counterpoint. The even treatment suggests slow progress and creates the impression that due to our ingrained automatism events cannot develop according to their own tempo. Alas, there is no way to rush things; everything must wait for its turn.

Tempo in itself is of little importance; instead, what matters is the intrinsic order of things that deserve our respect. And this patient approach generates tension that reveals the restraining force of expectation. For we cut down on speed before reaching a crucial stage, like an aircraft before landing or an elevator before stopping. More important than tempo, a constant surge, a flow accumulating strength with each step becomes an essential component, almost independent of the inner tempi of specific building blocks. With consistent discipline, Kaurismaki allows this ironic and wise rhythm to take over.

Similarly, in the *The Man without a Past* (2002), which won the grand prize at Cannes, all building blocks represent equal value. Even as the slow simmer of the narrative kept on the back burner heats up on occasion (such as in the wild bank robbery scene), the essential mode of operation is defined by its relationship to the story's bare essentials, the axioms of its simple origins and consequences. All is treated with deliberate restraint in a mundane setting; here, for instance, the scandal (robbery and police intervention) is resolved with a glass of beer drunk at a bar counter.

Although he is the victim of horrific physical blows, the hero goes through life like anyone else. He constructs his existence piece by piece. Collecting small objects, he creates a home for himself, finds love at the side of the unattractive and lonely Salvation Army employee (tenderly, with a soft, stolen kiss on her cheek), looks for a job, performs some good deeds, gets in trouble again, and finally gains his due: the girl and the horrendous project building—proceeding all along in a single, uninterrupted march.

What appears to be impassiveness is in fact a most self-evident quest for a livable life and survival, indeed an attempt to fulfill ambitions. He steers Salvation Army musicians in the direction of "modern" music and organizes parties. He acts silently, without passion, and injects his intention into the entropic scene through his sheer presence. The man without a past is constructive, looks forward and generates action, albeit in his quiet, unassumingly diligent manner. He is like a slow river that finds its destination, embedded in totality. A counter-play or changing scale, if you like. When cooking, sitting down to a dinner of poorly made roast, or sitting around aimlessly on the sleazy couch is the central event, we arrive at a vegetative state replete with comical and dense (yet unexploited) opportunities that create an atmosphere with the cheeriness of unrealized potential. Thus absence becomes the aura itself, the gripping symbol of slowly inching vitality.

When the man returns to his former wife, the non-event, the abandoned fight with the new lover charges the scene. They stand, haplessly facing each other. "So that's all?" the desperate lover wonders. And he just nods silently, "That's right." No fuss, no tussle. Due to their quiet ways, a friendly handshake and departure (without a sudden acceleration of action) are more appropriate and telling than any loud scene would have been.

Our square-shouldered, hefty character is a man of slow movement. Whether he works, is locked up in prison, or is on duty, he expresses the same quality of emotion with equanimity. Whatever comes his way he must bear it in silence; whatever the task at hand, he must execute it—to the very end, all the way to love. And even that is expressed in a warm, homely gesture—gently laying his arm around her waist.

Kaurismaki's other actors create the same atmosphere by using the power of the motionless human face and a resolute bearing. As a result, the graceless heroine is transformed in the radiance of her stiff motions and dreadful dresses. The composition is finely modeled with the complete elimination of all contingency. The seemingly impassive performance generates a unique dramatic tension with its quiet, restrained and restraining tempo. Much detail may be observed within the accurately drawn, stunning scenery.

"I believe there are too many sounds, images and words in the world," Kaurismaki said in an interview.[4] Due to its banality, today's reality cannot be represented, either by beautiful cars or ravishing landscapes, Kaurismaki says. That is one reason why he returns to the ambiance of bygone ages avoiding, for instance, the hackneyed scenes of middle-class marriage. Work, people at work, the displaced and marginalized have more vitality and deserve more attention. In his laconic presentation, nonsense raised to the level of the grotesque proudly mixes with features of the road movie and the melodrama. That is why he so eagerly goes for "bad" music, or old-fashioned authentic and imitation blues, making fun of worn-out evergreen songs. In a gesture that is simultaneously mocking and genuine, he manages to bring together a wide variety of forms, including jazz, rock, tango, Carlos Gardel—the multifunctional elements of a complex culture.

Kaurismaki is a serialist, as if he only recognized the simple juxtaposition of things. Yet, he is also a minimalist; while quiet indignity and truly warm feelings are held at the same level, they contain but a few elements. Instead of accretion, he opts for reduction.

What Does Boredom Hide?

Of course, this minimalist, apparently dry narrative has a rich historic vein. Let us recall Marco Ferreri's *Dillinger Is Dead* (1969), the most provocative representation of ennui and alienation. The hero, whose job is designing gas masks, returns home after a day's work and tries to kill time. It is hot, the middle of the vacation season when one struggles just to get some air. Furnished for convenient consumption, the decent middle-class home surrounds him like a seamless and tight envelope. Without being luxurious, the house is smartly appointed with careful attention for comfort, with porcelain figurines, spice containers, electronic gadgets, and works of art covering every inch of space. Ferreri does not attempt to exaggerate the objects' uselessness: the glut of objects is enough to make us wonder what their function might be in the mostly abandoned house. He applies but a single trick—the color composition of the scene. The home is bathed in soft shades of purple/pink and the syrupy atmosphere makes everything sticky, as if covered by honey. Later, in the scene where Piccoli fondles the maid, Ferreri will use the effect of honey as a poignant metaphor.

The narrative is developed along two parallel lines that complement each other with increasing irritation. The protagonist, Michel Piccoli, does nothing else for ninety minutes but prepare with utmost concentration and precision for two essential tasks: consumption and destruction. First comes the dinner, the aesthetic and gourmand preparations for culinary pleasures that must be complemented by a variety of other forms of entertainment (deploying all the wonders media has to offer). The other is the finding, dismantling, and assembly of a handgun to prepare it for firing/murder. The two tasks are pursued with the same attention to detail and devotion; the two actions overlap and approach completion simultaneously.

Everything created by the protagonist is destined for destruction. Whether he eats from it or not, the beautifully arranged plate represents ephemeral value; sooner or later it will turn into waste to be disposed. The gun to be used for murder is the only useful and durable object. This explains the endless care expended: he takes it apart, cleans it, immerses it in oil, and after assembling it even decorates it. He paints dots on the gun to make it more attractive.

Ferreri's zest for stylization is inexhaustible. With endless patience, he takes us through each phase of every pleasure. Nothing misses his attention. He demonstrates the aggression of things as they demand to be used. The availability of electronic appliances is not a simple offer but an active temptation. Each one must be tested, one after the other. There is something irresistible in the slide, the sequence of steps as he plays out all possibilities—the pleasure of the moment followed immediately by nausea, driving him on in the hope of more gratification. For our hero things can only be experienced through objectification, where the object is god incarnate. The fine china and utensils, the sacred objects of a modern kitchen piled high, exotic spices and their colorful receptacles, and a tiny, agile lizard, perfectly suitable for tickling and scaring the sleeping wife—these are equally stimulating aspects of the environment, dominating time and space. Indeed, in another category of objects, the wonders of home entertainment are all meant to generate heightened sensation. As these conjure events that had already happened elsewhere at another time to someone else, they not only suggest that an event recorded on film has more weight than any personal memory, but also that communication with the world happens exclusively through the use and application of these objects. This is the only chance for today's man to "experience himself."

If the scene described above has an arc and a drive, it is due to none other than the methodical implementation of destruction. Let us not forget that our protagonist is a gas mask engineer/designer. His job is to render these brutal objects more aesthetic and more suitable to wear. The gun is also an object of beauty in need of proper presentation. The odd solo show performed by Piccoli over an entire night turns all action into an act of substitution before it arrives to the last truly significant act—murder. This chain of action followed through with patience and consistency becomes the most powerful exposition of Ferreri's satire.

Chantal Ackermann's *Jeanne Dielmann,* made a few years later (1976), has also become a veritable reference work for modern, minimalist scriptwriting with its actionless scenario sustained for two-and-a-half hours. Delphine Seyrig performs a housewife's most tedious chores with unfailing routine to arrive in the end at the similarly detached murder scene. The chilling effect is inseparable from radical reduction, from the brutality of mechanical, robotic repetition. The long shots and barely moving camera articulate the stylized time that appears natural only at first sight, placing the scene in a solid framework. These are tools not to create fluidity but to accentuate duration.

I believe that Mike Leigh's prize-winning *Naked* (1993) is the most radical critique of apathy and aimlessness. The film's philosophizing and vegetating hero is ready to stretch the hopeless game of contingent argument and killing time ad infinitum. It is not only the structure of the flow of various episodes that holds our interest. Instead, responding to my theme, a thoroughly new approach presents the viewer the option of rejecting old rules and discovering new solutions. I am thinking of the exceedingly long night scene where the young protagonist wanders the streets of London penniless, thrown out of a pub, looking for shelter at the entrance of a huge office building. Of course, the security guard stops him and bars his entry. And there, in the monumental and brightly lit space where he is obviously not welcome, he embarks on an endless argument and even a dialogue with the guard, a "forbidden" discussion that ranges from theoretic reasoning through the most personal exchange. I repeat, the discussion exceeds all "reasonable" proportion. Resistance and rapprochement, encounter and understanding followed by departure all color the duel. However, the scene does have a point but it has little to do with what we actually hear. True, we get a glimpse of the protagonist's tortured thinking and troubled mind, as much as we see the guard's lonely widowhood, his search for faith and his disappointment, but the essence of the scene lies in length and duration. Both must kill empty time, both experience the chance of letting loose a torrent of words as a rare adventure. Not surprisingly, the scene has no denouement, it doesn't lead anywhere: neither the guard nor the young man receive a further clue in their "quest" for the meaning of their lives. We experience in "real time" their need in its formless fashion. And this sense of disproportion, this insatiability becomes the unexpected essence of the culminating scene, its psychological and social core past all specific and direct contexts.

Thus extension and distance may also be filled with words, with the "useless" flow of surging arguments, and yet or because of that they have the force of revelation, keeping the viewer on the edge despite the unusual technique and rhythm. As we know, few are able to successfully represent the ennui of apathy, loneliness, and abandonment without committing the sin of becoming boring themselves.

Ironic Serenity

The classic interpreters of humdrum existence, like Ozu and neorealism's other masters, taught us to accept the unhurried tranquility of tempo with tender and intimate representation. Their determined modesty in selecting characters and rendering scenes is effective because they avoid all high-flown phraseology. In these works we get a sense of the serenity and meditative attention of ordinary people. The complex web of family relations, the gentle melancholy of solitude and aging may rise to the surface only through such a slowly advancing pace. The almost soothing tenderness of quiet unfolding became the very texture of their work. They worked without the tension of overcharged, loud outbursts and the anxiety of attendant fast-paced action sequences and clashes. The dramatic effect is always reached through gentle attention and acknowledgment; after the event, after all have run their course. Umberto D., the pensioner walking his dog in his ragged Sunday best, or Ozu's heroes following the passage of seasons under the sun of late summer and early fall, savoring the subtle taste of sake, rice, or green tea, live on a scale of their own, amid small pleasures and quiet sorrows. Widower fathers and their daughters close to spinsterhood, or parents visiting from the country, radiate this imperceptible sense of poetry that goes through life with uncomplaining heroism, an almost cheerful acknowledgment of its limitations.

Again, the apparent simplicity is misleading. For, if the story were not spiced with subtle irony and the surrealism of things lurking just beneath the surface, we would soon sink into sentimentality. And there is nothing more tedious than cheap emotions. But in these works we constantly encounter the unexpected,

Jiri Menzel, *Closely Watched Trains,* 1966

masked by the routines of daily existence. This is why slow elucidation has the force of revelation: we experience the giddy folly
of sudden, unforeseen developments or the distortions of specific
practices—without all the razzle-dazzle, however. And the absence of much commotion is promptly accompanied by a unique
temporality, the illustration of a broader perception caused by
distancing. Thus, individual destinies are placed in a larger context, allowing the viewer to be more forbearing and accepting in
a gently mocking manner.

There is no need to deny, as I mentioned above, that here
again the best works are attempts at unraveling the secrets of
ennui. The demonstration of powerlessness in the face of phenomena, and the illustration of struggling, mechanical reactions
(for lack of anything better), became rewarding subjects for the
artist meditating on the absurd.

Think of the comedies of Jiri Menzel and Milos Forman, who

had the courage to create "boring," ploddingly evolving stories by violating all the standard rules of the genre. Starting with *Closely Watched Trains* through *The Loves of a Blonde*, from the inane gaping of *Black Peter* to the glorious mediocrity of *Capricious Summer*'s pensioners, the defiantly slow action is shaped by an insignificance raised to center stage and the weird reflections of a distorting mirror. Amid the infantile, almost senile pleasures of passing time, the characters in *Capricious Summer* have the patience not only to watch the rope dancer's stunt (in the virtuoso performance of Menzel himself), but in their primitive fashion they are even ready to "root" for him. Is it not a classic example of absurd comedy when, tugging at the wooden pole holding the rope with increasing agitation, they keep warning the fearless acrobat about his imminent fall until the inevitable happens? There is a gaping hole between the best of intentions and foresight here.

In Ivan Passer's early short masterpiece, *A Boring Afternoon* (1964), literally nothing happens save the active and intense boredom of its main characters. Potbellied, exhausted average citizens sit around a table in a pub-like room. They nurse their drinks, may even push around some cards, and, for lack of anything better to do and without the slightest inclination to engage in a discussion, they sing softly to themselves. We have rarely seen a world with such a thick atmosphere, presented to us in such "intimate lighting." Time appears to have come to a standstill; it drags on imperceptibly, and only the emphatically reserved tempo and unperturbed apathy show any signs of life, with their measured heartbeat and quiet regularity.

The British director Mike Leigh's comedies *High Hopes* (1988) and *Life Is Sweet* (1990) hover at the edge of mocking intimacy and a slightly crueler lampoonery. This refreshingly novel mix of register and sound animates his films, which are often built on disciplined improvisation. Thus, gestures are born before our eyes in their organic immediacy, revealing clumsiness, good will, or sudden eruptions of unbridled egotism and vanity. When caring for an old mother is both a chore and an inexorable duty and birthday parties inescapably turn into fiascoes, the scenes come across as the trivialities of daily existence and integral parts of family life. And since Leigh exposes in a bright light these scenes and his protagonists' fumbling and guaranteed defeat in "heavy" situations, we laugh and sympathize, even have fun at their expense, but never quite deny them the solidarity they deserve.

When the tall, disheveled woman finds herself in close intimacy with her meek, warm-hearted, motorcycle-messenger husband, who is two heads shorter than she is, she finally has the chance to reveal her heart's desire. They talk about a child they could not support and bring up in luxury for the time being, but that has little effect on their longings and their search for often missing closeness. Days pass without a trace, mechanically, including the family obligations referred to above, so how touching it is when once, before she goes to bed, we see the wife crouching at the feet of her husband, caressing, warming each toe with a tenderness that gives expression to genuine erotic desire. Of course, they cuddle up at the end, and this endless, warbling-whispering attempt at intimacy memorably conjures the aura of an entire way of life.

If later we were to visit Marx's tomb in the cemetery, the sight of the two lonely figures in front of the large, intrinsically grotesque bearded statue only intensifies the absurdity of the scene: we experience the pretensions of small lives for some greatness in an eerie setting never seen before. Thus the deliberately leveled rhythm of the unfolding story doesn't mean any pallid lack of inventiveness, but on the contrary, it brings viscerally close to us not just a lifestyle but the emotion-filled gaze of the author as well.

However, the most unexpected success of the past few years is *The Straight Story* (1999), a film by the persistently subversive American director David Lynch, an almost sacrilegious example of an eventless road movie in reverse.

At the twilight of life, sick and exhausted, Mr. Straight decides to have a last dramatic encounter with his brother, whom he has not seen in decades, following a quarrel the cause of which has long been forgotten. Receiving news that the brother may be on his last leg convinces him to visit his brother and finally make up. With no means of adequate transportation, he is forced to cover the distance between Laurens, Iowa and Mount Zion, Wisconsin on a 1966 lawnmower, making painfully slow progress, while suffering from arthritis and impaired vision.

Nothing could be more implausible, moving, and ambivalent than the undertaking of this long journey where all component elements, circumstances, characters, and stylistic patterns work against each other. The noble pathos of the old man's mission and its grotesque, amusing/earnest yet simple execution clash head-on. And yet, in the end, it all works out charmingly. We progress step by step through various pitfalls and a series of friendly and hostile encounters that demonstrate our protagonist's wily wisdom and enduring optimism. Vicariously, we experience the nature of "the prose of life" through the generosity and small-mindedness of ordinary men and women and the all but interminable and exhausting duration of the journey.

And we must accept the eventual encounter between the brothers with the equanimity of the old man: it came about as it was predestined to transpire and this too will soon be over, just as their fate draws to a closure. Instead of fast takes, Lynch's narrative is "lubricated" by resolute action and the lurking presence of irony. We must surrender to the story's serenity.

A final note: as usual with Lynch, we cannot be absolutely certain how much of the presented modesty is in deadly earnest and how much belongs to the realm of the absurd. Often we must wonder whether the sky is not too blue, the landscape not too verdant, or the war confession, obviously made to the first stranger encountered, not too involved. For me this ambiguity is an essential component of the "seasoning." Exaggeration demands its counterpoint and banality must be raised to another power; the confluence of often unidentifiable flavors guarantees the work's sumptuousness.

The Evidence of Existence

In his famous short essay on serenity, Plutarch asserts that looking for divine providence in the most humble natural phenomena is in fact a spiritual exercise available to stoics alone. His anecdotal parable is most telling: "It is said that once Marcus Aurelius, chewing at a piece of bread crust and examining its tiny cracks, noticed that the mere sight of this baked and well-encrusted piece of dough acted upon him as a source (surrogate) of enjoyment. In this instance, he recognized divine nature in this manifestation of surfeit."[5]

In Lynch's film and Mr. Straight's journey, similar encounters and moments of recognition represent opportunities for man to find joy and quiet disappointment, and at times stunned amusement and strength, in that peculiar excess that visits him occasionally in the disguise of pleasure.

However, we can give the term "divine providence" a more prosaic interpretation. Instead of a miraculous, superhuman benevolence that blesses ordinary mortals with some kind of spiritual gift, one might think of the commonsense, practical moderation shared by the majority of men, with which they endure the drudgery of daily existence.

I find no better way to illustrate the significance of this film than by quoting the skeptical wisdom of the late Hollis Frampton: "A specter is haunting the cinema: the specter of narrative. If that apparition is an Angel, we must embrace it; and if it is a Devil, then we must cast it out. But we cannot know what it is until we have met it face to face."[6]

Abbas Kiarostami, *The Taste of Cherry,* 1997

9 Endgames

The Open End
Retardation or Delay
Unexpected Epiphany
Enigmatic Border Crossing
Emotional Flashback
Finale
Ritornello
Suspense and Surprise

Working out the end is always a serious test of efficient rhythmic design, provided the artist wants, or is able, to avoid a hasty resolution that, acting like a short circuit, can "extinguish" the entire work. He may choose an accelerating crescendo, leading to turbulence, or on the contrary dare to apply a retardation or prudent slowness in order to offer a poetic flow and closure.

Introductions have their own complex strategies, but the rhythm and methodology of conclusions or resolutions are just as varied and intricate. Following Aristotle, we hold that in the Fable or Plot, we are looking for the end and purpose of the tragedy, "and the end is the chief thing."[1] Or in the words of Kermode, "In the journey [of the end] the episodes are related internally: they all exist under the shadow of the end."[2]

To further illustrate the way this "shadow" works, Peter Brooks says: "It writes the beginning and shapes the middle . . . only the

end can finally determine meaning, close the sentence as a signi-
fying totality."[3]

The way an artist approaches this closure is a most intimate
confession of his or her experience and vision of the world. As
Ricœur reminds us, working out the plot belongs definitely to
the family of "reflective judgement" and as such it allows various
forms of experiments and playing with time.

Since the ending has the charge to sum up the whole, it does
make a difference what layers of time—events of the past, the
present, or the future—are lined up to ensure that the story can
unfold in its full meaning. It also makes a difference whether the
extension of time flowing is real or imaginary, for it can be the
hero's, and even the artist's, last chance to act or to shed the light
of interpretation on the triumph or the failure in the end.

The Open End

To leave a story unresolved requires the kind of courage that has
for a long time been considered an unacceptable audacity. For,
as discussed earlier, the narrative creates catharsis, shock, and
relief primarily by its ability to intimate answer(s) regarding the
background complexities. Whether the ending calms or upsets, it
provides something rarely found in real life: it finishes its adventures.

Yet, the portentous, open-ended conclusion became increasingly popular in more modern and sophisticated films because it
meant a relief from artifice or the forced happy ending. Consider
François Truffaut's *The 400 Blows* (1959), a film that was the most
famous product of the French New Wave and that has become a
most-quoted example since. We follow relentlessly the long run
of an adolescent boy who has escaped from a reformatory school
and is now making his way toward the sea. The movement is
from left to right, and we have the impression that it approaches

us, or that it is inching closer to some more fortunate end. Still, we cannot shake a sense of anxiety and uncertainty. Is it possible that he could succeed in the midst of all this heartlessness and insensitivity? Is there enough justice on earth to save this basically innocent, unfortunate kid from evil? Truffaut's solution is complex in its simplicity. The boy reaches the sea, he wades in. Now we see only his back; for a moment the idea arises of death, of drowning, then he turns to face the camera, and looks at us. It is a long, steady stare. Innumerable shades of emotions cast their shadows on his face: exhaustion, dread, hope . . . . Then the face, a face seen in close-up, freezes and stays with us as a photo so ominous that it inescapably conjures up the image of a police mug shot.

In other words, we don't know what will happen to the boy, what kind of life lies ahead of him, but the implication of the image is that he'll be watched, he "has a record," since running away is a crime. It doesn't matter that he had been detained for an act of silly, childish complicity in the first place. We can sense from this image that from now on he is a marked man, and we know what this means in a society ruled by indifference, rigid bureaucracy, and strict laws of punishment. I should point out that this open ending could not be so effective if it hadn't been played out with such patience and at such unusual length, down to the tiniest detail. The hero's face, his uncertain fate, stays with us for a long time in this ambiguity. We are watching anxiously, contemplating, and pondering unpromising alternatives as we hold that still image frozen in time. No closure could be more effective than this open ending. We don't know what the future may bring.

Wim Wenders in his *Sky over Berlin* (1987) deliberately leaves open the intricate play of many characters, and even the story of the lovers. It is the texture, the city itself that interests him more than the all-deciding, finalizing gesture. At the end of the film an unusual sign appears in the sky, "TO BE CONTD." Wenders confesses he included the sign "because it seemed odd to me that I had

made a film that starts in earnest only at its end . . . I just wanted
to go on telling this story. . . . If one imagines that there are cities where there is no 'to be contd.' . . . it is only fitting that this
should appear in the sky over Berlin. Berlin is a city that cries for
a continuation."[4]

Wenders's argument is made exciting and thought-provoking by the wide scope of his interpretation of openness. Instead
of applying it to the end merely, he uses it to revolt against the
convention of all-too-closed stories. "Some films are like closed
spaces," he said in an interview. "There is not a single crack between the images that would allow us to see something other
than what the film wants to show. There is no chance for the eyes
or the thoughts to wander. One cannot give from oneself, cannot
contribute any of one's emotions or experiences to it."[5] Airiness, a
more spacious, more relaxed structure can make room for a little
dreaming. In fact, it also helps the viewer in identifying with the
fates of the characters presented. It leaves open possibilities for a
deeper, more personal involvement.

In the famous closing scenes of Michelangelo Antonioni's
The Eclipse, (1962), the ending that strives for a kind of opening
shows a different inspiration, and naturally it also creates a different atmosphere. Its brilliant, exquisite, and thrillingly mysterious
images seem virtually inexhaustible. With these images Antonioni
also challenges viewers, but his approach and methodology differ
from those of Wenders.

The first striking difference is the conspicuous absence of
our heroes in the last seven-minute-long succession of scenes.
The expanded and emptied world we have entered has already
left them behind. Objects and details do appear, reminders of a
shared past, since we had been here with them before. A wooden
railing; a barrel, with a twig and a discarded box of matches mysteriously swimming in it; the barren scaffolding of a construction
in the distance; the intersections of wide, empty roads—all these

speak to us differently now. Especially because the gradual wan-
ing of light—the solar eclipse—literally shows everything in a different light. The eclipse is a concrete material metaphor since it is
indeed about the disquieting disappearance of the light, and we
know that disappearance is never free from the actual and complete vanishing, from death. Hence its somber force.

Thus the end, thanks to Antonioni's perspective, does indeed
gain a cosmic dimension. Going beyond the fate of our heroes,
the end points toward something more universal, and by the
power of poetic intimation it projects the image of a cold, alien,
and ominous future. Besides familiar details, occasionally more
contingent visual compositions appear: a close-up of a man reading his newspaper, and foliage moving in the wind. These also
serve to expand the vision so that the image of the gradually increasing shadow can be even more effective. Leaving behind the
notion of an individual ending, we have transcended the realm of
the personal and entered the dimension of an unfamiliar, abstract
time.

Finally, we encounter another, poetic variation of open ending in Theo Angelopoulos's *Landscape in the Mist* (1988). The
journey of the two children searching for their father ends in misty
ambiguity. Having lived through all the adventures, growing
pains, failures, and hopes of the great journey, they arrive at a real
geographical border, which in our age—and in Angelopoulos's
thinking—is the place and embodiment of defenselessness, of
the threatening experience of not belonging anywhere. It is dark,
and in this no man's land where they are hiding out the sound of
gunshots is heard; from the top of tall watchtowers searchlights
are combing the space below. Our heroes are skulking on the
bottom of a flatboat. We don't know what's happening or what's
happened so far with them. Then, after the complete fade out,
we suddenly see them in a new setting: they are running happily
through an empty field toward a wondrous, magnificent tree.

The tree is obviously a symbol and a tangible object at the same time, a veritable mirage: it symbolizes the father's promise, and more generally, it holds out the possibility of a more fairytale-like life. Yet, at the same time, it also stands for complete uncertainty, a stage in the childish, dreamy mission that pleases with its beauty rather than with its concrete reality. The tree is a recurring theme in Angelopoulos's work. Here, it is the liberating symbol of a hovering yet uplifting arrival that presents the viewers, as well as the heroes, with an illusory sense of fulfillment.

Retardation or Delay

When the artist's intention is to extend a present that practically rules the entire film, and so he foregoes a rapid closure, we often see another solution applied in a slowing down of the last episode that stretches it out to a great length.

In films like Arthur Penn's *Bonnie and Clyde* (1967), or Terrence Malick's *Badlands* (1973), we enjoy the longer lasting, delayed ending, but we are filled all the while with anxiety, dread, and irrational hope. Are these cases of abuse, a shrewd twisting of our nerves, or just a deliberate stretching of time necessary for the director to create his intended effect? In the case of *Bonnie and Clyde,* the famous ending is justified by the clever redefinition of the entire genre, or by its "hybridization," to use the modern terminology. With an intentional romanticizing use of slow motion, Penn elevates the death of the two criminal protagonists to mythical heights. The ballet, shot with four cameras, suggests the playful, fairytale-like survival of the legend. This is why there is so much emphasis on the delay of the last moment, death itself, and its choreographic, poetic form. Real slow unfolding stresses the showing of close details, such as the bullet-riddled vest and clothing, and the aesthetic quality of the radiance and movements of the beautiful protagonists in order to ensure a complex emotional effect, the paradoxical experience of "pity and fear."

In *Badlands* this stalling is simpler. After the capture of the boy there is a chance to stay with him once again for a while. This lets the killer-victim, surrounded by policemen, appear in a different light in the scenes shot on the airplane and afterward. He is charming and funny. It's not for nothing that he is a James Dean lookalike; his escorts too come under his spell. There is an air of near complicity, a winking recognition in the scene, and somehow we too experience the magic. Thus the friendly chat, logical but perhaps unnecessary, draws a more cheerful aesthetic aura around the finish, not unlike the sympathy in the case of *Bonnie and Clyde*.

Among more recent successful films, there is one that already has the reputation of a masterpiece: Abbas Kiarostami's *Through the Olive Trees* (1994). It's probably no accident that, like Ozu's films, this one too has its roots in traditional oriental culture. The film is remarkable for its unusually patient presentation of a story unfolding in the present. With its sheer length and consistency, it surpasses every customary expectation.

Kiarostami is never stingy with detailed narration. In *Through the Olive Trees* he tells us the story of a film shooting in an area destroyed by an earthquake. In this film within the film the local youths, the actual victims of the catastrophe, are supposed to play themselves. In this web of complications, the young man playing the young husband does indeed turn with fervent longing toward the girl playing the brand-new wife. The scenes, to be rehearsed many times over and over, fill up with all his expectations, imploring, hopes, heartaches, and sadness. No matter, the girl is deaf to his pleas. She doesn't even lift her eyes, let alone return his gaze. When the shooting is over, they both set out to return home through the gently rolling hills, sparse woods, and olive groves. This is the boy's last chance, his final attempt to sweeten up the girl before they part ways for good. We witness one of the most beautiful and memorable endings in the history of film as we watch the unhappy, somewhat boorish boy with the two tin jars in his hands following his heartthrob doggedly to make her change her mind. But the girl is inexorable. They move across the landscape. The camera follows them from a distance—it does not want to intrude. The sequence is notable for showing us the choreography, the "dance" of the couple: two barely visible figures in a vast natural space. Now the boy gets closer, now he falls back, as the girl occasionally quickens her pace or as he, struggling with his humiliation, draws closer with a sudden determination. But the girl won't look back, won't give the slightest sign of encouragement or reason for hope.

Thanks to the director's sensitive skill, we begin deeply identifying with this couple as they endure various stages of undulating emotions, human intentions, and tense drama. This escorting scene goes on and on, and its openness speaks so directly to the heart that we wish it never to end. We too are anxious and expectant, desiring with all our heart that the boy's plea be heard. As long as the march continues, there is hope. This is why the defiantly long scene, running more than ten minutes, can keep us spellbound. They keep on marching and we follow them, paying no heed to the *slow* pace. Every gesture, blade of grass, shadow, and light gains a larger dimension. And, of course, there is no clear answer waiting for us at the very end. Kiarostami leaves it all open. Since we are looking on from afar, we can see only that the boy at one point turns around and starts walking back. Has anything happened? Was he given any encouragement? Or did he turn around because he had had enough of this futile imploring or of the girl's offensive indifference? The music, at any rate, slides into a different mood: it becomes livelier and more hopeful. Even if we don't know what precisely has happened, we care about their fate. Through the boy's sorrow we have experienced everything that love means with its anguish, joy, and uncertain outcome. There is a faint intimation regarding the future: nothing is over yet. But to get here, it was necessary to have the kind of patience and most sensitive lingering that can be associated only with the finely wrought ritenuto of great works of music, where the emotional content and essence of the entire work is summed up in the tension of a consciously withheld conclusion, in moments of suspended time.

With the endings of Hitchcock's or even Woody Allen's films there is a quite different sort of patience or impatience created in the viewer. Here, we have to wait for the unfolding of a web of complexities, for the resolution of unexpected problems before getting to the final end. It is not so much the method of the slow pace in itself that is effective here as the intentional unpredictability, chance happenings, and seemingly inexplicable actions, since all these contribute to stretching the finale, where inventiveness and hidden contingencies play an essential part. But for all that, the emphasis here, too, is on retarding the closure, a move that multiplies many times over the well-deserved sense of relief.

The excruciatingly long ending of Marco Bellocchio's *Fist in the Pocket* (1965) is truly tormenting in its excess. The retardation gains here an unusual sense: it becomes the emotional dispensing of poetical justice, to be sensuously troubling. His method is a shivering *tour de force*. If he wanted to express the fatality and tragic nature of the murdering young boy's madness, he needed all the minute detail to depict the disturbing experience of this ambivalence. The length of this closure surpasses all expectations. Under the power of the romantic music of *La Traviata*, first the boy betrays a kind of liberation: they are left alone with his beloved sister, the house is empty, free for their own use. But then, rather fast, the inebriation goes to his head; he loses control and has no command of his body: there is no way to stop his epileptic fit. Carried along by the howling record-player we follow him to his bitter end. The arrival of his death comes slowly, torturing his distorted body in terrible convulsions, while the music endlessly screams. Bellocchio spares neither his hero nor the spectator. It is a punishing, yet illuminating end. The director implies that para-doxical character of the boy's tragedy could be found only in this extreme fashion

In *North by Northwest* (1959), Hitchcock makes use of the strategy of "stalling" in two different ways. One is emotional, re-lated to the gradual unraveling of the initially unfathomable rela-tionship between the two protagonists, Cary Grant and Eva Marie Saint. It is a process studded with unexpected moments, since the woman plays a seductive spy who, we find out only at the very end, actually does carry out the seduction for a good cause. At length, they can have their somewhat ambiguous happy end-ing. But Hitchcock has still another way of creating tension, and this will put our heroes into situations of physical danger. Here too, we have to root for them all the way to the end; yet another twist, another almost fatal moment of their escape from their pur-suers fill the time before we are granted the sense of triumph.

In Woody Allen's films and especially in *Annie Hall* (1977), the complications are bewildering and intractable, not so much due to the force of external events but as a consequence of the hero's inner uncertainties, mistakes, bad conscience, and dreams. As a result, the closing gesture cannot be free of a mixture of contradictions, requests, and errors so that the ending can be a lengthy, not immediately obvious one. The ritenuto concentrates on demonstrating a field of forces pulling in many directions, in-stead of offering quick solutions.

Unexpected Epiphany

Throughout the film *Thelma and Louise* (1991) Ridley Scott uses the classic patterns of speeding and chases, but at the end he em-ploys an interesting solution. He articulates the chase in obliga-tory detail, which thus appears to take place in almost real time, leaving time for a long "stop" that has the power to suggest the

Miklós Jancsó, *Red Psalm,* 1972

dignity of farewell, of the moving commitment to friendship, and of the resolve to die, while all this is underlined by the beauty of the landscape and the long, almost speechless, demure silence of the two characters. And he tops this with an ending stretched to an impossible length. The image of the car running into the abyss gets frozen in time; it keeps hovering forever between earth and sky. The destruction is held back, cannot be seen. There is a little room left in our imagination for dreams, for hope by which we can avoid the tragic end. Of course, the image is a metaphorical one, placing us outside immediate physical reality: it helps to realize a wish, but in such a vivid manner that it gives a different, more poetic tone to the entire story, and allows the viewer a different emotional satisfaction.

We cannot avoid reminding ourselves of the miraculous closing scene of *Miracle in Milan,* where the liquidation of Bidonville and the carting off of the inhabitants in paddy wagons is frustrated by some angelic intervention. Arriving in front of the Dome of Milan, our heroes break out of their rickety wooden prison, and hopping on broomsticks, fly away toward the open sky, "toward a world where 'good morning' will actually mean good morning." It is an enchanting, funny, playful, and heartwarmingly mischievous idea. The joyous and deserved redemption of our heroes takes us into the paradise of fairytales.

And here we come to an entirely different group of end-solutions that I would like to term the "unexpected epiphanies." The two funniest and most playful examples of this are in John Cassavetes's *Minnie and Moskovitz* (1971) and Marco Ferreri's *Dillinger Is Dead* (1969).

Cassavetes, as usual, is full of restlessness and boisterousness, and in this piece too he tirelessly drags his characters up and down on the roller coaster he has built for them. In spite of the mismatch between the man and the woman, which forms the subject of the entire comedy, he finishes off the story with a spectacular happy ending. Of course, he does this only to hyperbolically enlarge this bizarre contingency and then to toss it mockingly into an excessive constellation. The fairytale-like end functions as an epilogue, and with its countless children, clowning parents, and celebration of sweet grandmothers it is a defiant grimace. The obvious exaggeration of this impudent farce is the height of impossibility—and it is charming as such. What we didn't, or rather wouldn't want to believe—the happy union of the beautiful, slender Gena Rowlands, who comes from a good family, and the old, scruffy hippie, Seymour Cassel—is, lo and behold, more wonderful than a glorious fairytale. As a result of this impossible encounter the world's happiest and most harmonious family is born.

Undoubtedly, the solution is ironic, we must take it with a grain of salt; the grimace, however, throws light on many things. Cassavetes is obviously an iconoclast. He is not interested in commonly valued things. He rejects every a priori value judgment. This is why he dares to stress that his heroes, in spite of their ecstatic nature, are average people, even if with this commonality there is quite a bit of hysteria and craziness mixed in that makes them equally vulnerable. The stylized end of the epilogue demonstrates that Cassavetes has no intention to form intelligent opinions about truth and order. Instead, he wants to jump right into the middle of the muddy waters of inexplicable complexities and to follow their absurd undulations.

Ferreri's *Dillinger,* like most truly extraordinary films, can be approached only from its end. This defiantly "boring," drily antidramatic work suddenly changes its tone and style at the end to sail (literally!) out to the waters of high-kitsch romanticism. Our relentlessly unimpassioned killer—thanks to the kindness of a gorgeous young woman, owner of a yacht that just happens to float by in the deep blue sea—is able to leave behind his entire sordid life by skipping away under full sails and in the shadow of a gigantic red sun toward the paradise of Tahiti.

The shift is so drastic that we must pause to ponder the ambiguity of the ending. We can view the last ten minutes of the film as a freestanding epilogue, a coda after the end. Does this miracle with its dreamlike feeling really happen, we ask in disbelief? Is this all-forgiving apotheosis conferring total freedom on our serenely indifferent killer-hero really possible? We watch the color of the images, the exotic, erotic, seductively smiling girl, and the windblown yacht running out to the open seas in the shadows of an eternal sunset. The romantic illusion is so overwhelming and the kitsch is so perfect that we may reasonably doubt its reality.

But is it really important to know whether all this is a dream, a figment of the imagination defying reality, or an accidental event? After all, the fiction has elevated the entire story to the symbolism of a cautionary tale. Precisely because its narrative style is characterized by the driest objectivity, and precisely because Ferreri concentrated his energies on detailing the dead moments, the contradictory style speaks for itself. His aim is not to entertain but to shock. To shock us into recognition.

If liberation is a fantasy, there is significance in where the escape route leads: in the direction of classic kitsch, the sultry brilliance of picture postcards, or somewhere else. At any rate, here the combination of the two textures yields an effective disharmony. Although in their respective moods and devices they stand clearly opposed, quotidian boredom and the fantasies it triggers have a common source: they form two sides of the same philistine life.

The essential ambiguity of kitsch, however, makes further interpretations possible. For, if we stop to think about it, the liberating escape might as well be real. What would stand in the way of this escape in our brave new world? It's not impossible that every other luxury yacht hides a similar criminal happily sailing, by fate's inexplicable grace, toward perhaps another act of gangsterism. Ferreri suggests nothing less than that the probability of this moral scandal might be quite high.

Two contrary examples of unexpected epiphany are the end and the last chapter of Martin Scorsese's *Taxi Driver* (1976), and the wildly surreal, symbolic play of Jean-Luc Godard's famous *Weekend* (1967).

On a first reading, *Taxi Driver* is a story of returning to normalcy and its realization on a higher level. De Niro, in contrast to the fervent and restless moments of the opening images, and especially to the long, horrible, bloody massacre scene, continues driving a taxi, but now, it turns out, as a celebrated hero who saved the life of an innocent girl. He also gets to meet the beautiful blond woman whom he pays back for his former humiliation by refusing to forgive her. Happy end? Is everything back in its proper place? Perhaps, but another possible interpretation remains open, and this lends the whole unexpected ending a unique sense of uncertainty and ambiguity. The last phase of the shooting and the police action ends on a peculiarly emphatic note: De Niro lifts his two fingers to his blood-soaked temple, a sign used to indicate a deadly or suicidal shot, leaving open the consequences of the gesture. Was he killed? Did he kill himself? Did he say farewell to the world after what he had seen? We can't tell. Thus the epilogue following the fade-out on the screen does indeed become ambiguous. It surprises us not only by everything suddenly returning to normal but also by leaving behind justified questions: is this for real or just a fantasy? The wish-fulfilling dream of the last moment? The stylized image produced in the calm before death? The director leaves it to us, the viewer, to decide, to ponder the possibilities, and by this he presents us with further food for disturbing thoughts.

Godard's *Weekend,* one of his more popular films, plays with a drastic shift in its last movement. After the almost-realism of the first parts we are suddenly presented with Godard's most daring images of fantasy on the loose: revolutionaries in costumes, and the orgiastic festival of cannibalistic rebels and social outcasts. He not only conjures up metaphorically the threatening danger of a possible future, but makes sure to express the political content verbally as well. From the cruel and grotesque reality we step up to the stage of pure play; the beating of drums calls everyone to join, and the physical reality of the action, manifested for instance in the repellent pleasure of flesh-eating, apparently shuns no horrific (or just playfully exaggerated) effect. We have to spend a long time with every action of the characters.

As for the supposedly heartwarming ending of Pedro Almodovar's *Everything about My Mother* (1999), I would rather call it a mocking and fashionably subversive twist, in which the father finally found turns out to be a woman. This obviously quirky, bizarre discovery requires an appropriate response. This is why Almodovar dares to choose the starkest contrast. Our heroes are weeping and sobbing, and the effect of this veritable storm of tears depends equally on the impossible turning point and on the overdose of emotional details.

Enigmatic Border Crossing

The unexpected endings of Kiarostami's *The Taste of Cherry* (1997) and of Wong Kar-wai's *In the Mood for Love* (2000) appear embarrassing, however. The essence of Kiarostami's closing gesture is quite incomprehensible at first glance, but it is based on a thought-provoking surprise. The award-winning *Taste of Cherry* has a resolution that is so ambiguous, lending itself to so many different interpretations, that it's hard to guess the inspiration of the original intention. On top of this, it also contains a "jump" that doesn't even attempt to hold on to the idea of organic unity. Viewed from outside of the plot, from a different perspective that places everything in an entirely new context, it is more confusing than shocking, but in any case, it definitely provides solid food for thought.

Kiarostami's recurring preoccupation in his films is honestly befriending death; he is looking for its place in our lives with a characteristic lack of pathos, pomp, tragic shadows, and gloom. In fact, this time it's the bizarre nature of the narrative, in which a suicide candidate, Mr. Badi, attempts to find allies to his decision, and fails on three occasions.

In the film, the character appearing in the third encounter shows the beauty of the world to the protagonist, tells him about the taste of cherries, but to no avail, for this cannot divert the hero from his original intention. Yet the vitality of Kiarostami's conception apparently transcends the individual's fate. The film doesn't end with the image of Mr. Badi's grave. The epilogue contains a definitely different conclusion. After the grave's image fades into darkness on the screen, suddenly and rather surprisingly a colorful image appears out of nowhere. First we don't really understand what we are looking at, and then it turns out that we are privy to a filmmaking process: scenes of exercising soldiers (or extras?)

bring us back from metaphysics to a mundane reality. Among the characters we can recognize Mr. Badi himself. We have seen a tale then, a sort of mystery play; the performance is over and the actors take their bows at the end. Only this time, instead of the curtain, it is the visible presence of the film camera that reminds us of a play.

The emphatic presence and role of filmmaking in Kiarostami's films is always conspicuous and interesting, as if existence could show itself only through these doubly reflecting mirrors. The breathing and the force of things can break through the surface by making use of the talent of the recording camera. Life's talent suddenly becomes the camera's talent, the two merge together.

Here too, according to this ending, it is a film's business (or only its potential?) as a life-recording practice (and not a mere technique!) to hold on to the experience of continuing life. If life goes on, then it's thanks partly to the film camera's talent. What has been will stay and will be there in the future on the movie reel.

The ending's "inorganic" connection with the story cannot be arbitrary. The director, without much preparation, has intentionally put it in a seemingly inappropriate place: he wanted to call attention to an idea or a fact of life that he had considered important. So the role that film plays in this world is an essential or organic one after all, from its own point of view. The true and the artificial meet in this marriage, displaying for us simultaneously the archaic and the cutting-edge modern, accepting this odd match as perfectly natural.

This way, the ending is more than mere commentary. It places the confession about contemporary reality in a new and more spacious dimension.

Wong Kar-wai's end-solutions reflect an entirely different perspective. The recognizable pattern here is the principle of eternal continuity, the rejection of closure. It is as if the director wanted to intimate an endless process that can flow anytime in any direction. This is most noticeable in *In the Mood for Love,* where even after its natural end the actual story wanders on to realms of different ages and regions, losing the concentration on the film's original characters. He even has the courage to use some newsreel footage (for example, de Gaulle addressing a crowd) in order to give a sense of the march of historical time. To many people this continuation seems inorganic in the literal sense of the word, but in any case, the underlying intention definitely comes through; the intention of wanting to see, and have others see, this painful yet banal story in a larger dimension. Personal fate and its surrounding social and political circumstances will, with the passing of time, integrate into the larger whole by altering its original proportions. To achieve this, the film even alters its voice and style. It changes the lyrical tenderness of the film's texture to a cooler, more objective tone.

Emotional Flashback

The originality of the solutions mentioned so far lie in the fact that they can be valued mostly as projections or jumps into the future. Many decades ago, in the age of more traditional filmmaking, and especially under the direct influence of Freudianism, it was more common to resort to strategies whereby the past or its fragmentary elements would surface here and there in an enigmatic haze to throw more light on a deep-seated psychological trauma (Hitchcock's *Spellbound,* for instance). In general, nonlinear stories prefer to make use of details that, stepping out of the continuity of the present, turn to memories of the past for the sake of some comprehensive closure. As opposed to anticipation, in these narratives a piece of the conjured past, arriving through a sudden association or demanded by the emotions, clamors for admission into the finale, to serve as a key to the story or a solution to the puzzle, as it were.

Max Ophuls's *Letter from an Unknown Woman* (1948) is a film that tells its entire story through a voiceover narrating the text of a letter. Only by the end of the reading, by the tragic end of this unhappy love, does it become clear to the man whose person and what are really referred to in this sad story. At this point, fragments of old memories of his forgotten love flare up in his mind, images that are familiar to us from the woman's letter (and of course from the visual representations of the letter's details). This slowdown is very important from an emotional point of view, for it leads to the real end of the film: it helps the man in his decision to take up the challenge of the duel.

Ophuls makes use of various structural combinations. The parallel of the opening and the closing employs the method of the returning and forwarding frame, whereby the first scene shows the hero's preparation for the duel, while the last one, serving as the continuation of the first, as it were, shows the man's cart taking off toward the scene of the duel at dawn. The entire story takes place between these two "moments," occasionally interrupted by the reading of the letter, and by the scenes accompanied by the woman's voiceover. But this distance is an enigmatic one, for until the last minute we have no notion of the reason for the duel, or of the final decision to face possible death. Keeping the secret to the end, delaying its revelation is certainly part of a sophisticated game that, besides having an emotional effect, manages to maintain a mood of expectation and excitement. The last flashbacks I mentioned above have the further psychological significance of being the proximate cause of the hero's dramatic decision. By transcending a merely linear flow, the unorthodox participation of the elements of the past results in the end in a complex, emotionally rich, yet finally unsentimental flow of action.

Since the intervention of the past in current happenings is always essential and authenticating, the question is how to avoid oversimplified and didactic explanations. A modernist example, memorable in its simplicity, comes to mind. Michelangelo Antonioni in *La notte* (1961) also calls up from the past an essential memory for the melancholy, compromised reconciliation of the frustrated couple. His taste, however, forbids him to include any direct flashback. The surprise is produced by Jeanne Moreau's reading a long, anxiously guarded letter, which recalls the passion and harmony that once existed between them. Here, the provocative device is a dead object, a relic instead of the fortissimo of mutual accusations. We are not really surprised to see, and find it telling, that the writer-husband himself, Marcello Mastroianni, cannot recognize his own text; he doesn't know who the author of this confession might be, so deeply has he buried the memory in himself. The called-up past, then, is indeed a lifeless corpse at the same time. On the other hand, even though it can be resuscitated somehow (for it does lead to the couple actually falling into each other's arms), still, keeping in line with the great alienation, it remains astonishingly indirect.

Or what should we call the dramatic breakdown of Zampano in Federico Fellini's *La Strada,* when a fragment of a tune played on a crummy old trumpet reminds him of the half-witted and never rightly appreciated girl, Gelsomina. The memory makes him cry over his loss and solitude. With the tune an entire wasted past returns hauntingly, pointing at what is no longer and will never be again.

The almost opaquely lyrical final resolution of Alain Resnais's *Hiroshima, mon amour* (1959) affects us by the creative interpretation of space in which the departing lovers have to experience the beauty and pain of a farewell simultaneously. Here, Resnais chose the most unusual yet simplest writing: due to the softly gliding movement of his camera, Hiroshima and Nevers come to live in the continuity of a single space, as part of the reality of an impossible geographical unit. We are whisked, without any jerks, from one to the other in a way only the imagination can move:

conquering time-space limitations, with a dreamlike smoothness that can be experienced only deep inside us.

Finale

We know this type of closure from the stage and especially from the opera. This is where it's necessary to "tie up" all loose ends, to bring every motif to its endpoint. This is why it's natural in films with large casts that the characters of subplots arrange their fates, their stories, into some order, giving on the one hand a certain completeness to the conclusion and lending to it, on the other hand, an undeniably retarding character as well.

Altman, a master of plurinarratives, is always happy to deploy this game of clever complications. As we can see in his many films, arranging and tying together all the threads in these works is not a ready-made, simple task.

One of his French critics, Yanick Mouren, calls Altman's writing choral-like while emphasizing how much formal-technical inventiveness the films require and contain: for example, eight simultaneous soundtrack recordings, using microphones hidden in the clothing of the actors; complicated camera movements; and long sets using various camera positions, including the special zoom technique as well. Of course, this narrative technique that relies on such an extraordinarily large cast will yield rather stereotypical characters as a result, but this never means clichés or empty patterns.

As for tying up the end, Altman always finds it necessary to introduce some strong event or action of general public interest. In *Nashville* it is the murder of the woman singer, in *A Wedding* it is the death of the couple, and in *Short Cuts* it is the drama of the earthquake. These all add a darker tone to his colorful stories.

However, the gesture of such closures goes beyond the principle of "the whole is more than the sum of its parts." The strong final messages in these films, which don't come through in individual actions or concrete events, try to suggest a more existential totality. Félix Guattari calls this final tying up "collective existential territories," where we experience the catharsis by stepping over the threshold of the subjectivity of individual characters.

Ritornello

The ritornello, to use a more familiar musical expression, is, on the one hand, the concrete physical realization of some intentional return; on the other hand, as we have seen, it is undeniable that its use is justified mostly to the extent that some new, additional element can be detected in it.

With regard to the structural construction itself, most of the time it occurs in the form of a replay, serving as a frame of some sort. This too is "stretching," a further spreading that results in a slowdown, which, at the same time, can unite very effectively the fate-like character of the beginning and the end. This explains its popularity.

Perhaps the most classic example is the closure of Orson Welles's *Citizen Kane*. The often-cited sudden emphasis and lingering on the glass ball bearing the hero's last words, "Rosebud," has been the symbolic expression of the mysterious secret (that, of course, was taken to be the hidden essence of the character all along). After many attempts there is still no light thrown on the secret. But in the last scene, where the by now superfluous, vast estate has to be faced and reviewed in detail, the camera suddenly zooms in on the sled, once held within the glass ball, highlighting once more its comprehensive symbolic power. Thus the circle is closed, and it is part of Welles's greatness that, avoiding every trace of banality, he only uses the view of the sled to justify a kind of failure. Returning to the object doesn't supply any evidence to the investigators who cast it into the flames, but it does provide the viewers with an explanation, doubly underlying thereby the illusory nature of the belief that human life is easy to decipher. It affords us a view of a paradoxical success, enriching even more the experience of its audience.

Another classic example of framework closure is Akira Kurosawa's *Rashômon* (1950). In the closing scene the opening image of the towering, gigantic stone gate in the pouring rain returns, and places the entire drama we have just witnessed in a larger context and dimension. Now image and attitude exude a different atmosphere. The pouring rain is replaced by calm. The sense of peace, the wise acknowledgment of tragic contradictions, testify to the compassion and equipoise of the Buddhist vision. This closing even suggests hope in the acceptance of the responsibility of caring for the baby who, up to this point, has been the very symbol of neglectful abandonment. The four stories thus seem to be joined by another one that completes the rest and lends a larger, philosophical perspective to this richly textured drama.

The ritornello relies not on the elements of forms, materials, and ordinary meanings, but on emphasizing an existential motif embedded in a multifold and sensitive whole. As Guattari observes, "This ritournelle escapes beyond the strictly defined limits of space-time. With it time ceases to be external so that it can become the intensive center of *temporalisation.*"[6]

Luis Buñuel, in *The Exterminating Angel* (1962), also trusts his deepest message to a new beginning. The inexplicable curse and its even more inexplicable lifting gain their final meaning with the closing of this mysterious circle. In both cases people stand uncomprehending before what happened; these characters don't understand why it has to be them, and not others, who have to suffer the curse of being locked in. But if Buñuel wants to suggest that people live blindly and hypocritically, and furthermore that precisely for this reason they are helpless in managing their own lives, then it's clear that they deserve the repetition of the curse.

Everything starts again, or it may start, since nothing inside them has changed. An insincere life and its possible punishments cannot be carriers of deserved, well-merited changes.

It is in his characteristic puritanical, austere manner that Bresson provides a framework for Mouchette's fate in *Mouchette* (1967). He sums up and indicates the inevitable end by the revolving description of the opening images and by the return of Monteverdi's music. This life is unredeemably closed, yet the film is not stressing determinism. The hero has to go through a nonmechanical series of experiences and reactions before we can understand and live through the implied suicide. Since psychology is expunged from Bresson's vocabulary, the apparently simple surface stands before us only in the convoluted texture. This is why the girl's decision is not premeditated, but rather is dictated by social and physical conditions. It is always a circumstantial, minutely depicted, and changing reality that pushes the girl to the end. Her long rolling down the hillside looks almost like a game, but it's a game that has to lead to death. So, her present and her future meet in a loop from the very beginning in this laconically and elliptically related life story. The intensity of the ritornello vividly highlights the boundaries of Mouchette's life.

David Lynch's *Blue Velvet* (1986) returns at the end with a dry irony to the opening images. The idyllic family life, the glorious garden with the red tulips, and the peace that smoothes out everything, all these are restored. The film asks: Are we back in the same place we were before? The answer is a fine mockery of appearances: not at all. Everything is different, the time of innocence is over. Moreover, the lies too are now disturbingly transparent since even the chirping bird up on the tree is not real; it is "fake," and so are the smiles and other niceties. But this realization required the experience of *almost identity,* and the lengthy replay of everything down to the smallest details. This is how, in the end, we are afforded an insight into the chicanery, into the logic of the judgment.

Among the ritornellos of modernist films, Theo Angelopoulos's *The Traveling Players* (1974) with its reverse twist is probably the most thought-provoking.

The story of the film and its last images end where they
started: in front of the small town's railway station, only now we
are not in 1952 but in 1939! It is a startling jump in time. Every
character is present, including the ones that died and departed
in the course of the story's development. "Like in a large family
photo where the future has already marked them," says the director. "The entire film, (History, Time) is summed up in this last
image." This way time and memory visibly and spectacularly melt
together, not as sheer past but, Angelopoulos says, "as if everything happened in the present." For memories, just like myths,
legends, and poetry, belong to everyone. "The flashback is the
collective memory of the whole company," says Angelopoulos.[7]
The great forms of the tradition, the opposition and meeting of
folklore and tragedy, meant to him not merely a grand structure
(the film is four hours long), but also the free play of calligraphy,
and the freedom of going beyond the confines of the story. The
loss of chronology, its emphatic opposition can also be explained
by his conscious effort to destroy illusions. The odyssey leads us
back to where we began. The implication is that the essence of
travel is not the arrival but the journey itself.

This paradox of the future, which blends into the past, goes
back to the oldest wisdom as a character in another Angelopoulos
film, *Voyage to Cythera* (1984), puts it, borrowing from T. S. Eliot:
"In my end is the beginning."

Suspense and Surprise

Reviewing the various methods of endings it turns out that we
have two basic procedures at our disposal. Whether the defining gesture of the closure is the stretching of the present, the
fragmentary recovery of the past, or the intimation of some open

future, the structural principle can be classified as either suspense or surprise. They don't differ in quality or value, no matter how hard Hitchcock tried to devalue surprise. For there is nothing sinful about the deus ex machina; every theatrical tradition has made use of it. Of course, the question is how forced or emotionally unjustifiable are the unexpected and chance elements that we weave into the story.

If the end is really such a "chief thing," as Aristotle says, then it is easy to see that every work will get its full meaning from the closing paradigms that, regardless of their great variety, always hold out the promise of some rounded whole. An additional promise is that there will be no surprise without suspense; for in the absence of the tense waiting that precedes the surprise, lulled by the appearance of calm or equanimity, the suddenly released change couldn't have the necessary effect. And the reverse of this dialectic, this mutual presupposition is also true: without the occurrence of unexpected twists, ingenious associations, and unusual details the entire suspense strategy would remain ineffectual. For all maneuvers of delaying and waiting can be employed successfully only by intentionally highlighting witty, intricate, and remarkable things.

This combination is noteworthy because it shows clearly that without suspense even the most unexpected twist can be forced, and the other way around: tension, even if it "portions out" with the cleverest logic, will sooner or later make an unexpected ending mandatory.

Hitchcock's *Rear Window* (1954) also achieves its extraordinary effect by the endless stretching of our patience as we follow the unraveling of the secret. Here, the hypothesis and the "misleading" gathering of evidence intentionally employ different means. This time, the viewer knows nothing more than the hero or the other characters in the film. In many thrillers we know what to expect. Here, we are investigating alongside the hero, sharing his ignorance and false assumptions, and the attendant doubt and uncertainty make for a rather different sort of excitement. Still, we do get a surprise ending, not only because we encounter a totally different kind of danger and revelation, but also because the masterful play on our nerves—achieved here too by the gradually intensifying suspense-building that lasts almost throughout the entire film—prepares us for something else. Yet the surprise remains strong for it has the effect of an unexpected twist.

There is, then, no recipe for connecting suspense and surprise. It is certain, however, that in some way they mutually presuppose each other. A lot depends on the proportion between the two, but if the suspense is lacking, the surprise in itself will inevitably look cheap. The reverse of this is also true: if the suspense is unable in the end to deliver some odd or witty twist, then we remain disappointed.

The essence of film drama is not the employment of some mechanistic structure but a complex, heterogeneous, shifting structure that attempts to track the complexities of the human experience.

Andrej Tarkovsky, *Mirror*, 1975

10 Strategies of Time

Rhythm and Tempo
Opposites Intertwined
Festina Lente—Hurry Up Slowly

Rhythm and Tempo

I have attempted to review the complex relationship of rhythm and tempo and the peculiar interaction of fast and slow pace. It has turned out that a closer look at the problem of temporality leads to essential perceptions. The handling of time determines tone, style, and method. To put this in another way, the artwork's time structure is dependent on the very nature of the work. The comprehensive vision is present in the way time is articulated.

If the primarily music-related dictionary definition of rhythm can safely be applied to film, then it implies that this concept has a wider, more general meaning. Its interpretative role and its sensual-psychological effects are valid in other branches of the arts as well. The *American Heritage Dictionary*'s entry seems to be the most useful for my purposes: "[Rhythm is] the patterned recurring alternation of contrasting elements of sound [or speech]," but then it immediately goes on to say that "in painting, sculpture, and other visual arts, [it can be applied as] a regular pattern created by lines, forms, and colors" as well. The structure of a composition is characterized by the distribution of its successive beats or accents. It is this much-neglected relationship that I've always looked for in analyzing films.

Rhythm, then, is a basic shape organizing all the participating elements into an expressive whole. It is not only a temporal formation indicating duration, but, to continue the quote, "is the result of the interaction among the various aspects of the material." In other words, the melody (in our case, the sequence of events), the intensity, the tone-color, the texture, and, of course, the harmony, all these play a role in the rhythm. The point is that although the order of a recognizable pattern presupposes regularity, this consists of contrasting elements. A commitment to this idea and its elucidation was the starting point of my book. My further ambition has been to show that every dramatic device, including the physical movements of a film's actors, together with the alternation of light and shadow, the vitality of the camera, and, moreover, the elements of sound and silence, the accents and the beats, all express content and emotion, and these devices stand in a complex, dialectical relationship with each other. The sole ground of any richness is the tension within the ensemble of these dynamic factors.

On the other hand, tempo is subordinated to rhythm, for it is rhythm that first has a formative effect in response to inner, substantive needs. Rhythm, as applied to our field, is the dramatic design itself. It is a secondary matter whether the performance of this unique, characteristic pattern will be fast or slow. Musicians are also of the opinion that "while changes in tempo will alter the character of the music and perhaps influence our impression of what the basic beat is . . . tempo is not a relationship. It is not an organizing force. . . . Hurrying or slackening of tempo has no power to alter the rhythmic organization."[1]

Schoenberg, on the other hand, says that the fact of progression, as opposed to simple succession, always points toward some tangible goal, and this is what creates the rhythm. "Progression has the function of establishing or contradicting a tonality," he says.[2] Of course, once again I have to modify the narrower musicological sense of tonality. Still, one thing remains true: progression never happens simply in the sense of "establishing" a matter; it can also evolve in the form of "contradicting."

Progression is of course extremely important in dramatic narrative, for it determines the manner of development, anticipating its structural possibilities. The intonation of the opening scenes will signal this characteristic quality, the future shape that will function as the motor, the drive of the developing plot. It determines and anticipates the meaning of the events, leading toward the denouement. To name just one similarity: here too we can find ascending and descending progressions that will influence tempo formation. And the unfolding of the combination of harmonies depends on the nature and deeper sense of the premise, to the extent that it promises modulation, contrast, or reaffirmation. After all, as I have indicated before, we are not dealing here with a simple causal, rational logic, but with a wittier game that attracts attention and will fascinate the spectator with surprises. Isn't this what Aristotle's *peripeteia* is all about? For it too presupposes modulations, contrasts, and reaffirmations as the condition for complications that unravel the story through fortuitous difficulties.

At any rate, working out the difficulties and keeping the door open for unexpected possibilities will create suspense and complexity and, bypassing commonplace logic, will give rise to original combinations. This is why we can say that the complicated and interdependent relationship between rhythm and tempo and their expressivity is subordinated to the overarching whole. And in the distribution of turbulence and flow we, in fact, get to enjoy the peculiar interaction of fast and slow pace as well.

Opposites Intertwined

For the occurrence of turbulence, as is well known, can never be predicted. When an inner or external tension reaches the boiling point, the subsequent transition to a different dynamism can never be a mechanical affair, and especially not one constructed on the principle of purely incremental development. Even more important are, however, the various possibilities of the nature and process of the outbreak. To refer to a distant analogy: it is impossible to foretell the time of an earthquake or a volcanic eruption. Of course, when geologists today are able to give an accurate description of the famous eruption of Vesuvius that devastated Pompeii, they are recording something that already happened and that offers some useful lessons for us. Research shows that the process follows certain well-defined stages and that the volcano explodes when pressure from the frothy magma exceeds the strength of the plug whereby it overcomes the resistance of the crust.

This is how it happened. But did it necessarily have to happen this way and at that particular time? For, although increasing internal pressure leads up to the eruption, the mere possibility of the event, in other words the openness of alternative possibilities in general, is not less significant. "Many people picture a volcano's innards as a vertical tube like a straw drawing magma from a balloon-like well of magma which obligingly burbles out through a crater . . . [however, the process is more complex:] the same magma, in the same volcano, can either create a tremendous explosion or ooze forth sedately—called an effusive eruption . . . or they rise through irregular fissures."[3]

Not every accumulation leads to eruption. This is why all explosions are so unpredictable even if we are familiar with the nature of the process. At times, the fatal explosion fails to occur.

In cases when the magma rises slowly enough, the bubbles, like air in honey, do have time to expand, coalesce, and leak away through fissures in the earth. This is how it happens in ordinary, everyday existence: things can fizzle out, run out of steam, or be resolved through minor eruptions.

Drama discusses these processes on a magnified scale, and usually follows the inevitability of the eruption. But to show the place and role of "effusive eruptions"—as I tried to emphasize in my discussion of works inclined to deal with "streaming," in which the quiet flow has a deeper meaning—slower reactions in cracks and crevices, which reveal minor, modifying phenomena, are important here too, precisely because this process may offer a better understanding of the insidiously threatening character of natural and internal human processes.

"The creator's work has to take account of many rhythms," Calvino says in *Six Memos for the Next Millennium*. "Vulcan's and Mercury's, a message of urgency obtained by dint of patient and meticulous adjustments and an intuition so instantaneous that, when formulated, it acquires the finality of something that could never have been otherwise." "Vulcan is a god who does not roam the heavens but lurks at the bottom of craters, shut up in his smithy, where he tirelessly forges objects that are the last word in refinement. To Mercury 's aerial flight, Vulcan replies with his limping gait and the rhythmic beat of his hammer." Thus we live with both practices, "but it is also the rhythm of time that passes with no other aim than to let feelings and thoughts settle down, mature, and shed all impatience or ephemeral contingency."[4]

Festina lente—Hurry Up Slowly

In the chapter on quickness in *Six Memos for the Next Millennium*, Calvino refers to his favorite Latin motto, *Festina lente*, which he found in a Renaissance publisher's emblem. The illustration depicts the following enigmatic design: a dolphin is shown twisting itself in a sinuous curve around an anchor. "This elegant graphic sign represents the intensity and constancy of intellectual work . . . I've always liked emblems that throw together incongruent and enigmatic figures like in a puzzle," Calvino says. "A similar one is an illustration with a butterfly and a crab on it that illustrate Festina Lente in Paolo Givio's sixteenth-century emblem collection. Both of them, the butterfly and the crab have bizarre, symmetrical shapes, but there is an unexpected harmony between them."

Festina lente, hurry up slowly, is a paradoxical expression; it suggests trying to understand the law of duality, the tension of opposites. If haste is mere rushing about, then it cannot offer much excitement, no matter what measure of speeding we consider. But allying haste with a slow pace, matching and opposing the two, will create a challenge, a "bizarre harmony" that brings us face to face with the unfamiliar. Speed, like any other experience, has to be worked on, slowly, patiently discovering its nature, its inner secrets. If we do it quickly then we are not only committing the crime of superficiality, but we also lose the possibility of an intimate experience. After all, what else is poetic creation than approaching the familiar with the dissecting urge normally reserved only for the unfamiliar and, by this process of "defamiliarization," making others discover it?

There is a time for the thumping rhythm that leads to the climax, but then there is a time for patience that ends more quietly. We may enjoy dynamism and high speed but we cannot revere them as exclusive values. It's also good to lag behind, to review the past, to grasp alternative possibilities. We can pay closer attention to the mysteries of the present, or look back on the road traveled so far. Moreover, we can dream about what the future may have in store for us.

A carnival, to use Bakhtin's favorite concept, is undoubtedly a loosening of time, a stepping out of frameworks, and an intensification of rhythm. But this doesn't cover life itself as a whole. Bakhtin also calls the carnival "an alien world of adventure time" in his famous essay, "Forms of Time and of the Chronotope in the Novel."[5] The catastrophic speed of action, the vortex of events, and the dynamism of works of art do not amount to a victory over time. And Virilio's point, although somewhat exaggerated, is still well-taken: "If time is the story (itself), then speed is only its hallucination; perspectival hallucination that destroys the time of the narrative and of action in the sole interest of the sensational."[6] We should add: this at least is a danger we encounter only too often.

Of course, I don't wish to claim that everything that is painstakingly observant of and persistently focused on the trivial texture of everyday life is therefore good (good because it is slow). For banality remains banality if our attention extends only to a bare description of what exists. The repetition of commonplaces, or the highbrow, artsy self-indulgence on this side of the fence, is just as discouraging with all its pretensions as the cheap acrobatic productions we have seen accumulated on the other side. But it must be admitted that in our age we are far from having to see the greatest danger in too much restraint.

* * *

A storyteller is a gamester and a sculptor of time who not only lives and thinks in time, but who also, at the same time, and inevitably, speaks always of time. He interprets and investigates it, storming its expanse and depth. Time is made human by narration, to cite Ricœur's nice formula. For, we set ourselves against the unknown measure of time meted out to us; we face the finitude of our time with the help of stories, by gathering and passing on the lessons of our experience. This is what enables us to create what Lukacs called our "transcendental home."

But whether we are basing our stories on the traces of things past or heading toward an imaginary future, our sole playing field is the present. This here and now has taken quite a dramatic turn in the past few decades. The ways we project and record information, call up past experiences, and relate to knowledge, desire, and other emotions have all become threateningly mechanical. Direct, genuine communication is replaced by substitutes and simulacra. We no longer have to travel if we want to see Venice or the Himalayas; no longer have to go to libraries to consult books written by wise men of old; and the day is coming when a celebrated surgeon will use the Internet to perform an operation on a patient thousands of miles away. The wonderful new gadgets of technology make an escalated, almost limitless mobility possible. But is this really infinite mobility? Isn't there a good measure of imprisonment, immobility, and dependence on mediators involved here? And isn't this state of sensory saturation paralyzing after all? True, everything comes to our doorstep, everything is available, but our absorbing capacity does set a limit to the information flow. If our movement of thoughts, the speed of our reaction time, is lower than the speed of electromagnetic waves, and if the world we face through pictures moves faster than our mind that tries to take it all in, then we are really falling behind things and events instead of comprehending their essence.

"What are we going to be waiting for when we'll no longer need to wait for arriving?" asks Virilio. "When we ourselves will be the films, TV broadcasts for our distant partners. . . . There, where the real time of direct, instant broadcasting has an advantage over the actually covered real space; there, where consequently the image is more important than the thing itself and the physically present human himself, in such a world there is no longer room for a holiday, the essence of which is a steady sequence of day and night. The electronic day of telecommunication is not identical any more with the astronomical day of the ephemerides."[7]

Becoming the bewildered travelers of the information superhighways, being overwhelmed by this suddenly emerging world of eternal stimulation and oversaturation, perhaps it is permitted sometimes to take nostalgic walks on seductive forest paths, to stroll down quiet country lanes, to stop and rest where space and time measure their own pace, and where things still live nurturing their own unmistakable distinctness. I believe we have come to a time when we should start making some selections and some rejections of the ever more globalized offers we receive daily. After an extended binge we would do well with a little diet, and would do even better with a bit of fasting.

The respect of plurality, the need for a synoptic vision, and the openness to opposition all concentrate on quality. They aim at deeper levels and not at the fireworks on the surface. This common need strives for the ambition of complexity. How long are we to wait for that prudent, ever more sensitive attention that is able to parse time once again, to bring back variety and complexity, and, together with its restraint, make effectual and accessible to our mind and heart that which is by nature measureless because it is infinite?

Notes

Preface

1. Paul Klee, *Théorie de l'art moderne* (Paris: Folio/Essays, 1964), 27.

2. Ingmar Bergman, quoted in *Film: Montage of Theories,* ed. Richard Dyer McCann (New York: Dutton Paperback, 1966), 144.

1. Volatile Time

1. Henri Bergson, *Creative Evolution* (New York: Continuum, 2002), 172–73.

2. I. Prigogine and Isabelle Strengers, *Order out of Chaos* (New York: Bantam, 1984), 311.

3. Ibid., 312.

4. Ibid.

5. N. Katherine Hayles, *Chaos Bound* (Ithaca, N.Y.: Cornell University Press, 1990), 60.

6. Alfred North Whitehead, *Science and the Modern World* (New York: Free Press, 1967), 243.

7. In *Les Théories de la Complexité,* ed. Françoise Fogelman-Soulié, Véronique Havelange, and Maurice Milgram (Paris: Seuil, 1991), 295.

8. Antonio Damasio, *Looking for Spinoza* (Orlando, Fla.: Harcourt, 2003), 38.

9. Roland Barthes, *Image, Music, Text* (New York: Hill and Wang, 1977), 92–93.

2. Setting the Pace

1. Alvin Toffler, *Future Shock* (New York: Bantam, 1970).

2. James Gleick, *Faster* (New York: Pantheon, 1999).

3. Italo Calvino, *Six Memos for the Next Millennium* (Cambridge, Mass.: Harvard University Press, 1988), 35.

4. Umberto Eco, *Six Walks in the Fictional Woods* (Cambridge, Mass.: Harvard University Press, 1994).

5. Walter Benjamin, *The Origin of German Tragic Drama* (New York: New Left Books, 1977), 83.

6. Calvino, *Six Memos,* 35.

7. Jean Epstein, *L'Esprit du cinéma* (Paris: Jeheber, 1955).

8. Takeshi Kitano, interview in *Positif,* April 19, 2003, 19.

3. Intricate (Extended) Story Structures

1. Interview with Harmony Korine, in Richard Kelly, *The Name of This Book Is Dogme 95* (London: Faber and Faber, 2000), 197.

2. Interview with Fassbinder, in Rainer Werner Fassbinder, *Írások, beszélgetesek* (Budapest: Osiris, 1996), 238. First publication in "Die Städte des Menschen und seine Seele," *Die Zeit,* March 14, 1980.

3. Ibid., 246.

4. *Positif* (April 2003): 19.

4. Detours

1. Gaston Bachelard, *La Dialectique de la Durée* (Paris: Quadrile/PUF, 1950, 1993), 123.

2. Ingmar Bergman, in *Films and Dreams,* ed. Vlada Petrie (New York: Redgrave, 1981), 51.

3. Milan Kundera, *La Lenteur* (Paris: Gallimard, 1995), 45.

4. Alain Resnais, in *Esprit* (Paris, 1960), 936.

5. Chris Marker, notes sur Vertigo, in *Positif* (1982).

6. Jorge Luis Borges, *Labyrinth* (New York: New Directions, 1962), 45–50..

7. Susanne K. Langer, *A Note on the Film and Form* (New York: Scribner, 1953), 411.

8. *Les Cahiers du cinéma* 165 (1965).

9. Federico Fellini, interview in *Cahiers du cinéma,* 165 (1965).

5. Seeing in Time: *Quasi una pausa*

1. Paul Klee, "Schöpferische Konfession," 1922; quoted in *Paul Klee,* trans. Paul Gohman (New York: Harry N. Abrams), 97.

2. Ibid.

3. Walter Benjamin, *The Arcades Project* (Cambridge, Mass.: Belknap, 1999), 462.

4. Quoted in Bela Balazs, *Theory of the Film* (New York: Dover Publications, 1970).

5. Emmanuel Levinas, *Totalité et infini* (Paris: Livre de Poche, 1971), 203 and 211.

6. In Rene Prédal, "Alain Cavalier," *L'Avant Scène du Cinéma,* no. 440 (1995): 136.

7. Robert Bresson, *Notes on the Cinematographer* (New York: Urizen Books, 1977).

8. James Elkins, *The Objects Stare Back* (New York: Harcourt, 1997), 45.

9. Bresson, *Notes on the Cinematographer.*

10. Walter Benjamin, "The Work of Art in the Age of Technical Reproduction," in *Illuminations* (New York: Schocken Books, 1969).

11. *Positif* (2003).

12. Quoted in Emilio Ambasz, *Italy: The New Domestic Landscape,* 68.

13. Tadao Sato, lecture at the New York Ozu Colloquium, November 2001.

14. Paul Ricœur, *Temps et Récit* (Paris: Seuil, 1989), 13.

15. Alain Cavalier, *Carnet de travail, Les Rencontres Culturelles de la Fnac* (Paris:, 1989).

16. Jean Renoir, *Faire des films* (Paris: Éditions Séguier, 1999), 20.

6. Repetitions or Reprise

1. Søren Kierkegaard, "Repetition," in *The Essential Kierkegaard* (Princeton, N.J.: Princeton University Press, 1995), 103.

2. Ibid.

3. As offered in the fuller French version, *La reprise* (Paris: Flammarion, 1990), 67.

4. Robert Bresson, *Notes on the Cinematographer* (New York: Urizen Books, 1977), 7.

5. Ibid.

6. Vaclav Havel, *L'Anatomie du gag* (Paris: Éditions de l'Aube, 1992), 28.

7. *Cahiers du cinéma* (1979): 303.

8. Danusia Stok, ed., *Kieslowski on Kieslowski* (London: Faber and Faber, 1993), 113.

9. "Télérama, hors série," *La passion de Kieslowski* (September 1993): 5.

10. Jacques Lacan, *Le séminaire,* vol. 1 (Paris: Seuil, 1975), 19.

7. Odysseys

1. Joseph Gelmis, *Film Director as Superstar* (New York: Doubleday, 1970), 293.

2. Andrej Tarkovsky, *Sculpting in Time* (Austin: University of Texas Press, 1986), 66.

3. Ibid., 69.

4. Ibid., 121.

5. Ibid., 80.

6. Ibid., 57.

7. Michel Ciment, "Entretiens avec Angelopoulos," *Positif* 174 (1975): 11.

8. Fragment from a personal letter sent by the director to Y. B.

9. Reference to the well-known titles of Angelopoulos's films.

10. Bill Viola, *Reasons for Knocking at an Empty House* (Cambridge, Mass.: MIT Press, 1995), 78.

11. Quoted in John Walsh and Bill Viola, *The Passions* (Los Angeles: Getty Museum, 1995), 30, 57, 36.

12. Ibid., 19.

8. Everyday Rituals

1. "Lo scandolo Pasolini," *Bianco e Nero* 1976, no. 37: 1–4.
2. Ibid.
3. Ibid.
4. Contrebande, 1999, Paris, no. 5.
5. Plutarque, *La sérénité intérieure* (Paris: Rivage/Poche, 2001), 15.
6. Hollis Frampton, *Circles of Confusion* (Rochester, N.Y.: Visual Studies Workshop Press, 1983), 59.

9. Endgames

1. Aristotle, *Poetics* (New York: Hill and Wang, 1961).
2. Frank Kermode, *The Sense of an Ending* (New York: Oxford University Press, 1966), 5.
3. Peter Brooks, *Reading for the Plot* (New York: First Vintage Books, 1985), 22.
4. Wim Wenders, Interviews, in Osiris (Hungarian) source: "Find myself in a city to live in," *Quaderns* 176 (1987).
5. Ibid., source: The Urban Landscape, Lecture in Tokyo, 1991 Oct. 12, in Osiris, Budapest, 305 and 387.
6. Félix Guattari, *Chaosmose* (Paris: Galilée, 1992), 84.
7. Michel Ciment, "Interview with Theo Angelopoulos," *Positif* 174 (1975); Michel Ciment, "Interview with Theo Angelopoulos," *Positif* 194 (1977).

10. Strategies of Time

1. Grosvenor Cooper and Leonard B. Meyer, *The Rhythmic Structure of Music* (Chicago: University of Chicago Press, 1960), 3.
2. Arnold Schoenberg, *Structural Functions of Harmony* (New York: W. W. Norton, 1969), 1.
3. *New York Times,* Science Section, November 18, 2003.

4. Italo Calvino, *Six Memos for the Next Millennium* (Cambridge, Mass.: Harvard University Press, 1988), 48.

5. M. M. Bakhtin, *The Dialogic Imagination* (Austin: University of Texas Press, 1982), 89.

6. Paul Virilio, *Un paysage de l'événement* (Paris: Galilée, 1996), 123.

7. Ibid., 133.

Selected Bibliography

Adorno, Theodor W. 1963. *Philosophy of Modern Music.* New York: Seabory.

Agel, Henri. 1978. *L'éspace cinématographique.* Paris: Pierre Delargue.

Angelopoulos, Theo. 1985. *Études Cinématographiques.* Paris: Minard.

Aristotle. *Poetics.* 1961. New York: Hill and Wang.

Attali, Jacques. 1982. *Histoires du temps.* Paris: Fayard.

Aumont, Jacques. 1992. *Du visage au cinéma.* Paris: Cahiers du Cinéma.

Bachelard, Gaston. 1931. *L'intuition de l'instant,* Paris: Éditions Stock.

———. 1950. *La dialectique de la durée.* Paris: PUF.

Bakhtin, M. M. 1982. *The Dialogic Imagination.* Austin: University of Texas Press.

Balazs, Bela. 1970. *Theory of the Film.* New York: Dover Books.

Barthes, Roland. 1977. *Image, Music, Text.* New York: Hill and Wang.

———. *S/Z.* 1970. Paris: Éditions du Seuil.

Benjamin, Walter. 1960. *Illuminations.* New York: Schocken Books.

———. 1973. *Reflections, Essays, Aphorisms.* New York: Harcourt.

———. 1999. *The Arcades Project.* Cambridge, Mass.: Belknap Press.

Berger, John. 1985. *The Sense of Sight.* New York: Pantheon.

Bergson, Henri. 2002. *Creative Evolution.* New York: Continuum.

Blanchot, Maurice. 1981. *The Gaze of Orpheus.* Barrytown, N.Y.: Station Hill Press.

Bollas, Christopher. 1982. *Being a Character.* New York: Hill and Wang.

Bordwell, David. 1985. *Narration in the Fiction Film.* Madison: University of Wisconsin Press.

Borges, Jorge Luis. 1962. *Labyrinth.* New York: New Directions.

Bresson, Robert. 1977. *Notes on the Cinematographer.* New York: Urizen Books.

Brooks, Peter. 1985. *Reading for the Plot.* New York: First Vintage Book.

Burch, Noel. 1969. *Theory of Film Practice.* Princeton, N.J.: Princeton University Press.

Calvino, Italo. 1988. *Six Memos for the Next Millennium.* Cambridge, Mass.: Harvard University Press.

Cavalier, Alain. 1996. *Études Cinématographiques.* Paris: Minard.

Cooper, Grosvenor, and Leonard B. Meyer. 1960. *The Rhythmic Structure of Music.* Chicago: University of Chicago Press.

Damasio, Antonio. 2003. *Looking for Spinoza.* Orlando, Fla.: Harcourt.

Debord, Guy. 1967. *Commentaires sur la société du spectacle.* Paris: Gallimard.

Deleuze, Gilles. 1989. *The Time Image.* Minneapolis: University of Minnesota Press.

Eco, Umberto. 1965. *L'œuvre ouverte.* Paris: Éditions du Seuil.

––––––. 1994. *Six Walks in the Fictional Woods.* Cambridge, Mass.: Harvard University Press.

Eisenstein, Sergei. 1969. *The Film Sense.* New York: Harcourt.

Elkins, James. 1995. *The Objects Stare Back.* New York: Harcourt.

Epstein, Jean. 1955. *L'Esprit du cinéma.* Paris: Jeheber.

Fassbinder, Rainer Werner. 1996. *Írások, beszélgetesek.* Budapest: Osiris.

Fogelman-Soulié, Françoise, Véronique Havelange, and Maurice Milgram, eds. 1991. *Les Théories de la Complexité.* Paris: Seuil, 295.

Fraser, J. T. 1990. *Of Time, Passion and Knowledge.* Princeton, N.J.: Princeton University Press.

Frampton, Hollis. 1983. *Circles of Confusion.* Rochester, N.Y.: Visual Studies Workshop Press.

Gleick, James. 1999. *Faster.* New York: Pantheon.

Godard, Jean-Luc. 1972. *Godard on Godard.* New York: Da Capo.

Goffman, Erving. 1967. *Interaction Ritual.* New York: Pantheon Books.

Gregory, R. L. 1970. *The Intelligent Eye.* New York: McGraw Hill.

Guattari, Félix. 1992. *Chaosmose.* Paris: Galilée.

Hall, Edward. 1966. *The Hidden Dimension.* New York: Doubleday.

Hasumi, Shiguehiko. 1988. "Ozu." *Cahiers du cinéma.*

Havel, Vaclav. 1992. *L'Anatomie du gag.* Paris: Éditions de l'Aube.

Hawking, Stephen. 1988. *A Brief History of Time.* New York: Bantam Books.

Hayles, N. Katherine. 1990. *Chaos Bound.* Ithaca, N.Y.: Cornell University Press.

————. 1991. *Chaos and Order.* Chicago: University of Chicago Press.

Horton, Andrew, ed. 1997. *The Last Modernist.* Westport, Conn.: Greenwood.

Ishagpur, Yousef. 1994. *Les formes de l'impermanence.* Tours: Farrago.

————. 2000. *Le réel, face et pile.* Tours: Farrago.

Kelly, Richard. 2000. *The Name of This Book Is Dogme 95.* London: Faber and Faber.

Kermode, Frank. 1967. *The Sense of an Ending.* New York: Oxford University Press.

Kiarostami, Abbas, and Laurent Roth. 1997. *Abbas Kiarostami.* Paris: Cahiers du Cinéma.

Kierkegaard, Søren. 1995. "Repetition." In *The Essential Kierkegaard.* ed. Howard Vincent Hong and Edna Hatlestad Hong. Princeton, N.J.: Princeton University Press.

Klee, Paul. 1964. *Théorie de l'art moderne.* Paris: Folio, Essays.

Lacan, Jacques. 1977. *Écrits.* New York: W. W. Norton.

Langer, Susanne K. 1953. *Philosophy in a New Key.* New York: Scribner.

Lotman, Jurij. 1977. *The Structure of the Artistic Text.* Ann Arbor: University of Michigan.

Lukacs, Georg. 1972. *Soul and Form.* Cambridge, Mass.: MIT University Press.

Luria, A. R. [1932] 1960. *The Nature of Human Conflicts.* New York: Liveright.

Levinas, Emmanuel. 1971. *Totalité et infini.* Paris: Livre de poche.

————. 1991. *La mort et le temps.* Paris: L'Herne.

Lyotard, Jean-François. 1995. *Moralités postmodernes.* Paris: Galilée.

McLuhan, Marshall. 1964. *Understanding Media.* New York: Signet Books.

Marker, Chris. 1967. *Commentaires.* Paris: Seuil.

Menil, Alan. 1991. *L'écran du temps.* Lyon: Presses Universitaires de Lyon.

Merleau-Ponty, Maurice. 1945. *Phénoménologie de la perception.* Paris: Gallimard.

Moholy-Nagy, László. 1947. *Vision in Motion*. Chicago: University of Chicago Press.

Onfray, Michel. 1966. *Les formes du temps*. Paris: Éditions Mollat.

Pasolini, Pier Paolo. 1988. *Heretical Empiricism*. Bloomington: Indiana University Press.

Perez, Gilberto. 1998. *The Material Ghost*. Baltimore, Md.: Johns Hopkins University Press.

Prigogine, I., and Isabelle Stengers. 1984. *Order out of Chaos*. New York: Bantam.

―――. 1998. *Entre le temps et l'éternité*. Paris: Fayard.

Ricœur, Paul. 1983. *Temps et recit*. Paris: Seuil.

―――. 2000. *La mémoire, l'histoire, l'oubli*. Paris: Seuil.

Rorty, Richard. 1989. *Contingency, Irony, and Solidarity*. Cambridge, Mass.: Cambridge University Press.

Schoenberg, Arnold. 1969. *Structural Functions of Harmony*. New York: W. W. Norton.

Sklovski, Viktor. 1990. *Theory of Prose*. Elmwood Park, Ill.: Dalkey Archive Press.

Solomon, Maynard. 1995. *Mozart*. New York: Harper Perennial.

Sontag, Susan. 1966. *Against Interpretation*. New York: Farrar, Strauss, and Giroux.

Stam, Robert. 1989. *Subversive Pleasures*. Baltimore, Md.: Johns Hopkins University Press.

―――. 1992. *Reflexivity in Film and Literature*. New York: Columbia University Press.

Stok, Danusia, ed. 1993. *Kieslowski on Kieslowski*. London: Faber and Faber.

Szondi, Peter. 1969. *Theorie des modernen Dramas*. Frankfurt: Suhrkamp.

Tarkovsky, Andrej. 1986. *Sculpting in Time*. Austin: University of Texas Press.

Toffler, Alvin. 1970. *Future Shock*. New York: Bantam.

Virilio, Paul. 1995. *La vitesse de la libération*. Paris: Galilée, 1995.

―――. 1996. *Un paysage de l'événement*. Paris: Galilée.

Viola, Bill. 1995. *Reasons for Knocking at an Empty House.* Cambridge, Mass.: MIT University Press.

———. n.d. *The Passions,* with Peter Sellars, John Walsh, and Hans Belting. Los Angeles: J. Paul Getty Museum, in association with the National Gallery, London.

Vogel, Amos. 1974. *Film as a Subversive Art.* New York: Random House.

Whitehead, Alfred North. 1967. *Science and the Modern World.* New York: Free Press.

Filmography

8½ (Federico Fellini, 1963)
10 (Abbas Kiarostami, 2002)
The 400 Blows (*Les 400 coups*) (François Truffaut, 1959)

À nos amours (*To Our Loves*) (Maurice Pialat, 1983)
Accatone (Pier Paolo Pasolini, 1961)
Amarcord (Federico Fellini, 1973)
America, America (Elia Kazan, 1963)
Andrey Rublyov (Andrej Tarkovsky, 1969)
And the Ship Sails On (*E la nave va*) (Federico Fellini, 1983)
Annie Hall (Woody Allen, 1977)
Ariel (Aki Kaurismaki, 1988)
L'Atalante (Jean Vigo, 1934)
An Autumn Afternoon (*Sanma no aji*) (Yasujiro Ozu, 1962)
L'Avventura (Michelangelo Antonioni, 1960)

Badlands (Terrence Malick, 1973)
Balthazar (*Au hasard, Balthazar*) (Robert Bresson, 1966)
Barry Lyndon (Stanley Kubrick, 1975)
Battleship Potemkin (*Bronenosets Potyomkin*) (Sergei Eisenstein, 1925)
The Beekeeper (*O Melissokomos*) (Theo Angelopoulos, 1986)
Berlin Alexanderplatz (Rainer Werner Fassbinder, 1980)
The Bicycle Thief (Vittorio De Sica, 1948)
The Big Heat (Fritz Lang, 1953)
The Birds (Alfred Hitchcock, 1963)
Black Peter (*Cerny Petr*) (Milos Forman, 1964)
Blind Chance (Kryzstof Kieslowski, 1987)

Blue Velvet (David Lynch, 1986)

Bonnie and Clyde (Arthur Penn, 1967)

Breathless (*À bout de souffle*) (Jean-Luc Godard, 1960)

Café Lumière (*Kôhî jikô*) (Hou Hsiao-Hsien, 2003)

Calendar (Atom Egoyan, 1993)

Capricious Summer (*Rozmarné léto*) (Jiri Menzel, 1968)

Citizen Kane (Orson Welles, 1941)

Cleo from 5 to 7 (*Cléo de 5 à 7*) (Agnès Varda, 1961)

Closely Watched Trains (*Ostre sledované vlaky*) (Jiri Menzel, 1966)

Chunking Express (*Chung hing sam lam*) (Wong Kar-wai, 1994)

Come Back to the Five and Dime, Jimmy Dean (Robert Altman, 1982)

Comédies et proverbes (Eric Rohmer, 1980–1987)

The Conversation (Francis Ford Coppola, 1974)

Cries and Whispers (*Viskningar och rop*) (Ingmar Bergman, 1972)

Damnation (*Kárhozat*) (Bela Tarr, 1988)

Days of Being Wild (Wong Kar-wai, 1991)

Dead Man (Jim Jarmusch, 1995)

Dekalog (Krysztof Kieslowski, 1989)

Dillinger Is Dead (*Dillinger è morto*) (Marco Ferreri, 1969)

Diner (Barry Levinson, 1982)

Dogville (Lars von Trier, 2003)

La Dolce Vita (Federico Fellini, 1960)

Dolls (Takeshi Kitano, 2002)

Dolorosa (Bill Viola, 2000)

The Double Life of Véronique (*La double vie de Véronique*) (Kryzstof Kieslowski, 1991)

Drowning by Numbers (Peter Greenaway, 1988)

The Eclipse (*L'eclisse*) (Michelangelo Antonioni, 1962)

Early Spring (Yasujiro Ozu, 1956)

Elephant (Gus Van Sant, 2003)

Everything about My Mother (Pedro Almodovar, 1999)

The Exterminating Angel (*El Ángel exterminador*) (Luis Buñuel, 1962)

Faces (John Cassavetes, 1968)

Fallen Angels (Wong Kar-wai, 1995)

Fargo (Ethan and Joel Coen, 1996)

The Fiances (I Findanzati) (Ermanno Olmi, 1963)

The Fire Within (Le feu follet) (Louis Malle, 1963)

Fireworks (Hana-bi) (Takeshi Kitano, 1997)

Fist in the Pocket (I pugni in tasca) (Marco Bellocchio, 1965)

Gerry (Gus Van Sant, 2002)

The General (Buster Keaton, 1927)

The Gleaners and I (Les glaneurs et la glaneuse) (Agnès Varda, 2000)

Going Forth by the Day (video installation) (Bill Viola)

Goodbye, Dragon Inn (Bu San) (Tsai Ming-liang, 2003)

Goya (Carlos Saura, 1999)

La Grande illusion (Jean Renoir, 1937)

The Great Dictator (Charlie Chaplin, 1940)

Greeting (video installation) (Bill Viola)

Gummo (Harmony Korine, 1997)

Happy Together (Chun gwong cha sit) (Wong Kar-wai, 1997)

Head-On (Gegen die Wand) (Fatih Akın, 2004)

High Hopes (Mike Leigh, 1988)

High Noon (Fred Zinnemann, 1952)

Hiroshima, mon amour (Alain Resnais, 1959)

The Hole (Dong) (Tsai Ming-liang, 1998)

Husbands (John Cassavetes, 1970)

In the Mood for Love (Fa yeung nin wa) (Wong Kar-wai, 2000)

The Island (L'île nu) (Kaneto Shindô, 1960)

Jeanne Dielman, 23 Quai du Commerce, 1080 Bruxelles (Chantal Akerman, 1976)

La Jetée (Chris Marker, 1962)

Jonah Who Will Be 25 in the Year 2000 (Jonas qui aura 25 ans en l'an 2000) (Alain Tanner, 1976)

Julien Donkey Boy (1990)

Kes (Ken Loach, 1969)

The Lacemaker (*La dentellière*) (Claude Goretta, 1977)
Ladybird, Ladybird (Ken Loach, 1994)
Landscape in the Mist (*Topio stin omichli*) (Theo Angelopoulos, 1988)
The Last Picture Show (Peter Bogdanovich, 1971)
La Strada (Federico Fellini, 1954)
Letter from an Unknown Woman (Max Ophuls, 1948)
Libera me (Alain Cavalier, 1993)
Life and Nothing More (Abbas Kiarostami, 1991)
Life Is Sweet (Mike Leigh, 1990)
Loves of a Blonde (*Lásky jedné plavovlásky*) (Milos Forman, 1965)

Mamma Roma (Pier Paolo Pasolini, 1962)
Man without a Past (*Mies vailla menneisyyttä*) (Aki Kaurismaki, 2002)
The Marriage of Maria Braun (*Die Ehe der Maria Braun*) (Rainer Werner Fassbinder, 1979)
The Matchfactory Girl (*Tulitikkutehtaan tyttö*) (Aki Kaurismaki, 1990)
Minnie and Moskovitz (John Cassavetes, 1971)
Miracle in Milan (*Miracolo a Milano*) (Vittorio De Sica, 1951)
Mirror (*Zerkalo*) (Andrej Tarkovsky, 1975)
Mon oncle (Jacques Tati, 1958)
Mouchette (Robert Bresson, 1967)
Mullholland Drive (David Lynch, 2001)
Muriel (*Muriel, ou le temps d'un retour*) (Alain Resnais, 1963)

Naked (Mike Leigh, 1993)
Nashville (Robert Altman, 1975)
North by Northwest (Alfred Hitchcock, 1959)
La notte (Michelangelo Antonioni, 1961)

One Flew over the Cuckoo's Nest (Milos Forman, 1975)

Padre, padrone (Paolo Taviani and Vittorio Taviani, 1977)
La Passion de Jeanne d'Arc (Carl Theodor Dreyer, 1928)
Passions (video installation) (Bill Viola, 1991)
Peeping Tom (Michael Powell, 1960)

Persona (Ingmar Bergman, 1966)

Pickpocket (Robert Bresson, 1959)

Pickpocket (*Xiao Wu*) (Jia Zhang-Ke, 1997)

Platform (*Zhantai*) (Jia Zhang-Ke, 2000)

Play Time (Jacques Tati, 1967)

Le Procès de Jeanne d'Arc (Robert Bresson, 1962)

Psycho (Alfred Hitchcock, 1960)

Raging Bull (Martin Scorsese, 1980)

Rashômon (Akira Kurosawa, 1950)

Rear Window (Alfred Hitchcock, 1954)

Rebel without a Cause (Nicholas Ray, 1955)

Red Desert (*Il deserto rosso*) (Michelangelo Antonioni, 1964)

The Red and the White (*Csillagosok, katonák*) (Miklós Jancsó, 1967)

Red Psalm (*Még kér a nép*) (Miklós Jancsó, 1972)

La rencontre (Alain Cavalier, 1996)

Repulsion (Roman Polanski, 1965)

The River (*He liu*) (Tsai Ming-liang, 1997)

The Round Up (*Szegénylegények*) (Miklós Jancsó, 1965)

Run Lola Run (*Lola rennt*) (Tom Tykwer, 1998)

Saraband (Ingmar Bergman, 2003)

Satan's Tango (*Sátántangó*) (Bela Tarr, 1994)

Scene at the Sea (Takeshi Kitano, 1991)

Scenes from a Marriage (Ingmar Bergman, 1973)

Seisaku's Wife (*Seisaku no tsuma*) (Yosujo Masamura, 1965)

Seven Chances (Buster Keaton, 1925)

The Seventh Continent (*Der siebente Kontinent*) (Michael Haneke, 1989)

The Shining (Stanley Kubrick, 1980)

Short Cuts (Robert Altman, 1993)

The Silence (Ingmar Bergman, 1963)

Silence and Cry (*Csend és Kiáltás*) (Miklós Jancsó, 1967)

Sky over Berlin (Wim Wenders, 1987)

Sonatine (Takeshi Kitano, 1993)

Spring, Summer, Autumn, Winter . . . and Spring (*Bom yeoreum gaeul gyeoul geurigo bom*) (Kim Ki-duk, 2003)

Stalker (Andrej Tarkovsky, 1979)

The Straight Story (David Lynch, 1999)
Stranger Than Paradise (Jim Jarmusch, 1984)
Stromboli (Roberto Rossellini, 1950)
Sweetie (Jane Campion, 1989)

The Taste of Cherry (Abbas Kiarostami, 1997)
Taxi Driver (Martin Scorsese, 1976)
The Tenant (*Le locataire*) (Roman Polanski, 1976)
Thelma and Louise (Ridley Scott, 1991)
Thérèse (Alain Cavalier, 1986)
Through the Olive Trees (*Zire darakhatan zeyton*) (Abbas Kiarostami, 1994)
Tokyo Story (Tokyo monogatari) (Yasujiro Ozu, 1953)
The Travelling Players (*O Thiasos*) (Theo Angelopoulos, 1975)

The Ultimate Woman (*La Dernière femme*) (Marco Ferreri, 1976)
Umberto D. (Vittorio de Sica, 1952)

Viridiana (Luis Buñuel, 1961)
Vive L'Amour (*Aiqing wansui*) (Tsai Ming Liang, 1994)
Vivre sa vie (Jean-Luc Godard, 1962)
Voyage to Cythera (*Taxidi sta Kithira*) (Theo Angelopoulos, 1984)

Wanda (Barbara Loden, 1970)
We Won't Grow Old Together (*Nous ne vieillirons pas ensemble*) (Maurice Pialat, 1972)
Weekend (Jean-Luc Godard, 1967)
The Weeping Meadow (*Eleni*) (Theo Angelopoulos, 1985)
Werckmeister Harmonies (*Werckmeister harmóniák*) (Bela Tarr, 2000)
Wild Strawberries (*Smultronstället*) (Ingmar Bergman, 1957)
Where Is My Friend's Home? (*Khane-ye doust kodjast?*) (Abbas Kiarostami, 1987)
Wings of Desire (*Der Himmel über Berlin*) (Wim Wenders, 1987)
Woman of the Dunes (Hiroshi Teshigahara, 1964)
The World (*Shijie*) (Jia Zhang-Ke, 2004)

Yi yi (Edward Yang, 2000)

Index

Page numbers in italics indicate illustrations.

Abe Kobo, 116

Accatone (1961), 183–184

acceleration, 29–32, 37

Ackermann, Chantal, 194

Akin, Fatih, 135–136

Allen, Woody, 212

Almodovar, Pedro, 217

Altman, Robert, 49, 50, 51–52, 223

Amarcord (1973), 70–71, 95

America, America (1963), 106–107

American Heritage Dictionary, 231

An Autumn Afternoon (1962), 75–76, 131

And the Ship Sails On (1983), 95

Andrey Rublyov (1969), 158, 160, 161

Angelopoulos, Theo, 166, 227; The Beekeeper (1986), 118, 150, 164–166; Landscape in the Mist (1988), 162; The Travelling Players (1975), 162, 163, 227; The Weeping Meadow (1985), 150, 164–166

Annie Hall (1977), 212

Antonioni, Michelangelo, 70, 206–207, 222

The Arc of Passions (Bill Viola), 172–178

Ariel (1988), 73–74, 186

Aristotle, 203, 233

L'Atalante (1934), 43

Aurelius, Marcus, 201

L'Avventura (1960), 70

Bach, Johann Sebastian, 184

Bachelard, Gaston, 70

Badlands (1973), 208–209

Bakhtin, M. M., 236–237

Balazs, Bela, 108

Barry Lyndon (1975), 63–65

Barthes, Roland, 27

Battleship Potemkin (1925), 111

The Beekeeper (1986), 118

Bellocchio, Marco, 57, 211–212

Benjamin, Walter, 34, 106, 115

Berger, John, 54

Bergman, Ingmar, xi, 80; Cries and Whispers (1973), 91; Persona (1966), 91, 103–104; Saraband

(2003), 109; *Scenes from a Marriage* (1973), 109–110; *The Silence* (1963), 72–73; *Wild Strawberries* (1957), 26, 91, 92

Bergson, Henri, 3, 147

Berlin Alexanderplatz (1980), 65–67, 66

The Big Heat (1953), 24–25

The Birds (1963), 43

Black Peter (1964), 198

Blind Chance (1981), 142–144

Blue Danube (music) (Strauss), 154

Blue Velvet (1986), 226

Bogdanovich, Peter, 53

Bolero (music) (Ravel), 134

Bonnie and Clyde (1967), 208

border crossing endings, 218–220

boredom, expression of, 192–196

Borges, Jorge L., 11, 88

A Boring Afternoon (1964), 198

Breathless (1960), 23–24

Bresson, Robert, 112, 134–135, 226; *Notes on the Cinematographer,* 114–115, 135

Brooks, Peter, 203–204

Buñuel, Luis, 108, *111,* 225–226

burlesque, 36–37

Café Lumière (2003), 121–122

Les Cahiers du cinéma (magazine), 138

Calendar (1993), 139

Calvino, Italo, 32, 38, 235

Campion, Jane, 96

Candide (Voltaire), 38

Capricious Summer (1968), 198

Carne, Marcel, 117

Carver, Raymond, 52

Cassavetes, John, 53–54, 104–105, 214–215

Cassel, Seymour, 105, 214

catalyzer role, 22–23

Cavalier, Alain, 109; *La rencontre* (1996), 114; *Libera me* (1993), *100,* 107–108, 114, 122–123; *Thérèse* (1986), 107–108

chaosmose, 12

Chaplin, Charlie, 111

chronos, 10–11

Chungking Express (1994), 61–62

The Circular Ruins (Borges), 88

Citizen Kane (1941), 224–225

Clarke, Arthur, 152

Cleo from 5 to 7 (1961), 57–59, *58*

Closely Watched Trains (1966), 33, *197,* 198

Coen, Ethan, 71

Coen, Joel, 71

Columbine High School massacre. *See Elephant* (2003)

comedy in reprise, 136–140

contingent and "accidental" detours, 69–76

The Conversation (1974), 96

Cooper, Gary, 125

Cooper, Grosvenor, 232

Coppola, Francis Ford, 96

counterpoints, 41–42

"Creative Confession" (Klee), 101–102

Cries and Whispers (1973), 91

crossroad structures, 54–56
Cuny, Alain, 26

daily occurrences. *See* rituals, everyday
Dalio, Marcel, 123
Damasio, Antonio, 15–16
daydreaming, 91–95
Days of Being Wild (1987), 62–63, 96–97
De Niro, Robert, 41, 216
De Sica, Vittorio, 107; *Miracle in Milan* (1951), 113, 213–214; *Umberto D.* (1952), 196
Dead Man (1995), 185–186
deadpan, detachment of, 185–192
Decalogue (1989), 145
Deleuze, Gilles, 102–103
deliberation, 34
density, 37–38
detours: contingent and "accidental," 69–76; daydreaming, 91–95; dreams, 91–95; fantasy, 76–80; flash forward, 95–99; memories, 80–91
deviations, 73–74
digressions. *See* detours
Dillinger is Dead (1969), 192–194, 214, 215–216
La Dolce Vita (1960), 26
Dolls (2002), 55–56, 116–117
Dolorosa (2000) (installment), *173*
The Double Life of Véronique (1991), 142, 144–146
dreams, 91–95
Dreyer, Carl T., 104

Drowning by Numbers (1988), 147
duration, 67

Early Spring (1956), 74–75, *128*
Early Summer (1951), 131
The Eclipse (1962), 206–207
Eco, Umberto, 32–33
Egoyan, Atom, 139
8½ (1963), 91, 92–95, 107, 123–124
Eisenstein, Sergei, xi, 108, 111
Elephant (2003), *1* (facing), 6–10
Eliot, T. S., 227
Elkins, James, 109
ellipsis, 76, 135
emotional flashback, 220–223
End of Autumn (1961), 74–75
endings: about, 203–204; border crossings, 218–220; emotional flashback, 220–223; finale, 223–224; open end, 204–208; retardation, 208–212; ritornello, 224–227; surprise, 227–229; suspense, 227–229; unexpected epiphany, 212–217
epic narration, 63–65
epiphany endings, 212–217
Epstein, Jean, 39, 41
Everything about My Mother (1999), 217
existence, evidence of, 201
The Exterminating Angel (1962), 225–226

face (portrayal of), 103–110
Faces (1968), 104–105

Fallen Angels (1995), 61, 62

fantasy, 76–80

Fargo (1996), 71

Fassbinder, Rainer Werner, 16–21, *17*, 65–67, *66*, 120

Faster (Gleick), 31

Fellini, Federico, 94, 95; *8½* (1963), 91, 92–95, 107, 123–124; *Amarcord* (1973), 70–71, 95; *La Dolce Vita* (1960), 26; *And the Ship Sails On* (1983), 95

Ferreri, Marco, 192, 214–216

Festina lente, 235–237

The Fiancés (1963), 45–46

finale, 223–224. *See also* endings

Fire, Water, Breath (1997) (video installation), 172–174

Fireworks (1997), 117

Fist in the Pocket (1965), 57, 211–212

flash forward, 95–99

The Flavor of Green Tea over Rice, 131

flow, ix, xii

Forman, Milos, 197–198; *Black Peter* (1964), 198; *The Loves of a Blonde* (1965), 198; *One Flew over the Cuckoo's Nest* (1975), 156

"Les formes de l'impermanence" (Ishaghpour), 132–133

"Forms of Time and of the Chronotope in the Novel" (Bakhtin), 237

The 400 Blows (1959), 204–205

fragmentation, xii

fragmented narrative, 57

Frampton, Hollis, 201

"future shock," 30

Gabin, Jean, 123

The General (1927), *28*

The Gleaners and I (2000), 112–113

Gleick, James, 31

Godard, Jean-Luc, 23–24, 104, 216, 217

Going Forth by the Day (2002) (video installation), 175–178

La Grande Illusion (1937), 123

Grant, Cary, 212

The Great Dictator (1940), 111

Greenway, Peter, 147

Greeting (1995) (video installation), 175

Guattari, Félix, 12, 225

Gummo (1997), 60–61

Hackman, Gene, 96

haiku, 158–160

Hamlet (Shakespeare), 23

Haneke, Michael, 181–182, 182–183

Happy Together (1997), 97–99

Hartley, Hal, 112

Au Hasard Balthazar (1966), 134–135

Hasumi Shiguehiko, 131

Hayashi Hikaru, 134

Hayles, N. Katherine, 11

Head-On (2004), 135–136

hermeneutic codes, 27

High Hopes (1988), 198–199

High Noon (1952), 125–126

"hinge-points," 27

Hiroshi Teshigahara, 116

Hiroshima, mon amour (1959), 81–83, 222–223

Hitchcock, Alfred: *The Birds* (1963), 43; *North by Northwest* (1959), 212; *Psycho* (1960), 43, 112; *Rear Window* (1954), 228–229; *Spellbound*, 220

The Hole (1998), 68, 76–80, 117

Hou Hsiao-hsien, 121–122

hurry up slowly, 235–237

"Hurry up Slowly" (Bíro), ix

Husbands (1970), 53–54

In the Mood for Love (2000), 43–45, 218, 219–220

inciting incidents, 21–27

insertions, 74, 93

intertwined opposites, 234–235

Ishaghpour, Yousef, 132–133

Island (1960), 134

Jancsó, Miklós, 118–119, *213*

Jarmusch, Jim, 185–186, 187

Jeanne Dielmann (1976), 194

La Jetée (1962), 80, 81, 83–88, *84*

Jonah Who Will Be 25 in the Year 2000 (1976), 54

Josephson, Erland, 110

Julien Donkey Boy (1999), 60–61

Kaurismaki, Aki: *Ariel* (1988), 73–74, 186; *The Man without a Past* (2002), 74, *180*, 189–192; *The Match Factory Girl* (1989), 186–189; *Shadow in Paradise* (1986), 186

Kazan, Elia, 106–107

Keaton, Buster, *28*, 37

Kermode, Frank, 203

Kes (1969), 59–60

Kiarostami, Abbas, x; *Life and Nothing More* (1991), 115; *The Taste of Cherry* (1997), *202*, 218–219; *Through the Olive Trees* (1994), 107, 209–211

Kiekegaard, Søren, 129, 130

Kieslowski, Krysztof, 142–144, 144–146, *145*

Kim Ki-duk, 118

Kitano Takeshi, 67; *Dolls* (2002), 55–56, 116–117; *Fireworks* (1997), 117; *Scene at the Sea* (1991), 124–125; *Sonatine* (1993), 47–48

Klee, Paul, xi, 101–102

Korine, Harmony, 60–61

Kubrick, Stanley, 63–65, 151–155, 155–158

Kundera, Milan, 80

Kurosawa, Akira, 140–142, 225

La Motta, Jake, 40

labyrinths, 162–166

Lacan, Jacques, 147

Ladybird, Ladybird (1994), 41–42

Landscape in the Mist (1988), 162, 207–208

landscapes, portraying, 115–122

Lang, Fritz, 23, 24–25
Langer, Susanne K., x, 91
The Last Picture Show (1971), 53
Late Spring, 131
Leigh, Mike, 194–196, 198–199
Letter from an Unknown Woman
    (1948), 221
Levinas, Emmanuel, 108–109
Libera me (1993), *100,* 107–108,
    114, 122–123
Life and Nothing More (1991), 115
Life is Sweet (1990), 198–199
linear time, 13
Loach, Ken, 41–42, 59–60
Loden, Barbara, 105–106
Lotman, Jurij, 26
The Loves of a Blonde (1965), 198
Lynch, David, 79–80, 199–201,
    226

Malick, Terrence, 208–209
A Man Escaped, 112
The Man without a Past (2002),
    74, *180,* 189–192
Marker, Chris, 80, 81, 83–88, *84,*
    90
The Marriage of Maria Braun
    (1979), 16–21, *17*
Mastroianni, Marcello, 124, 222
The Match Factory Girl (1989),
    186–189
memories, 80–91
Menzel, Jiri, 33, *197,* 198
The Messenger (1997) (video in-
    stallation), 172, 174–175

metaphors, 32–33; carnivals,
    236–237; forest, 32–33, 34;
    staircase, 11; of time, 15–16
Meyer, Leonard, 232
Minnie and Moskovitz (1971),
    214–215
Miracle in Milan (1951), 113,
    213–214
Mirror (1975), 89–91, 158, *230*
Mon Oncle (1958), 138
monotony, 181–184
Monsieur Hulot Goes on Vacation
    (1958), 138
montage, xi
Morin, Edgar, 16
mosaic structures, 56–63
Mouchette (1967), 226
Mouren, Yanick, 223
Mullholland Drive (2001), 79–80
Muriel (1963), 83
Mystery Train, 185

Naked (1993), 194–196
Nashville (1975), 223
New Wave techniques, 57, 117,
    119
New York Times (newspaper), 234
Nicholson, Jack, 156
North by Northwest (1959), 212
Notes on the Cinematographer
    (Bresson), 114–115, 135
La notte (1961), 70, 222

occurrences, daily. *See* rituals, ev-
    eryday

odysseys: arc of passions, 172–178; labyrinth, 162–166; space solitude, 151–158; timeless time, 166–172

Olmi, Ermanno, 45–46

One Flew over the Cuckoo's Nest (1975), 156

open ends, 204–208

Ophuls, Max, 221

orchestration, 65–68

Order out of Chaos (Prirogine, Strengers), 3, 5

Ozu Yasujiro, 120–121, 196; *An Autumn Afternoon* (1962), 75–76, 131; *Early Spring* (1956), 74–75, *128*; *Early Summer* (1931), 131; *End of Summer* (1961), 74; *The Flavor of Green Tea over Rice,* 131; *Late Spring,* 131; *There Was a Father* (1942), 22–23; *Tokyo Story* (1953), 131; use of reprise, 129–130

pace: acceleration, 29–32; living in time, 32–35; rushing, 35–42; streaming, 42–48

parallel structures, 50–54

Pasolini, Pier Paolo, 183–184

Passer, Ivan, 198

La Passion de Jeanne d'Arc (1928), 104

Passions (2000) (video installation), 175–176

Penn, Arthur, 208

perception, relativity of, 47–48

permanence, 129–136

Persona (1966), 91, 103–104

Piccoli, Michel, 192

The Pickpocket (1959), 134

Play Time (1967), 136–139, *137*

plurality, 70, 239

Plutarch, 201

Polanski, Roman, 77–79

polyphony, 52, 57, 69–76, 108

Prirogine, I., 3

proaleritic codes, 27

Le Procès de Jeanne d'Arc (1962), 134

projection. *See* flash forward

Psycho (1960), 43, 112

quasi una pausa, 111

Raging Bull (1970), 40–41

Rashômon (1950), 140–142, 225

Ray, Nicholas, 112

Rear Window (1954), 228–229

Rebel without a Cause (1955), 112

Red Desert (1964), 70

Red Psalm (1972), 118–119, *213*

The Reds and Whites (1967), 118

relativity of time, 67

La rencontre (1996), 114

Renoir, Jean, 123

repetitions. *See* reprise

reprise: combinations and variety, 146–148; comedy of mechanism, 136–140; permanence, 129–136; "What if" and "As if," 142–146

Repulsion (1965), 77

Resnais, Alain, 81–83, 90, 222–223

retardation, 208–212

rhythm, 15, 36, 67, 231–232

Ricœur, Paul, 32, 122

ritornello, 224–227

rituals, everyday: detachment
    of the deadpan, 185–192;
    evidence of existence, 201;
    expressions of boredom, 192–
    196; ironic serenity, 196–201;
    monotony, 181–184

The River (1997), 117

Rohmer, Eric, 147

Round Up (1965), 118

Rowland, Gena, 104, 214

Run Lola Run (1998), 146–147

rushing, 35–42

Saint, Eva Marie, 212

Saint Augustine, 13

Saraband (2003), 109

Satan's Tango (1994), 166–170

Sato Tadao, 120–121

Scene at the Sea (1991), 124–125

Scenes from a Marriage (1973),
    109–110

Schoenberg, Arnold, 233

Scorsese, Martin, 40–41, 216–217

Scott, Ridley, 212–213

seeing in time: about, 101–103,
    126; the face of things, 110–
    115; the human face, 103–110;
    landscapes, 115–122; silence,
    122–126

Seferis, George, 163

serenity, ironic, 196–201

Seven Chances (1925), 37

The Seventh Continent (1989),
    181–182

*71 Fragments of a Chronology of
    Chance* (1994), 182–183

Seyrig, Delphine, 194

Shadow in Paradise (1986), 186

Shakespeare, William, 23

Shindô Kaneto, 133–134; *Island*
    (1960), 134

The Shining (1980), 155–158

Short Cuts (1993), *50,* 51–52, 223

silence, 122–126

The Silence (1963), 72–73

*Six Memos for the Next Millen-
    nium* (Calvino), 32, 38, 235

Six Walks in the Fictional Woods
    (Eco), 32–33

Sky over Berlin (1987), 205–206

slowness, 183

solitude, 151–158

Sonatine (1993), 47–48

Sottsass, Ettore, 120

*Spring, Summer, Fall, Winter . . .
    and Spring* (2003), 118

"St. Mathew's Passion" (music)
    (Bach), 184

Stalker (1979), 158, 161–162

story structures: crossroads,
    54–56; epic narration, 63–65;
    mosaics, 56–63; orchestration,
    65–68; parallels, 50–54

La Strada (1954), 222

The Straight Story (1999), 199–201
Stranger Than Paradise (1984),
    185, 187
Strauss, Johann, 154
Strauss, Richard, 152
streaming, 42–48
Strengers, Isabelle, 3
surprise endings, 227–229
suspense, 65
suspense endings, 227–229
Sweetie (1989), 96

Tanner, Alain, 54
Tarkovsky, Andrej: *Andrey
    Rublyov* (1969), 158, 160, 161;
    Mirror (1975), 89–91, 158, *230;
    Stalker* (1979), 158, 161–162
Tarr, Bela, 166–172, *167*
The Taste of Cherry (1997), *202,*
    218–219
Tati, Jacques, 136–139, *137,* 138
Taxi Driver (1976), 216–217
technology, 21–22, 35, 39,
    238–239
tempo, 231–232
temporal duration, 70
temporal layering, 36–37, 67
temporalisation, 225
temporality, xi
tempus, 11
The Tenant (1976), 77–79
Thérèse (1986), 107–108
Thelma and Louise (1991), 212–
    213
There Was a Father (1942), 22–23

things, portraying, 110–115
Through the Olive Trees (1994),
    107, 209–211
Thus Spake Zarathustra (Strauss),
    152
time: *chronos,* 10–11; complex-
    ity, 15–16; concepts of present,
    1–6; duration, 67; eternal now,
    x; inciting incidents, 21–27; lay-
    ers of the present, 6–10; linear,
    13; living in, 32–35; rhythm,
    15; and technological advances,
    21–22, 35; *tempus,* 11; timeless
    time, 166–172; vertical, 11–12.
    See also pace; seeing in time;
    time strategies
Time Image (Deleuze), 102–103
time strategies: about, 237–239;
    Festina lente, 235–237; inter-
    twined opposites, 234–235;
    rhythm, 231–232; tempo,
    231–232
Toffler, Alvin, 30
Tokyo Story (1953), 131
transitions, 67
The Travelling Players (1975), 162,
    163, 227
tree metaphor, 15–16
Truffaut, François, 204–205
Trust (1991), 112
Tsai Ming-liang, x; *The Hole*
    (1998), *68,* 76–80, 117; *The
    River* (1997), 117; use of fish,
    113–114; *Vive L'Amour* (1994),
    55, 117

turbulence, ix, xii, 42–43
2001: A Space Odyssey (1968), 151–155
Tykwer, Tom, 146–147

Ullmann, Liv, *100*, 103, 110
Umberto D. (1952), 196
Une partie de campagne (1936), 112

Van Sant, Gus, 6
Varda, Agnès, 57–59, *58*, 112–113
vertical time, 11–12
Vigo, Jean, *43*
Viola, Bill: *Dolorosa* (2000), *173;* *Fire, Water, Breath* (1997), 172–174; *Going Forth by the Day* (2002), 175–178; *Greeting* (1995), 175; *The Messenger* (1997), 172, 174–175; *Passions* (2000), 175–176
Viridiana (1961), *111*
Virilio, Paul, 238
Visible Man (Balazs), 108
Vitti, Monica, 70
Vive L'Amour (1994), 55, 117
Vivre sa vie (1962), 104
Voltaire, 38

Voyage to Cythera (1984), 162, 164, 227

Wanda (1970), 105–106
Webster's Seventh New Collegiate Dictionary, 15, 52
A Wedding, 223
Weekend (1967), 216, 217
The Weeping Meadow (1985), *150,* 164–166
Welles, Orson, 224–225
Wenders, Wim, 205–206
Werkmeister Harmonies (2000), 166, *167,* 170–172
"What if" and "As if," 142–146
Whitehead, Alfred North, 14
Wild Strawberries (1957), 26, 91, 92
Woman of the Dunes (1964), 116
Wong Kar-wai, x; *Chungking Express* (1994), 61–62; *Days of Being Wild* (1987), 62–63, 96–97; *Fallen Angels* (1995), 61, 62; *Happy Together* (1997), 97–99; *In the Mood for Love* (2000), 43–45, 218, 219–220

Zinnemann, Fred, 125–126

Essayist, screenwriter, and professor emerita in New York University's Graduate Film School, Yvette Bíro has worked on a dozen prize-winning films with noted directors (Jancsó, Makk, Fabri) in her native Hungary. Recent scripts that she has written include one based on Nobel Laureate José Saramago's *The Stone Raft,* and *Johanna.* Bíro has published numerous essays and ten books on film, including *The Metamorphosis of the Image, The Seventh Art,* and *Profane Mythology* (Indiana University Press, 1982). Her work has been translated into seven languages.

Books by Yvette Bíro

Le temps au cinéma: le calme et la tempête. 2007

Időformak: A filmritmus játéka (The Forms of Time: The Role of Rhythm in Film). 2005

Nem Tiltott Határátlépések: Képkalandozások kora (The Metamorphosis of the Image). 2003

To Dress a Nude: Exercises in Imagination, with Marie-Geneviève Ripeau. 1998. Translated into French, Italian, Slovenian, and Hungarian

Festina Lente (Siessunk lassan). 1997

A Hetedik Művészet (The Seventh Art). 1997, 1998, 2003

A Rendetlenség Rendjeá (The Order of Disorder). 1993, 1998

Filmkultura 65/67 (collection of essays). 1991

Profane Mythology. 1982. Also in Chinese, French, and Hungarian

Jancso. 1977

A Film Drámaisaga (The Dramatic Structure of Film). 1968. Translated into Czech

A Film Formanyelve (The Language of Film). 1964

Printed and bound by CPI Group (UK) Ltd, Croydon, CR0 4YY

13/04/2025

14656531-0001